CRITICAL PRACTICES IN
POST-FRANCO SPAIN

Hispanic Issues

HISPANIC ISSUES
VOLUME 11

CRITICAL PRACTICES IN POST-FRANCO SPAIN

SILVIA L. LÓPEZ, JENARO TALENS, AND
DARÍO VILLANUEVA
◆

EDITORS

UNIVERSITY OF MINNESOTA PRESS
MINNEAPOLIS   LONDON

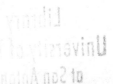

The editors of this volume gratefully acknowledge assistance from the Program for Cultural Cooperation between Spain's Ministry of Culture and United States' Universities; and the College of Liberal Arts and the Department of Spanish and Portuguese at the University of Minnesota.

Published by the University of Minnesota Press
2037 University Avenue Southeast, Minneapolis, MN 55455-3092
Printed in the United States of America on acid-free paper

Library of Congress Cataloging-in-Publication Data

Critical practices in post-Franco Spain / Silvia L. López, Jenaro Talens, and Darío Villanueva, editors.
    p.   cm. — (Hispanic issues : v. 11)
    Includes bibliographical references and index.
    ISBN 0-8166-2473-9 (alk. paper). — ISBN 0-8166-2474-7 (pbk. : alk. paper)
    1. Literature—Philosophy.   2. Discourse analysis, Narrative.
  3. Criticism—Spain. I. López, Silvia L. II. Talens, Jenaro, 1946 –   .
III. Villanueva, Darío. IV. Series: Hispanic issues : 11.
PN45.C73   1994
801'.95'094609045—dc20   94–1236

The University of Minnesota is an
equal-opportunity educator and employer.

Hispanic Issues

Nicholas Spadaccini
Editor in Chief

Gwendolyn Barnes-Karol
Antonio Ramos-Gascón
Jenaro Talens
General Editors

Jennifer M. Lang
Donna Buhl LeGrand
Associate Editors

Kuang-Lin Ke
Assistant Editor

Contents

Introduction
The Politics of Theory in Post-Franco Spain

Silvia L. López, Jenaro Talens, and Darío Villanueva

This volume presents a sample of contemporary critical work now being done in Spain. More often than not, "theory" is a word associated with France, Germany, and the United States. Seldom do we read how Spanish scholars are examining and using critical perspectives such as psychoanalysis, deconstruction, discourse analysis, text theory, or the aesthetics of reception. The essays presented here, submitted by professors of communication and literary theory in the Spanish university system, differ not only in their problematics but also in style and presentation from what one is accustomed to seeing in the United States. As editors of this volume, we believe that part of its value is to recognize difference in sameness. Foucault in Spain, for example, is not Foucault in the United States. Spain has traditionally been dominated by philological studies; the attention given to linguistic criticism there is comparable to the importance and recognition given to feminist criticism here. Accordingly, one of the objectives of the volume is to force readers to adjust their lens, to read what is not written for them, to find interests foreign to theirs, to see through the lens of the other—in other words, to remind the reader of the presence of otherness.

Like histories of criticism generally, the history of criticism in Spain is political. During the Franco years, literary criticism in Spain remained confined to what it had been since the end of the nineteenth century, namely, philological criticism. The important work of Ramón Menéndez Pidal and his school dominated the critical scene. It was only in the 1950s that a slightly broader concept of literary criticism emerged in the official circles of the university, when a *cátedra* (tenured chair) was created at the University of Madrid in "general grammar and literary criticism." For the next thirty years, this institutional space was devoted to research and curriculum in Spanish historical grammar and general linguistics. The slow and difficult development of something close to what we have come to understand as literary theory was evidence of the position held by the academy that nonpositivistic approaches to literature were questionable and ultimately irrelevant to the construction of a scientific discipline dedicated to literature.

This position did meet some challenges. Stylistics, for example, made its presence felt in the publications of some of the highly recognized scholars in the field (Amado Alonso, Alfonso Reyes, and Dámaso Alonso among them). However, such movements did not change the marginalization of literary theory within the official curricula. In 1952, for example, Carlos Bousoño published his *Teoría de la expresión poética* (Theory of poetic expression). This book, in all of its later versions, became a reference point for all those interested in the topic. Bousoño did not have an appointed tenured position in a Spanish university until the early 1980s, a few years before his retirement. For two decades, Bousoño's book and Wellek and Warren's *Theory of Literature* (translated into Spanish in 1951) were practically the only nonphilological texts read in the field.

The last years of the Franco regime and the years of the democratic transition saw rapid changes in this scenario. Modernization meant massification of higher education. More university positions became available as the number of students increased tenfold in some of the universities. This growth and opening up of the university system allowed a new generation of scholars educated in the 1960s to enter the profession. Along with the changes in the universities came a publishing explosion. New publishing houses such as Seix Barral, Anagrama, Ciencia Nueva, Comunicación, and others in Barcelona and Madrid devoted a great amount of energy to making available in Spanish most of the books that were at the center of the intellectual debates in Europe and the United States. During the period 1967–75, the works of Jacques Derrida, Michel Foucault, Gilles Deleuze, Roland Barthes, Umberto Eco, Emilio Garroni, the *Tel Quel* group, *Change,* and others became common currency among students and young scholars-to-be. Structuralism(s), semiotics, and psychoanalysis became political in the hands of that new generation of university professors. Outside the university, film criticism, film history, and similar disciplines began to develop their own space for research in nonacademic journals such as *La mirada* or *Contracampo.* Yet, like all explosions, this one had to subside, and it left few lasting effects. Things that happen fast generally don't last. Official curricula had changed little, and these new approaches continued to be considered trendy and unstable. In spite of all the visibility that theory had gained through the printing industry and the enthusiasm that it generated, theory in general remained, for professors seeking tenure, more an obstacle than an asset. Most positions continued to be defined in terms of the history of national literatures or languages. General grammar and literary criticism were spaces still dominated by linguists. In fact, to obtain a tenured position in Spanish literature, the field in which the majority of the new theorists found themselves, one had to demonstrate competence in either medieval or Golden Age literature. Contemporary literature and literary theory were still considered less "scientific": the first because of its proximity in time, and the second because of its abstract nature.

True university reform had to wait until the Socialist party won the 1982 general elections. It was only in 1985, when the University Reform Law (Ley de Reforma Universitaria, or LRU) was passed, that literary theory was declared an official discipline and was recognized as different from linguistics. The emergence of communication studies (even if limited to schools of journalism) opened up a new space for those who had been working on film and media studies. Thus, the ground for a more general and comparatist theory of discourse had been established. At the end of the 1980s and beginning of the 1990s, some universities, such as those of Valencia, Oviedo, and Santiago de Compostela, began to include film and media studies as part of the curriculum in new specialties devoted either to literary theory or comparative literature. Now, as we approach the turn of the century, it seems that finally literary criticism and textual criticism in general have found their institutional space. No longer will poststructuralism, semiotics, psychoanalysis, feminist studies, and film theory and history remain severed and isolated from each other.

Like all political histories, the history of criticism in Spain has provoked much debate. The stable position has been challenged, and the outcome of philology is not yet clear. Hence a volume dedicated to critical practices in Spain cannot present a complete and representative collection of texts. Furthermore, the editors of this volume recognize that such a task is not theoretically viable. All attempts to render completeness are marked by the exclusions that make such inclusiveness possible. This volume offers only a window onto the vast field of new discursive criticism in Spain, and the view from this window is always limited by its location and shadows.

The essays included in this book range greatly in their topics, styles, and critical concerns. Not all of them deal with strictly literary problems. Santos Zunzunegui, for example, shows us how to "read" the space of the contemporary museums of Europe, and Jesús González-Requena presents us with an analysis of the newscast as postmodern discourse. Jenaro Talens deals with the problem of translation. These essays reflect the concerns of young scholars for broader problems not limited to the strictly literary. Other essays, such as the contribution of José María Pozuelo-Yvancos, follow a more philological tradition. Pozuelo-Yvancos goes beyond that restrictive frame, however, by examining the pragmatics of lyric discourse. This approach is an example of the responses to the stagnation of linguistic criticism that developed during the structuralist hegemony of the 1960s and 1970s. Cristina Peña-Marín offers us an analysis of monologues in her application of Bakhtinian principles to *La regenta;* her essay is a practical example of the current challenges to structuralist narratological studies in Spain. Rafael Núñez-Ramos, following in the footsteps of Gadamer, addresses the problem of the reader and of aesthetic experience. Darío Villanueva attempts a redefinition of literary realism by bringing together phenomenology and pragmatics. Juan Miguel Company-

Ramón gives testimony to the presence of psychoanalysis in Spain by commenting on Jinkis's reading of Lacan's critique of the subject. And Manuel Asensi expands on his *Theoría de la lectura* (not yet available in English)—a series of reflections on a deconstructive theory of reading—in an essay framed by Derridean criticism.

Each chapter refers to a different problematic and, at times, reflects a different theoretical background. The editors of this volume do not want to hide these apparent gaps. On the contrary, we seek to make them productive, insofar as all of these authors desire to problematize the current established idea of literary criticism within the Spanish academic tradition.

Jenaro Talens broaches the problem of translation in his essay "Making Sense after Babel." In addition to the lack of recognition given to translators in the history of literature, Talens highlights an accompanying myth that has dominated that history: the myth of translation. The rendition of a text in translation is supposed to be a mechanical reproduction of the "original" into another language. Somehow in the process of translation that "original" is kept and simply recodified into a different language. Although translation practices have changed in history, from Cicero to Luther to the present, the core concept of translation as a reproductive immaterial activity has remained. From word-for-word translation, we have gone to what Nida and Taber call the "second translation system," consisting of (1) analysis of structure, (2) transfer of structure from a language a to language b, and (3) restructuring or synthesis to make the material comprehensible to the contemporary reader (Nida and Taber 33). Talens points out that this description of the activity of translation is "mental and abstract" and, though adequate for translation machines, fails to acknowledge that translation is not only a mental activity but a physical and emotional activity as well. The inscription of passions and feelings in literature affects the activity of the translator; they cannot be erased. The suppression of the body from the experience of translation accounts for the poverty of translation theory. Douglas Robinson, in *The Translator's Turn*, reflects on this problem and concludes that the artificial separation of translation theory from translation practice is the underlying reason for the low status of translation practice (xiii). Intuitive practices are seen as not belonging to the abstract process of theorizing, and theory is often considered an obstacle to the actual practice of translation. Robinson calls for a "physicalist" approach to translation. Talens aligns himself with this position when he recognizes that the dualism of reason and intuition does not and cannot hold in the practice of translating poetry.

Talens's concern with translation, besides addressing the problems of systematic translation models, lies also within the bounds of language itself. In the second part of his essay, he addresses Walter Benjamin's essay "The Task of the Translator," in which Benjamin affirms that any attempt to consider the problem of the receiver of a work of art is a failed attempt because no work of art is really intended for a receiver. The main problem of a translator is, according to Benjamin, not how to make the work contemporary for the receiver, but how to let the work speak through translation. Talens finds Benjamin's position idealist to the degree that it posits a "pure" language that shines through the practice of translation into other languages, and in that it ignores the communicative character of the text. The idea of a "pure" language reintroduces what Talens calls the "Babel ideology of language," and the displacement of the problem of the receiver evades the question of how to make the text contemporary to the translator's receivers. For Talens the task of the translator is to make the text contemporary: a task that requires a "dialogic process between poetry and doctrine." At the center of the problem of language and its function in translation is the question of what translation is. From Talens's perspective, translation is both creation and interpretation. A translation is creation in that it produces meaning in another language; in order to do that, the translator must first interpret. In short, in the process of translation, the mind and body meet to create an original from another original that is more than just a collection of equivalent words and structures in another language.

The importance of the discourses of the media in the creation of reality is elucidated in Jesús González-Requena's "The Television Newscast: A Postmodern Discourse." Through the production of those discourses we arrive at consensus on what reality is. The technologies involved in their production have changed over time to meet the exigencies of the present. The newspaper, for example, organizes a web of fragmented pieces of information into discrete and hierarchized narrative events. In a sense, our notion of the social is produced in this very process of selection, organization, and display. For this reason, Eliseo Verón maintains that "the news media are the place where industrial societies produce our society" (Verón in González-Requena).

The news discourse, whether in print, radio, or television, generates meaning at a macro level through the constitution of the occurrence as a conceptualized and narrativized event, and, more specifically, through the total presentation of events. In this article, González-Requena focuses on the way that newscasts operate within this general objective. The newscast differs radically from other forms of news discourse because it introduces a subject of enunciation. Traditionally, this subject of enunciation has affected European and American newscasts very differently. European newscasts have tried to hold on to the myth of objectivity by presenting the news anchor as simply a reader of the news. Such objectivist rhetoric ignores the powerful impact of the visual figure of the enunciator. González-Requena maintains that the enunciator functions as the one who stages the present: through the enunciator a sense of the present of the communicative act itself is rendered. In American newscasts, a much more highly personalized model of enunciation secures the bond between the viewers and the network.

Reality is reality only when it "submits to the order of discourse," that is, when it is actualized in an organized and predictable form for our comprehension and interpretation. All that is uncategorizable, chaotic, or irreducible, or that impedes the construction of meaning, González-Requena labels as the "real." His thesis is that the split between reality and the real is more pronounced in our times than in the past. Although now we have more semiotic means by which we can produce our sense of "reality," this sense is more fragile than ever before. The more our world lacks cohesion, the more we will attempt to construct it, although the threat of the "real" is there in all its force.

At the heart of the increasing rift between reality and the real is the problem of time. In a world where "time is unhinged," the newscast often fails to give us a complete sense of coherence. According to González-Requena, who bases his argument on Lyotard, this is a characteristic of our postmodern condition. As we question the myths that have traditionally supported the grand narratives of history, our sense of the past loses its certainty. Similarly, as the future grows unknowable, the present produced by our information discourses finds itself incapable of discursivizing time in relation to either the past or the future. The television newscast is an example of our incapacity to discursivize time in a postmodern world.

In "Architectures of the Gaze," Santos Zunzunegui offers us a historical analysis of the space of the museum from its origins in the ideology of the Enlightenment to its contemporary form. However, his article is much more than a description of how the space of the museum has served different social functions throughout time. Zunzunegui analyzes the transformation of the museum from a cognitive space into an aesthetic space, from a space dominated by a disciplinary practice of seeing to a space of aesthesis where only aesthetic judgment reigns. The most recent designs for museums in Europe actually subvert the ideology of the museum as repository of the great works of art. The work of Santos Zunzunegui follows closely the work of other contemporary European analysts of space such as Krysztof Pomian, Paolo Santarcangeli, and Michel Foucault.

The idea of the right to contemplate great works of art in public spaces is a product of the Enlightenment. From the sixteenth to the eighteenth century the great works of art were held in the private chambers of collectors. With the advent of the museum, artworks became public property. As an institution the museum fulfilled specific functions in what we can call the disciplining of sight. The museum was a total space with a specific organizational logic displayed in the idea of the tour or traversal. The museum was one of many institutions in the nineteenth century, including schools, prisons, and hospitals, that aided in the disciplining of the body of the citizen.

Classical museums are structured as predetermined mazes. Although one can get lost in the museum, its labyrinthine structure always offers a way out, both physically and metaphorically. The "minotaur" or high point of the museum's tour is the arresting moment—for example, *Las Meninas* in the Prado Museum. Visitors make the route as indicated, find what they are supposed to find, and learn what they are supposed to learn and experience by submitting themselves to the pedagogical traversal of sight.

Modernist museums break from the classical paradigm, allowing for a more liberating experience of seeing. Their open and flexible space encourages direct access rather than access through a "guided visit." Paradoxically, this kind of architecture demands more work from the visitor, as there is no longer a spatial anchor design to ground the cognitive aspect of the experience. If modernist museums represent the liberalization of the museum space, more contemporary museums can be said to have "proletarianized" this space. Zunzunegui maintains that museums are no longer places for the lay rituals of culture, but that they have become instead a place of encounter for the multitudes. In a highly fragmented society the desire for participation in the spectacle of culture is enormous. The museum provides the experience of conviviality in the spectacle through the consumption of such goods as catalogs and reproductions of works. These objects become witnesses to the participation in the spectacle and are more important than the experience of the visit itself.

Contemporary museums such as the Art Museum of Catalonia, the Castelo Rivoli (Turin), the Museum of Gibellina (Sicily), and the Mönchengladbach Museum (at Mönchengladbach in the German Rhineland) explode the limits of the modernist museums. The goal in these museums is the creation of a spatial experience. No longer presented with an ordered display, visitors are challenged to reconcile themselves with the space on their own terms. Some of these museums blur the differences between inside and outside by opening themselves up as spaces and incorporating archaeological sites as part of their structure. They subvert the traditional conceptions of space and time and, therefore, of cognition. They invite visitors to an endless exercise of aesthetic experience free from the dictates of knowledge.

In his essay "The Immutability of the Text, the Freedom of the Reader, and Aesthetic Experience," Rafael Núñez-Ramos investigates the relationship between aesthetic knowledge and

language. If aesthetic knowledge supposes an "unmediated relation between subject and object" and if language mediates our
"relationship to the world, which intervenes between the subject and object of knowledge," is it not contradictory to try to
establish a relationship between the two? According to Núñez-
Ramos, there is a contradiction only if we consider language in
its everyday use, in its representative function. He maintains
that subjects, in order to express their aesthetic knowledge,
must create a language for its representation. This is a symptomatic language that acquires meaning "in the orbit of the subject
who inscribes it in his or her world." This language serves as a
function signifier that reacts "against the receiver's system of
values in order to acquire meaning." According to Lotman, this
language, which we may call literary language, produces a "semantization of the extrasemantic" elements of natural language
(Lotman in Núñez-Ramos). Rather than representational, this
language is presentational; it speaks directly to sense. Núñez-
Ramos maintains that the unity of the subject and the object in
aesthetic knowledge is to be found not in the correspondence of
an exact linguistic sign with its exact referent but rather in the
presentational character of literary language, which elicits the
integration of the multiplicity of textual elements.

In "Phenomenology and Pragmatics of Literary Realism,"
Darío Villanueva distinguishes between two types of realism:
genetic realism and formal or immanent realism. He identifies
two forms of genetic realism. The first assumes that behind every word there is an object that corresponds to it (Zola); the second, rather than finding reality reproduced through language,
finds it reflected through language (Lukács). In formal or immanent realism, reality is within the text itself, disconnected from
the referent. Villanueva sees both of these forms of realism as
extremes. He looks into literary reception, building on work by
Ingarden and Iser, as a third way of dealing with the problem of
realism.

The main problem, as Villanueva identifies it, lies in the dialectic relationship between the work as "schematic structure"
and "its concretization as aesthetic object." The role the reader
plays in the actualization of the aesthetic object is key to this
third option. Villanueva borrows two concepts from Husserl's

phenomenology, "intentionality" and "epoche," to add to the model of an aesthetics of reception. Intentionality is "the activity in which the cognizant 'I' extends toward the transcendental phenomenon in order to endow it with meaning" (Husserl in Villanueva). This is an important concept for a theory of literary realism. Phenomenology studies those things "which intentionally point toward an object, real or otherwise, which form a constituent part of the intentional entity of life"; literature qualifies as one of those things. As reality becomes meaningful through an act of intentional experience, so does literature through the apprehension of the world by the writer, the production of the text, and the reading of it by its audience.

The second concept that Villanueva borrows from Husserl's phenomenology is epoche, or phenomenological reduction: "the suspension of the belief in reality of the natural world and consequently placing in parentheses the inductions which it creates in order to exclusively abide by that which is given" (Husserl in Villanueva). Villanueva points to the similarity of epoche to the attitude that convinces the reader to accept "fictionality." He calls this attitude "literary epoche." When talking about literary epoche one needs to pay attention to several important issues: (1) the notion of game that is always implied when there is a suspension of disbelief, (2) the pragmatic question of which speech acts belong to literary communication, and (3) the "logico-semantic status of the fictional." When all of these are considered, we get closer to Villanueva's aim: a comprehension of realism "not from the author or the isolated text but from the reader." This concept of realism takes into account the phenomenological aspect that deals with the ontology of the literary work, that is, with the assumption that the literary work is not complete if it is not actualized. At the same time, it takes into consideration pragmatic questions regarding the dialectic between the enunciation, the reception, and the referent. Literary realism is "a fundamentally pragmatic phenomenon that results from the projection, over an intentional world that the text suggests, of a vision of the external world that the reader—every reader—possesses." In this definition Villanueva tries to mediate between the exigencies of the phenomenological method and the demands of a pragmatics of meaning.

According to Pozuelo-Yvancos in his essay "The Pragmatics of Lyric Poetry," poetry has until recently been ignored in the field of pragmatics. In part, that has been due to the special type of linguistic object that poetry has been considered to be, given its rhetorical-elocutive character. Most studies involving poetry remain at the level of syntax and semantics. Very few studies deal with the pragmatic level, addressing the poem as a communicative form.

In this essay, Pozuelo-Yvancos asks two questions: Does lyric poetry constitute a specific mode of relation, with particular features not possessed by narrative or drama? To what extent is the pragmatic identity of lyric poetry a phenomenon of normative poetics and to what extent has this character constituted itself diachronically into horizons of expectation in different literary cultures? Although the second question is very interesting, he limits himself to addressing only the first.

Basing himself on Stierle, Pozuelo-Yvancos affirms that the "identity" of a discourse is not dictated so much by formal rules as "by the process of realization of a speech act directed at a speaking subject," which also holds true for poetry (Stierle in Pozuelo-Yvancos). Like all literature, poetry is an "imaginary representation," not governed by the rules of credibility that govern other discourses; poetic communication is thus a special norm. The communicative activity of poetry involves imaginary expressions that are expressions of what is authentic but not real. The poet does not compose "a speech act but a representation of one" (Oomen in Pozuelo-Yvancos).

The central pragmatic question in poetry, then, is defined by Pozuelo-Yvancos as the question of the poetic speaker and of the immanent "I" in lyric communication. On one hand, this has involved the treatment of lyric poetry as "the realization of the expressive function"; the reader is supposed to identify the lyrical with the genre where the first person dominates. On the other hand, it involves "the value of the I-you relation in the poetic contexts" or what happens to that relationship when a poem is read. Pozuelo-Yvancos points out, in the tradition of Martínez Bonati, that the concept of expressivity poses particular problems. The lyrical does not constitute a speaking about the speaker but rather "the manifestation of the speaking with itself in solitude." Rather than having a communicative function, poetry constructs "a lived experience inseparable from its enunciation" (Hamburger in Pozuelo-Yvancos). The I-you relationship also poses serious difficulties because in poetry, according to Stierle, "the norm of transmitter and receiver has favored the discursivization of the text in such a way that if the subject of enunciation is a function of discourse in all communication, it so happens that it is also produced in lyrical communication and vice versa: the discourse itself comes to stand as a function of the subject of enunciation" (Stierle in Pozuelo-Yvancos). The same would be valid for the poetic you. The multiplicity of contexts in poetry goes beyond those of the lyric persons. The spatial and temporal contexts of poetry form a "space of perception" that liberates the reader from concrete "real" time and spatial coordinates. Given the complexities of poetic discourse and the difficulty of its defining elements, often more readily identifiable in narrative and drama than in poetry, it is not surprising that the pragmatics of poetry have been insufficiently studied.

In "Reading in Process, the Antitext, and the Definition of Literature," Manuel Asensi applies his reflections on what would be a *theoria* of literature to the definitions of literature and text. The assumptions underlying such a project contrast sharply with assumptions prevalent until the arrival of deconstruction. The author affirms that literary language differs from instrumental language in that the literary sign does not have the rigidity of the latter. The literary text, given its flexible character, is, in a strict sense, not a sign but rather a trace. The trace, according to Derrida, is that which allows the literary text into the place of the *différance* (Derrida in Asensi).

This strategy of distinction tries to avoid essentialist definitions of literature. There is no "literaturity" about literature. Such a notion, claims Asensi, is bound to our inherited conceptions of literature from the Jena romantics and from the assimilation of the poetic to the realm of theory (in a scientific sense). The concept of literature as autonomous language, developed by the romantics, finds its culmination in the quest of the Russian formalists for a demarcation of poetic language. During this century, under the influence of formalism, the specificity of the literary became an important question. The problem of a scientific method for literature has also had a prominent place in the history of literature. The simple fact that literature "is" poses the question of "how" it is, or in the words of Asensi, "the 'being there' definitive of the text is an obligatory pretext . . . for an empirical science." Linguistics has attempted to be this science, and literary theory has often sought to accompany linguistics in this project. In his essay Asensi does not explain why this effort by linguistics and theory has failed, a matter he believes has been already addressed, but concentrates on answering why the question "What is literature?" is in itself problematic.

The antiessentialist attempts at answering the question that have received the widest attention are pragmatics and the aesthetics of reception. Out of these disciplines came a historically determined concept of literature. Asensi maintains that these attempts are still inscribed in the logic of presence that answers the question of what "is" literature. Instead of an essentialist answer to this question, now we are faced with the historicization of an essentialist answer, even if it does not make claims to universality.

In this essay Asensi tries to theorize, in the manner of Nietzsche and Heidegger, that very question, without presupposing that literature exists there as it, as an object making itself apprehensible by theory. Asking "What is literature?" makes clear that the project of literary theory is still enmeshed in the logic of being of Western metaphysics. For Asensi, what can be rescued from the work of the Jena romantics is the concept of the literary absolute. This absolute cannot be equated with the concept of an object with limits, but implies an endless self-enclosed process. This notion is closer to the notion of trace that he borrows from Derrida to designate a highly unstable condition that reveals hidden elements that he calls the "betweens." These betweens form the space of the antitext, "a space with neither borders nor edges."

In his *Teoría de la lectura* (*Theoría* of reading), Asensi addresses the paradoxical relationship between text (T) and metatext (MT) in the movement of identity and difference. The metatext can never saturate the text and because of this constant movement cannot claim to control the polysemy of the text. Is literature the text? It cannot be, for behind the appearance of the empirical text is the antitext, which can be identified only through the movement of the trace. The antitext denies the existence of something external to the text and at the same time denies the identity of a self-enclosed text. The betweenness arises "from the separation of literaturity from the literary text, a separation carried out by a reading in process by means of a displacement of general order." The question of "What is literature?" is permanently displaced, and all that we are left with is not literature, not the text, but simply the "between."

Cristina Peña-Marín's essay, "Subjectivity and Temporality in Narrative," is the only one in this collection that applies some of the theoretical models of narrative discussed to a text very well known among Hispanists, Clarín's *La regenta*. This article treats the problem of the relationship between temporality and subjectivity in a text in which the subject who carries out the narrative addresses himself/herself and is the protagonist of his/her own story.

Contemporary narrative theory distinguishes between the time narrated and the time of the narration. The clear separation of these two temporalities is linked to the speaker of the text. In *La regenta*, however, such a distinction becomes problematic because it is difficult to differentiate between the discourse-producing subject and those characters whose feelings and actions are reported to us. The polyphony of characters is associated with a free, indirect style or represented speech. At first sight this discourse seems to be written in indirect style, meaning that the signs of time and person correspond to the discourse of the speaker. Yet in its semantic and syntactic structure it is full of properties of the enunciator, that is, full of the discourse of the character. As Bakhtin has shown, in these cases it becomes impossible to tell the two voices apart.

Peña-Marín studies several examples of represented speech in *La regenta* not only to point to the temporal problematic but also to show another complexity that is introduced when represented speech deals with the story a character has constructed for himself/herself about his/her own past. The construction and options of identity are very much linked to this autobiographical narrative. In her analysis of *La regenta*, the author shows how the construction of identity is not a process, but rather a continual displacement of elements that the subject recognizes or dismisses in the narration depending on what he/she wants to become next.

Finally, Juan Miguel Company-Ramón discusses, in "Subject and Language: Reflections on Lacan and Jinkis," the epistemological basis of psychoanalysis and the implications of its understanding of the subject for our understanding of discourse and its sources. For a long time the epistemological basis of the human sciences has rested on the formulation that "man talks"; since the coming of psychoanalysis this epistemological premise has been questioned by proposing that "man" is rather a "talked-about being." What this means is not that "man" is the unified subject in control of his utterances—a notion we have inherited from the rationalist tradition in Western philosophy—but rather that when "man" speaks something else is speaking through "him."

The unconscious is the greatest contribution of psychoanalysis to a new theory of the subject. Lacan's part is to have proceeded from a linguistic basis to show the split of the Cartesian cogito and the constitution of the subject in language. "Psychoanalysis reveals that the enunciation that takes into account linguistic analysis is enunciated by the enunciation of the subject as defined by the dimension of the unconscious" (Jinkis in Company-Ramón). This means that " 'I' names the subject of enunciation, but it does not signify it," so who speaks when we say "I"? "There is always an 'I' that initially surfaces . . . but it is always the Other who answers." This divided subject is always marked by the desire to overcome its own split, and it is always marked by the lack of that unity. Company-Ramón explains the workings of the unconscious through a discussion of the mechanism of the joke as explained by Freud and gives us a sense of the workings of desire by analyzing Hitchcock's *Vertigo*. The relevance of psychoanalysis and of a new theory of the subject cannot be disputed:

> Every text is intended to be a parapraxis of writing, a
> radical nonmeeting between the object and its
> expression. To theorize such a split between the subject
> of enunciation and the subject of utterance was
> indispensable in order to define the space from which

this work's primary discursive source emerges as well to undertake further argumentation.

Neither being nor reading has been the same since Freud's great discoveries.

The window is open for you to venture through.

Works Cited

Benjamin, Walter. "The Task of the Translator." In *Illuminations*, trans. Hannah Arendt. New York: Schocken Books, 1969. 69–82.

Derrida, Jacques. "La Différance." *Marges de la philosophie*. Paris: Editions de Minuit, 1972.

Husserl, Edmund. *Die Idee der Phänomenologie*. The Hague: Martinus Nijhoff, 1958.

Ingarden, Roman. *Das literarische Kunstwerk*. Tübingen: Max Niemeyer Verlag, 1965.

Iser, Wolfgang. *The Implied Reader: Patterns of Communication in Prose Fiction from Bunyan to Beckett*. Baltimore: The Johns Hopkins Univ. Press, 1974.

Jinkis, Jorge E. "Una distinción tópica: el sujeto de la enunciación y el yo del discurso." *Cuadernos Sigmund Freud*. Vol. 1: *Temas de Jacques Lacan* (1971): 23–41.

Lotman, Juri. *La structure du texte artistique*. Moscow: Iskusstvo, 1970. Trans. Anne Fournier, Bernard Kreise, Eve Malleret, and Joëlle Yong. Paris: Gallimard, 1973.

Martínez Bonati, Felix. *Fictive Discourse and the Structures of Literature: A Phenomenological Approach*. Trans. Philip W. Silver. Ithaca: Cornell Univ. Press, 1981.

Nida, Eugene, and Charles Taber. *The Theory and Practice of Translation*. Published for the United Bible Societies. Leiden: E. J. Brill, 1969.

Oomen, Ursula. "On Some Elements of Poetics Communication." In *Pragmática de la comunicación literaria*. Ed. J. A. Mayoral. Madrid: Arco Libros, 1987. 137–49.

Robinson, Douglas. *The Translator's Turn*. Baltimore: The Johns Hopkins Univ. Press, 1991.

Stierle, Karlheinz. "Réception et fiction." *Poétique* 39 (1979): 299–320.

Verón, Eliseo. *Construir el acontecimiento*. Buenos Aires: Gedisa, 1983.

Zola, Emile. *Oeuvres complètes*. Vol. 11. Paris: Cercle du livre précieux, 1968.

Representation

Chapter 1
Making Sense after Babel

Jenaro Talens

Translator in Nowhereland

Translators occupy the smallest print in the history of literature. They are more than the impersonal, they are the anonymous. With few exceptions, the name of the translator appears in small type on the credits page; it rarely appears on the title page, and almost never on the cover. It is as if the act of reading a text in a language different from the original were a most shameful activity. "Good manners" are that institutionalized behavior that allows this shameful activity to be kept secret; everyone pretends not to see what everyone else knows (even the translator knows that they know!). To say that one has read Goethe or that the poems of Bonnefoy are moving can be in good taste. To say, however, that one has read them in translation makes one a second-class reader. It is not coincidental that the persona (the mask, in the original Greek sense) is constituted to a large extent through the residual material of that great phantasm we call "knowledge" (*saber* as opposed to *conocimiento*).[1] It is common practice to read authors in bilingual editions and then cite them in the original language. One tries to locate the phrase in the original language (a language one hardly knows) to be able then to cite it in the "original." We see this in critical and erudite works as well as in the work of antiacademic writers (ah, that academy outside the Academy!). The latter return to us the

3

inverted image of that which they pretend to negate. Institutionality has become second nature.

The recurring question of *traduttore/tradittore* will concern me here. In the prologue to his translation of Tacitus, the encyclopedist D'Alembert maintains that one should not expect much from a translator. Translators are faithful to the original if they produce an approximate and legible text. Eliot used to say that the importance given to Poe in France at the end of the nineteenth century was the product of the imperfect English of Baudelaire and Mallarmé. It is true that in Baudelaire's translations there are unorthodox semantic displacements. They have, nonetheless, not interfered with his translations. Often they have been richer than their counterparts in the text of the American author. The problem we face does not reside there. How many versions of Shakespeare have been deemed adequate although it was always understood that one could start all over again? Does not each period of time, then, have its own contradictions, and, therefore, need its own translations? Is it not the task, then, to re/produce the original rather than to respect it?

The problems of faithfulness to the "spirit" or to the word, of literalness versus nonliteralness, are generally absent from the questions that face the translator. If writing consists of producing one (symbolic) space for, and through, discourse, translation consists of a similar process: to trans-late, in its broadest sense, a poetic object from its own inherent individuality to a different system. One of the components of that individuality is the usage of a language different from the one into which it is being translated and outside whose coordinates the object ceases to exist as such. Translating presupposes more than a mechanical decanting from one vessel to another; it implies rewriting the object, which itself is only a part, decontextualizing it from its own poetic space to begin a new writing. Translating produces not a similar space but a different discursive and textual space, whose relationship to the original, although all-encompassing, misses the original text in its materiality. Language/language-system;[2] language-system/literature; language-system/cultures; form/sense, are not heterogeneous and dissociated terms. A text is a proposed whole that exceeds the strictly textual linguistic limits and imposes on the translator the need to translate it as such a whole.

The reading of a translated text should be understood not as an illustration or as an explanation but rather as the actual realization of the possibilities of meaning of the original text, which the translation tries to reproduce through a new textuality. It is a new point of departure, not an arrival point, because a translinguistic space supposes the I-here-now of itself. It requires a shifter that operates all possible displacements and provides possibilities of meaning for each new reader, even though language ages in space, time, and history.

In 1969 Eugene Nida and Charles Taber proposed a model ("the second system of translation") as an alternative to what they call "the first model" (word-for-word translation), consisting of

> a more elaborate procedure comprising three stages: (1) analysis, in which the surface structure (i.e., the message as given in language A) is analyzed in terms of (a) the grammatical relationships and (b) the meanings of the words and combinations of words; (2) transfer, in which the analyzed material is transferred in the mind of the translator from language A to language B; and (3) restructuring, in which the transferred material is restructured in order to make the final message fully acceptable in the receptor language. (33)

In this statement they deal with translation as what we may call "a mental and abstract process," as something that goes beyond the personal restraints of the individuals who are doing the work. This is why their model has been useful for translation machines. But if we are dealing with literature (that is, with inscriptions of passions, feelings, experiences, and bodies in a text), the passions, feelings, experiences, and bodies of the translators cannot be erased easily. The translator acts through what has been vaguely defined as "intuition," connecting with the text as a living other with whom the translator establishes a dialogue. There is no abstraction in reading a poem. If it touches us it is not because a mechanism for touching is already there, waiting to be put to work, but as a result of our reading. Its presence is always a posteriori. The opposition between "reason" (abstract) and "intuition" (irrational) does not work at all in this matter, as anyone who has translated poetry knows.

Translating as Re/Writing

Usually the work of translation has been understood from three possible perspectives, often considered exclusive of one other:

1. Translation as the transmission of content.
2. Translation as transmission of formal structures.
3. Translation as *glosa* or new text created from the model provided by the text to be translated.

The translators of the first group consider the essence of their task to be the rendering of a specific content. That content, which supposedly is something separate from the form, is what should be retained and not lost in translation. The result is that it is translated into another language-system, whether or not it is translated into another language. As an example we could mention here the translation of a classical text (in medieval English, French, or Spanish) into a modernized language. The translators of the second group, seeking to render the formal structures, face substantially the same problem, with similar theoretical presuppositions.

The second group privileges in the polar-opposite way from the first group. Agustín García Calvo chose the second option for his bilingual English-Spanish edition of Shakespeare's sonnets. In his translations he tries to maintain the consonant rhyme and adapts the iambic pentameter of the original to the Spanish hendecasyllable. As an example of erudition the result is brilliant. From a poetic perspective, however, it is disappointing to the same degree. An apparently contradictory example to this way of translating is Joan Triadú's Catalan versions of forty sonnets. Let's look at an example where both Triadú and García Calvo seem to be trying to maintain the formal devices previously discussed. Here is the first quartet of sonnet 113:

Since I left you, mine eye is in my mind,
And that which governs me to go about,
Doth part his function, and is partly blind,
Seems seeing, but effectually is out;

Joan Triadú translates:

Tinc, des que us vaig deixar, els meus ulls a la ment;
i allò que em dirigeix per moure'm a la vora,
fa en part el que ha de fer, pero en part cegament.
Sembla que miri enllà però l'esguard és fora.

Here is the corresponding translation by García Calvo:

Desde que te dejé, mi ojo en mi alma está,
y lo que me gobierna para echar el paso
en parte aún funciona, en parte ciego va;
parece ver, pero de hecho no hace caso.

We can see that the word choices are not equivalent. García Calvo translates "mind" as *alma* (soul), not *mente* (mind), which is not a well-justified semantic displacement. *Mente* instead of *alma* would imply in Spanish verse an added syllable, once the *sinalefa* (metrical elision) used in the couple *mi-alma* is taken out. That constriction, however, would be recovered in the French alexandrine utilized in this version, displacing the license to the couple *mi-ojo*, in which the actual structure would count three syllables instead of two had he used *mente*. Besides this, the grammatical sense is respected. The consonant rhyme obliges him to translate "to go about" as *echar el paso* and "is out" as *no hace caso*, which is somewhat odd in Spanish. The choice of blank verse would have perhaps allowed him to renounce the rhyme, to inscribe the meaning in other elements of the phrase and not necessarily in the form of equivalent phonemic groups at the end of the lines.

Triadú moves in a different way. It is true that the mono-syllabic structure of Catalan allows for an easier adaptation of the English rhythm than Spanish, which has a bisyllabic base and paroxytone accentuation. This fact explains why Catalan translations of English poetry usually "sound" better than Spanish ones (we remember T. S. Eliot's *Four Quartets* in the Catalan version of Alex Susanna and the Spanish one of Vicente Gaos, for instance), although both may be equally correct in grammatical and poetic terms. However, the differences in the two translated versions just quoted cannot be reduced to the specific characteristics of Spanish and Catalan. In fact, Triadú works more deeply by personalizing and subjectivizing Shakespearean imagery. "Mine eye" becomes "Tinc els meus ulls" ("I have my eyes"); "about" becomes "per moure'm a la vora" ("to move myself closely around"); "Seems seeing" becomes "Sembla que [jo] miri" ("It seems that I am looking at"). Obviously, the kind of work we have here goes beyond the repetition of the stanza and of the preservation of the rhyme. This work is a critical re/writing of the Shakespearean text that brings the translated text to life. In it, understanding the preservation of formal characteristics is secondary. It seems, after all, that Triadú's work cannot be classified within the second option.

Let's go to the third model of translation. Within this model we would have to distinguish between two groups: the first one (C_1) is made up of translators for whom the principal aspect of the work—beyond the problems of forms and contents—is to deal with that "something" mysterious (García Lorca used to define it as "goblin" [*duende*]) and untranslatable. These translators, faced with the impossibility of decanting one text into another, of simply reproducing, choose to do a reading *on* and not *from* the original text. Let's mention here, as we speak of Shakespeare, some of Leon Felipe's adaptations of Shakespearean plays (such as *El asesino del sueño,* based on *Macbeth*) or some of Leandro Fernández de Moratín's adaptations of Molière. Many critics maintain that in these cases the strong personality of the translator prevails over the text, resulting in a personal "new" author's work, rather than a translation. It is rarely accepted that the presence of the translator is always as inescapable as it is necessary. This presence is accepted as an "inevitable sin" when the translator is a well-known writer; but the translator is present in every good translation, for all good translators are writers even though they may have no production recognized as "original" and therefore cannot be socially classified as "writers." When I say that a good translator is always, at the same time, a good writer, I am referring to an operational way of describing work, not to a social or professional label. It is quite curious how often those who applaud the translations of Octavio Paz or Luis Cernuda vehemently attack those who dare work in a similar fashion without having the "institutional" literary stature of the former. It is as if the question resided in the mystique of social prestige rather than in the use of particular premises and operative methods of writing. This happens because underneath this glorification of the signature, instead of the analysis of the discursive device called subject-translator, what is at work in this kind of approach is the myth of "language" (both the one used in the "original" text and the one used for the translation) as a mere vehicle, as an empty form to be filled with contents.

The history of translation—where one can see how the very concept of translation is historical—uncovers this myth. Henry Meschonnic has shown how, in European culture and in the Near East, paraphrasing preceded translation. Targum (translation) was a mixture of paraphrasing and literalness. In the Middle Ages translation became a religious practice, and the question of literalness was avoided because the word itself was the locus of the sacred. The Renaissance, once it freed itself from the omnipresence of the word of God, moved toward a concept of "semantic equivalence," using paraphrasing for group effect. Fray Luis de León's translations of the Latin classics are a splendid example. During the seventeenth and eighteenth centuries, European culture came back to the Greek and Latin classics' idea of rewriting foreign works. Opposing "precision" to "beauty" was the inheritance of a Christian Western aesthetic of the dualism between "word" and "spirit." Romanticism, with its tendency toward individualism and particularism, brought literal translation, and toward the end of the century, this option became more emphatic in translations of the erudite type. This historical evolution of the work of the translator, marked by the evolution of the role and the function of translation, is usually dismissed by the mythification of the notion of language as a neutral vehicle, not to be transgressed except when the fetish of "social signature" offers an alibi. On the contrary, in contemporary twentieth-century literature we find the tendency to work toward a translation that is not literal, erudite, or a paraphrase. It is a creative type of translation that emphasizes the production of new meaning, that is, of a new text. This kind of work—which we should call "re-creative writing" in order to remain close to the ambiguous concept of "creation" that seems to define the "original"—constitutes a second typology (C_2), one that differs from C_1 not in its presuppositions but in the way used to solve the problems at work in translating.

For the translators belonging to this group, translation is a function in which both critical discourse and writing participate. To translate involves the textual interpretation of the text to be translated. This is what we should call "re/writing." It would be appropriate to clarify here that a re/written text, while constituting itself as different from the original, has no intentions to replace it—not out of modesty, but out of a theoretical and practical impossibility. What translation does is to displace and re/locate a text, making it a new element of the cultural universe where it is now inscribed; thus, translation makes the "original" contemporary for the present as well as for the space of its reading. To some extent, we could say that to write is to translate. In other words, it is to produce meaning while transforming actual actions and objects (concrete or abstract ones) into "discursive" actions or objects, or rather, into elements of a language-system. Therefore, while the so-called writing is always offered the possibility of being reworked in order to become a contemporary text for the reader, that privilege does not apply institutionally to translations, which are always dated. This circumstance has to do primarily with economic rather than with semantic reasons. In the end, it is a problem related to copyright, that is, to the introduction of the concept of private property into the territory of meaning. However, there are other arguments, somewhat less linked to the symbolic patterns of money, to justify this different treatment of the translator within social patterns of acceptance.

As I have discussed elsewhere, the object defined as "original" is an "open textual space" whereas the translation is a "closed text" (Company-Ramón and Talens). As such, it is a construction, the result of a process of interpretation/transformation of the possibilities offered by the textual space, and it is forced to remain within the semantic limits imposed by the latter. The room for the translator to operate has specific and clear borders that we can define in terms of *semantic restriction*. By this notion I refer to the need to take into account what the "original" actually means within a particular cultural and historical tradition to particular cultural and historical individuals. If we have to translate from medieval Spanish the word *aparescer* (to appear), we cannot forget that in that time this word meant "to be born." In this sense, one might say that the phantomatic connections we could establish around the use of this verb in a particular context must be left aside if we are translating. The multisignificance inscribed in a word can allow us to accept the drifting nature of the reading, but cannot erase the historical inscription of a historical meaning. This does not imply that this "meaning" belongs to the word. Rather, it belongs to the historical function of the word in a particular text. In this sense, the deconstructive approach is right in not accepting any hidden meaning within a text, as usually happens in hermeneutics, but at the same time, this absence of a hidden meaning does not eliminate the fact that a text had a particular function in a particular time. That historical function is what imposes semantic restrictions on an interpretation when we are translating. These restrictions are absent when we write an "original": we can feel free to move from one meaning to another, even if we are wrong in doing so. Most poems had their origin in misunderstandings. If a translation misunderstands, it can be a good text, even better than the original, but it is not a translation anymore. If the label were not so awkward, we should speak of a sort of deconstructive semiotics in order to deal with the problem of translation.

These considerations, although not eliminating the freedom of translators to integrate themselves into what they translate, do demarcate certain limits. To assume those limits or not is the difference between the two groups (C_1 and C_2). In both cases the results are personal texts of those who translate, but with the first group (C_1) the original remains, even if changed, incorporated to a new cultural context, and transformed. With the second group (C_2) one could hardly speak of "translation" because the "original" has practically disappeared.

We find the difference between translation and criticism in the object produced. Criticism develops its interpretation meta-linguistically and remains outside the textual space it is analyzing; translation constitutes itself through the same language-system of the original and substitutes for it. Let's look at two aspects of the problem in concrete examples, taken from my own work as a translator, so that we do not fall into the pretense of generalizing and being objective.

The first case is a poem by Georg Trakl, "Gesang des Abge-schiedenen." The word *Abgeschiedenen* appears twice in the poem, once in the title and once in the last line (the first time in the genitive singular and the second time in the genitive plural). The German term alludes to the condition of "being separated from," which implies a first literal value of "lonely" (separated from living beings) and a second symbolic value of "dead" (separated from life). Which one should one choose? Trakl does not specify, although one could speculate that the value of "lonely" would be lexically more precise. One could not make that first value obvious because it articulates the poem. When Ernst Edmund Keil and I translated this poem into Spanish in 1971 we opted for including "lonely" in the title and "dead" ("those who died") in the last line. This, we thought, enriched the meaning from the point of view of Spanish textuality. Both values combined; solitude is a form of death, and vice versa.

The second example deals with the incorporation of the translator as subject and as writing into the translated text. In 1972 Denis Roche published three versions (from poems by Ezra Pound, e. e. cummings, and Charles Olson) under the title *Trois pourrisements poétiques*. A year later two versions of Olson's poem "The Kingfishers" appeared in Spanish; one was published by Guillermo Carnero in the literary magazine *Trece de nieve* and another one by me in the section "Material inventari-able" in my book *El vuelo excede el ala*. If we compare the different options chosen in each case, perhaps they will shed some light on what I have been saying so far. The opening of the poem is a good case in point. Olson's line says:

What does not change / is the will to change

The three translations cited say:

(a) Ce ni que ne change pas / c'est la volonté de changer (Roche)
(b) La voluntad de cambio / es lo inmutable (Carnero)
(c) Lo que no cambia / es el deseo de cambiar (Talens)

From a lexical and syntactical point of view, all of them can be adapted to the Olson "original"; they are all within the pertinent limits imposed by the English text. However, there are elements that situate each option in a different space of meaning. The dynamic character of the verb form [Olson and versions (a) and (c)] is replaced in (b) by a static expression ("to change" for *de cambio*) and the concrete action by an abstract concept ("what does not change" for *lo inmutable*). From a lexical point of view, (a) and (b) translate "will" as *voluntad* and (c) translates it as *deseo*. Syntactically, the structure of the English "original" subject-verb-predicate is ambivalent because "what does not change" can be the subject and "the will to change" its predicate, or the other way around. This twofold possibility is maintained in (b) and (c) but disappears in (a), where the introduction of the *ce* (*c'est*) changes "the will to change" (*la volonté de changer*) into a subject. Generally, in ambivalent cases, the order privileges the value of subject for the term in the first position; (b) does this with *la voluntad de cambio* ("the will to change") and (c) with *lo que no cambia* ("what does not change"). As one can corroborate, "literalness" or "fidelity" toward the original means very little in this context. The three versions are "literal," but they do not have the same exact meaning. Roche published his version at the same time as *Le mécrit*, a work in which he announces his abandonment of poetry because of its own impossibility to exist ("La poésie est inadmissible / d'ailleurs elle n'existe pas," as he had written in a poem from 1968 included in *Le mécrit*). He pointed to the narrative collage as the only alternative to poetic discourse (his next book, *Louve basse*, provided a good example of it). In Carnero, the abstractions and the reduction to statism and privileged stature given to "will" as *voluntad* are coherent with his "original" writings of the time: *Variaciones y figuras sobre un tema de La Bruyère*, already finished but still unpublished when his version of Olson's poem came out, and the poems that later would become part of his book *El azar objetivo*. The tendency to abstraction as a form that allows us to overcome the impossibility of poetry to express ourselves (*El azar objetivo* contains the lines "In the emptiness / we engender no discourse / but only consciousness of emptiness") was at work both in his poetry and in his translations. Facing a similar kind of problematics, my *El vuelo excede el ala* and the poems later included in *El cuerpo fragmentario* proposed not to accept the abstraction and inhumanness of language but to try to disperse it by introducing in it the presence of consciousness as will and of the body as desire. Although the same poem was being translated, each translator was speaking from his own problematic and from his own perspective.[3]

The Master's Silence; or, Who Cares about Pure Languages?

Walter Benjamin, in an article published in 1923 as prologue to his German translation of *Tableaux parisiens* ("The Task of the Translator"), treats the problem in a different manner:

> [To allow the pure language to shine upon the original all the more fully] may be achieved, above all, by a literal rendering of the syntax which proves words rather than sentences to be the primary element of the translator. For if the sentence is the wall before the language of the original, literalness is the arcade. (79)

For Benjamin the concept of translation as vehicle is present, although he denies it explicitly—this is why he uses the word "transparent." He speaks of "pure language" (of which real languages would be nothing more than imperfect imitations), to which translation aspires. Translation "serves the purpose of expressing the central reciprocal relationship between languages" (72), and, therefore, "it is the task of the translator to release in his own language that pure language which is under the spell of another, to liberate the language imprisoned in a work in his recreation of that work" (80).

Benjamin's thesis is founded on the premise that "languages are not strangers to one another, but are, a priori and apart from all historical relationships, interrelated in what they want to express" (72). Thus, he opens his reflections with this explicit declaration of principles: "In the appreciation of a work of art or an art form, consideration of the receiver never proves fruitful" (69).

In Benjamin's opinion, any preoccupation with an "ideal" receiver of the work is detrimental to a theoretical approach to art. A poem, a symphony, a picture is never intended for a reader, a listener, or a beholder. In the same way, translations are not meant for readers who are not familiar with the original.

From the very beginning of his essay, then, Benjamin establishes a theoretical frame that locates the problematic of language within language itself. He is concerned very little with what is usually considered the "essential" character of a work of art: its meaning. In effect, when asking what a literary work "says" or what it communicates, Benjamin argues that for him a text "tells" nothing, or at least nothing relevant to those who understand it. Its essential quality is not based on the transmission of information. Thus, if a translation is made with the intent of reconstructing the meaning of a text, the process of translating constitutes the performance of something inessential.

However, Benjamin's arguments do not defend any essentialism such as "the mysterious," "the unfathomable," or the "poetic," which would lead us to the acceptance of the general idea that only a poet can be a good translator, because a poet is the only one able to serve the reader. Moreover, at the core of his essay we find the conviction that the more the translator recreates, the worse the translation is. The reason is clear: if the original does not exist for the readers' sake, why should the translation?

Benjamin tries to solve this kind of impasse by pointing to the difference between what he calls "objects intended" and "modes of intention." Crucial to his argument is the presupposed "translatability" of every human linguistic creation, even if no one should prove able to translate it. Translatability is an essential feature of a work; it indicates an intrinsic quality of the object, a specific significance inherent in the original that manifests itself in the translation. This quality, however, is not natural but cultural, not a quality that allows the original to survive in the historical process: "just as the manifestations of life are intimately connected with the phenomenon of life without being of importance to it, a translation issues from the original — not so much from its life as from its afterlife" (71).

This idea of life and afterlife should be regarded, Benjamin argues, with an entirely unmetaphorical objectivity, as the "range of life" is to be determined by history rather than by nature. Good translations — those that try to be more than a mere transmission of subject matter or meanings — come into being when the original has reached its fame in the course of its historical survival, when the translatability of the original has allowed the work to continue to exist even after its time is over. In this sense a good translation does not serve the work but exists only because of it. At the same time, it is in the translation that the life inscribed in the original attains its ever-renewed flowering.

If, according to Benjamin, all manifestations of life have their end not in life itself but in the representation of its significance, the translation ultimately serves "the purpose of expressing the central reciprocal relationship between languages." It is important to highlight that Benjamin refers here to a kind of higher and primordial Language, one that is pristine and universal, that differentiates itself from the known languages, and that underlies and grounds the historical languages as we know them. This primordial Language allows historical languages to differ in their manifestations but to agree in their essence. In arguing this way Benjamin is implicitly introducing the biblical metaphor of Babel as the locus where the one common language given by God to humans began its disintegration. Translation, thus, is a kind of task related to the discovery of the translatability of the work, or, in other words, of the reminiscences of that primordial language within the multiplicity of languages arisen after Babel.

This is why, as Benjamin points out, that "study appears to rejoin, after futile detours, the traditional theory of translation." If "the kinship of languages is to be demonstrated by translations, how else can this be done but by conveying the form and meaning of the original as accurately as possible?" (72). It is interesting, however, to note that Benjamin understands translating in dialogical terms, as a dialectical process in which both the language of the original and that of the translation are transformed:

> While a poet's words endure in his own language, even
> the greatest translation is destined to become part of the
> growth of its own language and eventually to be
> absorbed by its renewal. Translation is so far removed
> from being the sterile equation of two dead languages
> that of all literary forms it is the one charged with the
> special mission of watching over the maturing process of
> the original language and the birth pangs of its own. (73)

The relatedness of two languages, the possibility of communication between two linguistic systems that allows translatability, Benjamin says, does not reside in the similarity of words or of literary texts but in the intention underlying each language as a whole, "an intention, however, which no single language can attain by itself but which is realized only by the totality of their intentions supplementing each other: pure language" (74).

This idea of a "pure language," existing beyond all historical, concrete languages, is what allows the establishing of relations there where they did not previously exist, because "while all individual elements of foreign languages—words, sentences, structure—are mutually exclusive, these languages supplement one another in their intentions" (74). Here Benjamin establishes the previously mentioned distinction between "intended object" and "mode of intention." The words *Brot* and *pain,* for example, are different modes of intention because *Brot* means something different for a German than *pain* for a French speaker (or "bread" for a speaker of English). Both words, however, "intend" the same object and can therefore mean the same thing. The object here is complementary to the intention. If we leave aside the dialectical relationship between the "intended object" and the "mode of intention," the meaning can remain hidden in the language; that is, it is "there" somewhere in the language, but remains unperceived.

In my opinion, the extreme idealism of Benjamin's proposal resides in the implicit assumption about the existence of a meaning proper to each word, a meaning that can remain hidden in the language to which it belongs. In effect, signification for him is less the result of a historical process of reading than a quality to be discovered through a sort of "revelation," a flash, an illumination that comes to be when two languages come into contact and their elements conflict. For this reason, the use of the notion of history in the epistemological basis of his argumentation is paradoxical. With the term "history" Benjamin seems to indicate "diachrony," that is, merely a linear progression in time.

A word may have lost its original meaning with the passing of time; its connotative or sensory value may have deteriorated through use (what linguists call "lexicalization"). To rediscover its primordial value through a translation does not mean to historicize (contextualize) the use of that word, but to let surface something like the word's "real" value tarnished by time. Thus, Benjamin's assumption is that signification is not the product of a historical usage, but an intrinsic quality of the object, one that finds its raison d'être in someone's "intention" to signify a specific thing for a specific subject (social or individual). In his argumentation he does not explain either where to locate such intention as an objective mark or in which particular notion of "subjectivity" this intention inheres. The task of the translator therefore consists "in finding that intended effect (Intention) upon the language into [which] he is translating which produces in it an echo of the original" (76).

For this reason, the task of the poet and that of the translator are, for Benjamin, two definitely differentiated activities. The former cherishes a spontaneous, primary, and graphic "intention." The intention of the latter is instead derivative, ultimate, and ideational. He points to Luther, Voss, and Schlegel as examples of the superiority of the translator's accomplishment compared to that of the creator. The opposite is true in the case of Hölderlin or Stefan George.

We can notice in Benjamin's essay the assumption of a hierarchy in the two poles of "creation" and "translation," and although he explains that such a differentiation is based on what appears to be "use values," his argumentation is nonetheless articulated around the notion of "exchange values." In effect, what authorizes us to consider an "original" text superior to its translation but the social power of the signature, or, more concretely, what is called in modern times the copyright? The essential difference between Hölderlin's *Archipelago* and his translation of Sophocles lies in the fact that the former presents itself as an original text and the latter as a translation. How would the latter be considered if the original author had not been Sophocles but an unknown author whose existence had been known to Hölderlin alone, and if the translation had therefore been presented as an original text?

When Benjamin quotes Mallarmé—"The imperfection of languages consists in their plurality, the supreme one is lacking: thinking is writing without accessories or even whispering, the immortal word still remains silent; the diversity of idioms on earth prevents everybody from uttering the words which otherwise, at one single stroke, would materialize as truth"—and affirms as a comment that "translation, with its rudiments of such a language, is midway between poetry and doctrine" (77), he is proposing an important hypothesis that not only will remain undeveloped but will be diluted until it eventually disappears. In effect, to conceive of translation as an intermediary stage (here I am understanding "intermediary" to refer not to something that is "in between" but rather to a dialogic relation that operates in two directions at the same time) presupposes the introduction of the notion of work, of the production of meaning. That is, it means to locate translation and the so-called creation at a (relatively) similar discursive level. Thus an original text would produce meaning starting with the writer's work on shapeless material [personal or collective memory, imagination (another form of unconscious memory), reports, readings of other writers, and so on]. A translation would do the same but under more structured and defined constraints, which are imposed on the translater, as we argued before, by the already-fixed textual space of the so-called original work. The production of meaning, however, would function according to the same mechanism. All this seems to contradict the previous hypothesis that assumes that what translations do is not to produce a new original in a different language—a new referential universe, a new culture—but to discover the hidden, universal, and immanent meaning that underlies all originals, compared to the pure language before Babel.

In the arguments of his essay, Benjamin seems to take for granted the basic, elementary notion of "creation." "Creative writing" is, therefore, a historical or cultural label defining not a natural status of production but an institutionalized form of reception. To create, as a biblical term (as "Babel" itself is), means to make something out of nothing. This is the sense underlying the opening of Genesis. In the beginning was the Word—a sentence that, Benjamin says, applies to translating. In this way the writer becomes, as it was said in the nineteenth century, a metaphor for God. Translation in this context can be only a secondary task, like that of the interpreters of the Holy Scriptures. A translator cannot produce meaning but can only discover the hidden one.

This is why one of the theoretical problems arising in the discussion about translation is related to the dichotomy of fidelity and license. Benjamin explicitly denies the pertinence of this dichotomy but for very different reasons:

> The traditional concepts of any discussion of translations are fidelity and license—the freedom of faithful reproduction and, in its service, fidelity to the word. These ideas seem to be no longer serviceable to a theory that looks for other things in a translation than reproduction of meaning. (78)

In the translation of individual words, Benjamin argues, fidelity can almost never fully reproduce the meaning that words have in the original. Yet it is self-evident that in reproducing the form—what he calls "a literal rendering of the syntax"—fidelity hinders the rendering of the sense. Hölderlin's translation of Sophocles is again used as a paradigmatic example. Thus, for Benjamin, literalness can never be based on a desire to retain the meaning. On the contrary, what the language of translation has to do is "to give voice to the *intentio* of the original, not as reproduction but as harmony, as a supplement to the language in which it expresses itself, as its own kind of *intentio*."

Here again, as with the notion of creation, Benjamin takes for granted the notion of "original." To analyze what an original would mean, let us use the example offered by George Steiner at the beginning of his voluminous *After Babel: Aspects of Language and Translation*. Steiner analyzes the monologue by Postumo at the end of act 2 of Shakespeare's *Cymbeline*. Convinced that Iachimo has possessed Imogene, Postumo attacks the woman with anger:

> Is there no way for man to be, but women
> Must be half-workers? We are all bastards,
> And that most venerable man, which I
> Did call my father, was I know not where
> When I was stamp'd. Some coiner with his tools
> Made me a counterfeit: yet my mother seem'd
> The Dian of that time: so doth my wife
> The non pareil of this. O vengeance, vengeance!
> Me of my lawful pleasure she restrain'd,
> And pray'd me oft forbearance: did it with
> A pudency so rosy, the sweet view on't
> Might well have warm'd old Saturn; that I thought her
> As chaste as unsunnéd snow. O, all the devils!
> This yellow Iachimo, in an hour, was't not?
> Or less; at first? Perchance he spoke not, but
> Like a full-acorn'd boar, a German one,
> Cried "O!" and mounted; found no opposition
> But what he look'd for should oppose and she
> Should from encounter guard. Could I find out
> That woman's part in me—for there's no motion
> That tends to vice in man, but I affirm
> It is the woman's part: be it lying, note it,
> The woman's: flattering, hers; deceiving, hers;
> Lust and rank thoughts, hers, hers; revenges, hers;
> Ambitions, covetings, change of prides, disdain,
> Nice longing, slanders, mutability;
> All faults that name, nay, that hell knows, why, hers

In part or all: but rather all. For even to vice
They are not constant, but are changing still;
One vice, but of a minute old, for one
Not half so old as that. I'll write against them,
Detest them, curse them: yet 'tis greater skill
In a true hate, to pray they have their will:
The very devils cannot plague them better.

When we deal with such misogynous statements, are we really reading the "original Shakespeare"? What does "original" mean in Shakespeare? He wrote his play around 1611 and never published it. The first folio edition is dated 1623 and was probably written by using the manuscripts that someone—an actor, spectator, or friend of the author—gave to the publisher. The quarto edition differs in punctuation, distribution of lines, and even in words. The text Steiner quotes is taken from J. M. Nosworthy's edition in Arden. Here again there are variations in relation to both the folio and the quarto editions. The editor, throughout the text, substitutes whatever he believes to be a mistake in the *princeps*. He obviously follows some explicit guidelines, a certain logic. But what logic? The logic used to perform a critical edition, as it has been argued (see McGann, and Spadaccini and Talens) presupposes a certain truth, inscribed by the author in the author's original. When this original is missing, as with Shakespeare's plays, the *intentio auctoris* continues to be the scope of the editors, even if it is nothing but a construction institutionalized by historical and cultural interpretations about what had to be, in this particular case, the meaning of certain words and certain puns in seventeenth-century England.

Let's take, for example, following the line of Steiner's analysis, the interesting association established in the monologue between "stamp'd," "coiner," "tools," and "counterfeit." The connection between these words by their syntagmatic position in the text presents us with a flow of explicit and implicit significations. They are related both to the sexual and the monetary and at the same time to the connections that usually are at work in the innermost grounding of human behavior. The crook gives false money to the printing press to be stamped. The movement of printing-press parts can remind one of the movements of bodies during sexual intercourse. "Counterfeit" means to falsify, to feign, to pretend to be another. The *Oxford English Dictionary* quotes a different use for this word in 1577: "to adulterate." The mixing of "adulterate" (change) and "adultery" sounds possible, even if not etymologically correct. "Tools" has also a very rough sexual resonance. May there exist an echo of the word "stamp" in what the OED defines as having a double meaning in 1598: "movement of the hand when using a mortar" and, simultaneously, "to inflate when pumping"? "Pudency" means "susceptibility to shame." "Rosy pudency" is a blushing chastity. Moreover, the sexual connotations are at stake. "Pudenda" means at the same time "shame" and "sexual occasion for shame."

What exactly did Shakespeare have in mind? Aware of the repeated allusions to sexuality throughout his works that we, as readers, perceive, we can argue that he is presenting us with both possibilities at the same time. But this can only be the result of our perception. Even if these multiple and simultaneous interpretations are based on the agreement of many critics at different times, does that allow us to conclude that this was the specific meaning Shakespeare intended? Who cares about what Shakespeare had in mind? We deal with texts, not with minds. We try to understand what a text is saying to us through the dialogue we establish with it, but a text is always mute; we have to force it to speak. Our position, then, is that of an interpreter. If we deal with mystic poetry, for example, or with biblical texts, such as those of Solomon or David, can we say that they are metaphorical erotic texts? We are explaining with our own language and our personal ideas about the world in which we live what a silent page is unable to say. In other words, we are projecting over the text our own system of comprehending in order to make it comprehensible. Understanding is, then, a construction. So is writing; so is translation. To understand, Steiner argues, means to translate. It means to write, we can add, as well.

The case does seem to be different when the "author," that is to say, the person who gives her or his name as a signature to a text, sanctions with authorial authority the text as we know it. But what authorizes us to infer from this that what the author says or had in mind is what the text is saying? If we can translate an anonymous text—where the authority of the signature is absent—it is because there is no other authorial voice than the one we construct through reading and interpreting a text in order to allow it to make sense.

In her article "Genderizing Translation," for instance, Giulia Colaizzi, analyzing the problems of gender she found when translating into English one of my own Spanish poems, states how she was forced to deal with inscriptions I never thought could be present, even if her work demonstrates they were. What supposed intentional "authority" was she "discussing"? What allows me to be the "owner" of the final meaning, even of the English translation, but the institutional existence of the copyright?

The belief in a general truth coming from a primordial language that every writer is supposed to assume underpins Benjamin's argumentation. Because this primordial language is beyond history, Benjamin's analysis erases historicization in the process of signification.

In the last pages of his essay, we find something quite interesting in Benjamin's approach to the problem, something that goes beyond the limits of his almost theological conception of language. He deals with the idea that the interrelation of languages is an endless process of transformation and quotes Rudolf Pannwitz's observations in his *Die Krisis der europäischen Kultur*, ranking them, together with Goethe's *Notes* to *Westöstlicher Divan*, as the best comment on the theory of translation ever published in Germany until that time (1923):

> Our translations, even the best ones, proceed from a
> wrong premise. They want to turn Hindi, Greek, English
> into German instead of turning German into Hindi,
> Greek, English. Our translators have a far greater
> reverence for the usage of their own language than for
> the spirit of the foreign works. . . . The basic error of the
> translator is that he preserves the state in which his own
> language happens to be instead of allowing his language
> to be powerfully affected by the foreign tongue.
> Particularly when translating from a language very
> remote from his own he must go back to the primal

elements of language itself and penetrate to the point
where work, image, and tone converge. He must expand
and deepen his language by means of the foreign
language. It is not generally realized to what extent this
is possible, to what extent any language can be
transformed, how language differs from language almost
the way dialect differs from dialect; however, this last is
true only if one takes language seriously enough, not if
one takes it lightly. (80–81)

This is, probably, the most useful comment we find in Benjamin's essay. The expansion of the limits of the recipient language through the inclusion of foreign structures can operate even if the ghost of a primary God-like language before Babel does not appear in the horizon. In any case, going back to Benjamin's hypothesis about the similarity of languages, I believe that a translation has to begin with the assumption that languages are always foreign to each other and not only in an a priori manner. First, one cannot overlook the historical relations because they give meaning to language; they form it and deform it. Words are not empty signs but always refer us to a reality that they construct and make intelligible through linguistic formulations. Thought does not exist outside language; our capacity to know is linked to the possibilities language offers to create ways of knowing. These ways are always in language, through it, and for it. If we leave history aside, we leave language aside, because its signification and meaning are always historical. Today when we read a Góngora poem we are not reading what Góngora read while he wrote, nor do we read what a reader at that time read. We interpret from our time the words written at that time. Part of the signification field works in an unconscious manner in relation to the role of the word in its concrete historical context. The possibilities of understanding that role disappear if we ignore its given time-conditions. This is why any encounter with the past is never complete, but rather is always an encounter through the "thickness of the centuries" (Paul Zumthor). If this happens within the history of one language, how can we not apply it to the relationship of two languages and their respective histories?

In Benjamin we read that "it is plausible that no translation, however good it may be, can have any significance as regards the original" (71). From our previous explanations we can accept this premise only if we define translation as a neutral work of decanting. If, on the contrary, we think of it as re/writing, Benjamin's assertion would have little relevance. For better or for worse—that is an altogether different question—the translation does not "mean something for the original"; it "is" the original, made contemporary, revitalized, and offered from a new textuality.

Notes

Most of the ideas developed in this article were first present in the introductions to my Spanish translations of expressionist poetry (Stadler et al., 1972) and Hölderlin (1980). Giulia Colaizzi closely read and discussed this final version. I thank her for her criticism and suggestions and for allowing me to have access to her manuscript "Genderizing Translation."

1. By *saber* I mean accumulation, not always useful, of data; by *conocimiento*, a structured knowledge. English does not allow a distinguishing between these two Spanish terms, so I am using the only one I can.

2. By "language" I mean *lengua* (English, Spanish, German, and so on). By "language-system" I mean *lenguaje*, the semiotic concept of an articulated system of signs.

3. See the concept of "somatics of translation" in Douglas Robinson's highly challenging book *The Translator's Turn*, to which I did not have access until after this article was written.

Works Cited

Benjamin, Walter. "The Task of the Translator." In *Illuminations*, trans. Hannah Arendt. New York: Schocken Books, 1969. 69–82.

Carnero, Guillermo. *El azar objetivo*. Madrid: Trece de Nieve, 1975.

_____. *Variaciones y figuras sobre un tema de La Bruyère*. Madrid: Visor, 1974.

Colaizzi, Giulia. "Genderizing Translation." Paper presented at MMLA Annual Meeting, Chicago, 14 November 1991. Now in Spanish translation in Giulia Colaizzi, "Postestructuralismo y crisis de la modernidad." Diss., Univ. of Valencia, 1992.

Company, J. M., and J. Talens. "The Textual Space: On the Notion of Text." *M/MLA*, 17.2 (1984): D'Alembert.

Eliot, T. S. *Cuatro cuartetos*. Trans. Vicente Gaos. Barcelona: Barral, 1970.

_____. *Cuatre quartets*. Trans. Alex Susanna. Barcelona: Cuaderns Crema, 1982.

Hölderlin, Friedrich. *Las grandes elegías*. Ed. and trans. Jenaro Talens. Madrid: Hiperión, 1980.

McGann, Jerome. *The Textual Condition*. Princeton, N. J.: Princeton Univ. Press, 1991.

Meschonnic, Henry. *Pour la poétique.* Vol. 2. Paris: Gallimard, 1973.

Nida, Eugene, and Charles Taber. *The Theory and Practice of Translation.* Published for the United Bible Societies. Leiden: E. J. Brill, 1969.

Olson, Charles. *Los martín-pescadores.* Trans. Guillermo Carnero. Madrid: Trece de Nieve, 1973.

Robinson, Douglas. *The Translator's Turn.* Baltimore: The Johns Hopkins Univ. Press, 1991.

Roche, Denis. *Le mécrit.* Paris: Editions du Seuil, 1972.

_____. *Trois pourrissements poétiques.* Paris: L'Herne, 1972.

Shakespeare, William. *40 sonets.* Ed. Joan Triadú. Barcelona: Edicions Proa, Ayma, 1970.

_____. *Cymbeline.* Ed. J. M. Nosworthy. London: Methuen, 1955.

_____. *Sonetos.* Ed. Agustín García Calvo. Barcelona: Anagrama, 1974.

Spadaccini, Nicholas, and Jenaro Talens, eds. *The Politics of Editing.* Minneapolis: Univ. of Minnesota Press, 1992.

Stadler, Ernst, Georg Heym, and Georg Trakl. *Poesía expresionista.* Ed. and trans. Ernst Edmund Keil and Jenaro Talens. Valencia: Hontanar, 1972. (2d ed., rev. Madrid: Hiperión, 1981.)

Steiner, George. *After Babel: Aspects of Language and Translation.* New York: Oxford Univ. Press, 1975.

Talens, Jenaro. *El vuelo excede el ala.* Las Palmas de Gran Canaria: Inventarios Provisionales, 1973.

Zumthor, Paul. *Langue, texte, énigme.* Paris: Editions du Seuil, 1977.

◆ Chapter 2

The Television Newscast: A Postmodern Discourse

Jesús González-Requena

(translated by Silvia L. López)

Today's News Discourse

The production of reality today—that is, the production of those discourses that constitute it and that make consensus possible—demands enlargement and adaptation of the technology of the past into today's "mass communication media."

The reason is unmistakable: the expansion of the capitalist market, the Industrial Revolution, and the progressive antagonism of scientific discourses in the configuration of reality accelerate the transformation of reality itself. The expansion of forces of production and the multiplication of specifically scientific and technological codes constitute two aspects of a movement that expands the order of the commodity into the most unimaginable segments of the real (the prolific taxonomies in the novels of Jules Verne are witnesses of this process).

In this process of permanent acceleration, the present becomes a ceaseless crossroad: that of the constant rediscursivization of reality. The newspaper originated in the construction and expansion of the capitalist market and was firmly established with the Industrial Revolution. Its function is to consolidate the multiple discourses, or at least the echoes of the multiple discourses, that exist in the social space, in the production of an image that validates the present. The structure of the newspaper itself, a web of relatively hierarchized fragmented discourses, is an expression of its function. Eliseo Verón refers to this when he affirms that "the news media are the place in which industrial societies produce our reality" (xi).

One should clarify here the definition of news discourse that we have today. It begins with the newspaper and then is affirmed through radio and television. Today's news discourse aims to produce the social present through the promotion of systematic, discursive, and narrative events. In this sense we can say that the present — its time and rhythm — are the effect of the structural sense of today's news discourse. The fundamental operation through which this process takes place is the selection of certain events (located in the space of the real) and their conversion into social events initiated in a process of discursivization and narration that makes "the news."

Today's news is the field in which a particular semiotic apparatus (the languages and codes with which a collectivity configures its present) and the undifferentiated flux of the events of the real meet. The semiotic apparatus presents real events — which in themselves are absolutely singular and therefore insignificant — and names them, categorizes them, makes them significant through conceptualization and narrativization, and connects them through syntactic chains that are simultaneously temporal and causal. This is how a discourse that chains social events is generated. The news discourse generates meaning at two levels:

1. The micro level: the occurrence is constituted as event (conceptualized and narrativized).
2. The macro level: the present results from the totality of events. The present's cohesion depends on its being intelligible, which in turn depends on the rhythm (and time) and on the dramatic quality of its representation.

We can say that the existence of the present presupposes a certain notion of the present: the present as a dimension essentially changeable, submitted to a rapid transformation. The explanation is obvious. When today's news discourse did not exist or when the world was smaller — as we know, the "size of the world" is an economic question: the world gets bigger as the market gets bigger — then time was lived as possessing a slower and more stable rhythm.

The Newscast: Staging and Enunciation

The name "newscast" itself reveals, in its many versions, a journalistic origin. The newscast discourse emerges daily to present us with systematic information about today's world. But this discourse differs fundamentally from its journalistic ancestors, in precisely the same way in which reporting differs from a documentary—and on an even bigger scale from the difference between the cinematic tradition and the television tradition. This difference lies in the emergence of a subject of enunciation.

As we know, the newspaper reserves codified spaces, including designed spaces, for the discourses articulated in subjective enunciation, such as the spaces for "editorials" and "opinions." The rest of the paper, 90 percent or more of it, is dedicated to nonsubjective enunciation. That is the dominant norm. It is a double norm, in which the nonsubjective enunciation predominates and expresses the separation of "informational space" from that reserved for "commentary." Upon these spaces the press has constructed the ideology of objective information that many journalists and researchers still anachronistically try to use to conceptualize the functioning of televised news.

Historically, state television stations in Europe have sought to organize themselves around this model and have tried to frame the discursivity of their newscasts in terms of nonsubjective enunciation. The facts, and not the people announcing them, were supposed to play the main part in the discourse. To a large extent, the old European states staked their entire image of seriousness, rigor, and austerity on this premise.

In complete contrast to this is the dominant formula of the American newscast, which is essentially organized around the personalization of the informative act. In this type of newscast, news anchors explicitly assume for themselves the powers of interpretation, investigation, or dramatization explicit in the facts.[1]

However, even in the old objectivist European model, the form imposed itself only at the level of speech. The texts were, without doubt, written within the objectivist rhetoric of the national press. The visual texts were organized in terms of subjective enunciation. The word, adjusted and written within the objective canon of the press, was being read by someone to the camera. The visual figure of the speaker emerged not only on the surface of discourse but became from the first moment, through its systematic reappearance, the axis that structured the newscast in its entirety.

Even if one were to prohibit newscasters from interpreting the events that are being narrated, or to stop them from embodying a narrating subject, they would still manifest themselves as the ones who make an appeal to viewers—looking into their eyes and offering them information. Furthermore, in the various types of news reporting prior to the newscast, the figure of the reporter was inscribed as the one who ordered, told, interpreted, questioned, and dramatized the facts. Reporters never enjoyed their own space in the visual universe of the report because their universe is always the universe of facts, which always points to the referential context. In the newscast, however, news anchors walk amid the space of events through exchange with correspondents, reporters, and others with whom they explore the different universes that configure the present. In this way newscasters inhabit, in a stable fashion, their own space. This space is radically different from the space of events and, for that reason, impermeable to the logic of those events; it is a constant space that, because it is the space of the newscaster, presupposes the direct staging of the communicative context.

In the traditional European model, the presence of the narrator did not personalize the discourse of the news because this personalization would have contradicted the model's objectivist rhetoric. On the contrary, the objective was the depersonalization of the text read by the narrator to the camera. The body language and voice were supposed to be controlled, the clothes simple, and all unnecessary body movement suppressed. The message was: "I, the narrator, do not speak. I read. I am the spokesperson of a discourse that has been produced somewhere else, not by a human being but by an essentially objective machine."

Why, then, have a narrator physically present in front of the cameras? Why employ a subjective visual enunciation when the person embodying the enunciation is prohibited from making

physical gestures and comments? Why have such a high percentage of repeat images of the narrator in a set devoid of information when the objective is to offer the greatest amount of information? The answer is simple, but to attain it, we must
recognize a problem of staging.

The problem lies in how to stage the present. Someone could
say that it is simple: just transmit live. But this position ignores
the fact that what is live is determined only by the viewer. When
someone says, "We are transmitting live," the viewer can decide
to believe this statement or not. This points us to an ontological
question, to the question of the temporality of being that is
shown. Concretely, the problem, independently of whether
transmission is live or not, is how to produce the effect of being
live. How should the discursive be configured in order to produce the effect of the feeling of being live? The news offered on
the newscast is already past, even if only from the immediate
past (days, hours, minutes). For that reason, to submit those images to the newscast is to submit them to the register of the past.
Yet the idea of the newscast is to name the present, to affirm itself in it. This is why it is crucial that a subjective enunciation
allow the presence of the discursive in the present of the enunciation. The fact that the absolute present of the event is impossible is not important, so long as the discourse is organized
around the absolute present of the enunciation of the event, the
present of the communicative act itself.

In the European newscast the narrator is there not so much to
personalize it as to allow for a staging of the communicative context as an expansion of the present of the enunciation.[2] The narrator is the one who gives testimony to the "live" character of
some segments of the broadcast. From the position of the testi-
monial present, the narrator can announce the live character of
the segment that follows. This operation is achieved through a
cessation of the word and the image because the present belongs to the one who owns the word; that is, it can be accounted
for only by the word. Granting the present to the images that
follow is basically granting a person—the reporter—the use of
the word and of the image.

The newscast is organized around the systematic articulation
of two essentially heterogeneous spaces: (1) the space of the

world or the referential context and (2) the news space or the communicative context. The former is the space where the events take place; the latter is the space where the events are named and offered, constructed and in-formed.

An obvious difference exists between these spaces. The space of the events is always changing, multiple, and heteroclitic; the space of the enunciation of those events, in contrast, is always constant. Rain or shine, whether at Christmas or during an international economic crisis, the space of the enunciator is always constant. This constancy vis-à-vis a world in continuous transformation and conflict constitutes a guarantee of stability. Events occur rapidly, but the order of information is maintained. This tranquilizing effect is not the only one deducible from this asymmetry, that is, this opposition between the variability and elusiveness of the space of the world and the constancy and identity of the news space. The space of the world is the space of singularity (fleeting, unrepeatable images of the world); the news space is the space of the conceptual. In the latter, the word is privileged over other significant parameters, such as narrator and set. This privileging of the word comes about through the neutralization, by the word's constancy, of the other significant parameters; with a constant newscaster and set, variation only occurs at the verbal level through the new information communicated. And in the news space, the images that appear function as visual concepts of one sort or another— symbols, emblems, graphics, maps, and so on. The news space, like the space of the event, is captured by the concept. It is made intelligible. The news is born and the absolute present that this space generates is precisely the present of the produced news. In fact, the most characteristic scenographic traits of the newscast are eloquent in this produced sense: it is a space that is deconstructed, open, and flat, in which nothing is in the way of the display/appearance on the screen of the lights illuminating the newscasters or the dark and undecorated areas of the set. It is a space completely organized for the cameras, which often bring attention to themselves; far from hiding, they are exhibited and thus exhibit at the same time the production process of the newscast itself.

In the news images (where the traditional ideology of media says that the event manifests itself in the most direct way), contemporary newscasts present themselves as manipulative spaces, as discursive articulation. In this radical gesture the image is presented as image, as something different from the reality that visual technologies make possible. The images appear to move toward the spectator. Modern news discourse clearly states that the news image offered to the viewer does not represent the real. Rather, it is an image that is manipulable and manipulated and that approaches the viewer from a distant transmitter.

The difference in enunciative strategies between the traditional European televised discourse and the American one is not so much the subjective modality of enunciation but the degree of personalization that the latter expresses. The American model emphasizes the individualized performance of the star reporter: the anthropomorphization of the instance that carries out the informing act, which in doing so almost inevitably strengthens the imaginary bond between the television and the viewer. In the European model, on the other hand, the transmitting institution demonstrates its performance above the concrete subjects that embody its word, making explicit the discursive character of the informing act.

In any case, the informing space is presented to us as a realm in which the news—that is, the different segments that constitute the newscast—is articulated in order to configure a global discourse about the present. Although the segments of this discourse are necessarily narrational because they correspond to the diverse news of the day, the discourse in itself is not narrational. The newscast is in this sense like a synchronic cut of the multiple open narratives in the social fabric. The verbal formulas that newscasters use to pass from one news item to another are very expressive of this: "Meanwhile in Melbourne . . . ," "In the meantime, on the other side of the ocean . . . ," "Also in Europe. . . . "

We do not mean to say that the present is born there; we only affirm that that is where the production of the present is staged. Even if the present continues to be a discursive question, it is already born in other, sometimes secret, spaces.

Fragmented Reality

Reality is the realm of an organized, categorized, predictable world, where the singular obeys the law, where meaning reigns. In other words: the reality of the world exists only insofar as it is submitted/subject to the order of discourse. This is the reality principle of Freud.[3]

In opposition to it we have the real, which is the realm of the uncategorizable, of the chaotic, of the unpredictable, where the singular is affirmed in all its irreducibility, in its radical capacity to make meaning impossible. The real escapes the order of discourse. The split that separates one from the other, which delineates the threat of the real, is in our time more pronounced than it was in past times.[4] The reason is the debunking of all mythic narratives—religious, philosophical, utopian—that gave cohesion to reality. What is perhaps the most radical paradox of our time is thereby produced. Although we find ourselves with more codes, more discursive apparatus, more specialized fields of knowledge—in sum, a more refined semiotic apparatus to configure reality—at the same time we find ourselves in the most fragile reality of times, more and more threatened by shadows than at any other time in history. Thus, in spite of all the discursive richness, in spite of all the symbolic and technological power we have over it, our present world lacks the symbolic dimension that could bring cohesion to the whole.

The enrichment of the semiotic apparatus (the totality of all of the codes by which we operate around the real) generated by a proliferation of scientific and technological findings runs parallel to a very accentuated crisis of the symbolic dimension of discourse. In the absence of this dimension, the discourses of science and technology, as well as the discourses of common sense, become functionalized, limiting themselves in their semantic realm strictly to criteria of efficacy and in this way emptying themselves of any transcendental dimension. The emblem of communicative function, of efficacy in operation, is translated into a demand for maximum transparency. This is the last common space that the ideologies of communication share.

Here an important doubt arises: the demand for a transparent world, lacking in opacity, fully intelligible, embodies a fantasy of omnipotence as well as a paranoid rejection of the real. This could not be any other way. No matter how much reality expands under the order of the functional sign, so intimately related to the order of the commodity, and no matter how much its interventions proliferate on the order of reality, the real continues to be there. It is there even when its borders seem displaced and even when its radical opacity is in violent contrast to the discourse of transparency. The effect is inevitable: if reality lacks symbolic cohesion, it is found to be breakable, fragmented, even broken.

The Present as Threat

Jean-François Lyotard has described how the effects of this fragmentation are noticeable in the realm of historical discourses. Stripped of all mythical support, from all capacity to fabulate the future, history becomes full of uncertainty. And if the past, even when full of confusions, can retain a certain texture—few segments of reality are as evidently discursive as the past—the present becomes intolerable.

This result is inevitable, for if there is a realm in which the real threatens continuously to destroy the fabric of reality, that realm is, without a doubt, the present. The present is a space of the emergent, the new, the singular, and the unpredictable. If during the times in which mythic discourses used to inscribe on the origins or on the borders a determined symbolic number that permitted the cohesion of the past with the future, the present would be the hinge of time in a contemporaneity emptied of all symbolic notation. The present would become the rift where the past could at any moment dissolve. Something can always happen that can result in the emptying out of the meaning of the discourses of the past, that can destroy the models of intelligibility that constitute History.

The task of contemporary news discourses is delineated thus: to respond to this rift from which the real threatens the order of reality.

Scenography of a Postmodern Present

The newspaper was once the most characteristic medium of mass communication. It was the exemplary discourse of the Industrial Revolution. Its discursive structure, without precedent in the history of discourse, was fragmented in a mosaic of multiple news and yet hierarchized and ordered by a whole network of indicators that designated the magnitude and importance of each news item. In addition, the editorial line maintained a cohesion and manifested itself in a privileged space within the whole of the newspaper. This was ideal for confronting a reality continually subjected to accelerated change in the era of the commodity, science, and technology. Because of its fragmentation, this structure was particularly apt for rendering an account of the heteroclitic profusion of transformations to which reality was seen to be subject, and, at the same time, for realizing an opportune global rediscursivization of reality through the mechanisms of hierarchization and editorialization.

But those enlightened times have passed when the newspaper, looking at history, was certain that it was on its way toward the establishment of the rule of Reason. Gone too are the times of the Industrial Revolution, when the discourse of the newspaper announced the path to technological happiness. Also gone are the times of the party newspapers, in which the project of a new—or old—society allowed for the organization of discursive fragments. In semiotic terms, we can say that today's news discourse, whether in the press, on radio, or on television, lacks a symbolic dimension that would allow for an articulation of all the discursive fragments—fragments of reality—that constitute it. It needs to look for its isotopy, for the key to its semantic coherence, somewhere else: no longer in myth, or in the fabulation of the future, or even in the promise of (some) meaning that might be glimpsed on the horizon, but rather in the present itself. The present is the only isotopy that current news discourse has once reality has been broken.

But the present should be understood not as an epoch or a period, not even as a stage, but rather as an unstable threshold. Disjointed and confused reality does not find affirmation in the ideological realm, lacking semantic density and discursive cohesion; it affirms itself only in the incessant mutation, in the vertigo of its own acceleration.

If the newspaper was the exemplary genre of the Industrial Revolution, the television newscast is the genre of the postmodern world. This is essentially a scenographic question: the newscast is the medium that can produce the most complete mise en scène of the present. The deployment strategies of enunciative displacement are crucial in these media. The newspaper has an impersonal tone (nonsubjective enunciation); the newscast has multiple enunciative interventions, at least on the visual plane. In the newscast, while there is a proliferation of formal enunciative interventions, the space essential to the newspaper, the editorial space, disappears. The enunciative gesture of the editorial was of considerable semantic weight. With the disappearance of this space in the newscast, we are faced with the disappearance of the editorial line that determined the criteria of selection, magnitude, and treatment of each of the news fragments. The semantic weight that accompanied the gestures of enunciation is gone. This is why the role of the newscaster is not to take the word as if it were the speaker's own, as in an editorial, but to administer the chaotic profusion of words, signs, and events that reverberate in a confused world.

Even when the newscast tries to make intelligible each of its fragments, it fails, and it fails completely when it tries to make intelligible the totality of all the fragments.[5] Here we have the manifestation of the paradox once again: the reiterated presence of the newscaster, an anthropomorphic embodiment of discursive enunciation, guarantees the cohesion of the exclusively formal character of the newscast. But in the extreme it is only the present and its scenographic figures that formally give coherence to discourse (beyond which the reality of the world appears multiple, fragmented, and unintelligible).[6]

In the staging of the present the most formal characteristics of the newscast find their function: on one hand, the emergence of the figure of the newscaster, who directs the use of the word, and, on the other hand, the staging of a communicative space, from the transversal to the referential space, from which the newscaster interrogates the viewer. It is in this constant communicative interrogation that the present is given its name, or perhaps also constructed scenographically, utilizing the news, the events, the referential universe as an alibi, as that object that is offered "live" and in the present, independent of its relevance.

In light of this gesture of offering, the news is always old: it has happened already. Its time is the time of the utterance. The communicative space that promotes "live" interrogation is the space in which the spoken present is transformed into the key upon which everything rests.

Vertigo of the Real

The present that current news discourse produces is, as we have tried to demonstrate, a scenographic, enunciative, and syntactical present, but essentially a nonsemantic present. The hodgepodge of news, of fragments of the world, does not return to us a unified idea of the world. It does not construct a recognizable and constant narrative universe because the present of the news discourses lacks narrative dimension. It is as if time had dislocated itself while trying to give an account of it all.

The world has exploded into microworlds permeable to each other. Time has exploded into an infinity of asynchronic times. The television newscast is the best witness to our contemporary world's extreme incapacity to discursivize time. In the end, only a purely formal, scenographic, syntactic, rhetorical coverage unites the present of the world at the same time that it renounces any properly semantic construction and all efforts to endow it with meaning. With the loss, then, of any unified notion of time (such is the postmodern condition), the present that news discourse produces can no longer be a hinge between past and future because the past has become questionable and the future unknowable. The more opaque the world, the more spectacular it becomes.

Reality, confused and disjointed, and incapable of affirming itself in the ideological realm, affirms itself in the vertigo of its own acceleration. There is something very exciting about this. It is fascinating to observe the velocity of the newscast (of words, of news items, of different planes) independent of its content, the rapid movement of appearance and disappearance of the news items themselves, and also of the broadcasting of the news. These two cycles tend to be confused with each other. There is a certain enjoyment in the cadence and in the acceleration. That is right: the word is enjoyment. But this word is meant here not in a gratuitous, "metaphorical" sense: there is a certain enjoyment insofar as the real[7] is at stake.

As we have noted, beyond the effort to make every event intelligible by inserting it into a more or less flimsy narrative framework, there is an implicit renunciation of any attempt at making the newscast intelligible as a whole. Thus the world—and reality, since that is the topic of the newscast—is presented as fragmented, incoherent, broken, and somewhat opaque: that is, unintelligible and unmanageable. The real is, therefore, what is indicated here.

In this context the television image acquires an unexpected autonomy, by which it exhibits what within it escapes from the strictly informational order and from the whole economy of the sign. This is where the desire to know and the demand for an intelligible world tend to end. Another desire occupies their place: a desire for the spectacular. The spectacular (the capacity to satisfy a certain eminently visual desire) is part of an extrainformative variable of the news whose weight in news discourses increases progressively. On many occasions, the existence or nonexistence of visual material or its degree of visual attraction has a decisive influence on the place of insertion of the news into the informational chain. Consequently, visual material both affects the meaning and alters the dimension of the event. In a kind of boomerang effect, the real so systematically excluded from the entire spectrum of reigning television discourses makes its comeback through this crevice and feeds the other great information spectacle: that of the sinister, crime, suicide, war, and catastrophe.

The body thus becomes the great protagonist. This is not the symbolic body (conceptual, categorical), or the imaginary body (seductive, the body of identification). This is the body of the real, fiercely singular, wounded by time, marked by sexual difference, inexorably seized by death. And through this we can read certain peculiarities of the newscasters: their maniacal gestures, the unusual brightness of their eyes, the intensity of their words. . . . To the degree to which the newscast occupies the place of the circus, the newscaster is something of the ringmaster. News anchors speak from their space of security, which, like a decompression chamber, isolates but also protects us. From this space they announce that there is something beyond, in the world (in pieces of the world, to be more precise): the real, the fateful, the sinister. And the cameras, like the maniacal look of the newscaster, have captured that something.

Thus the newscast returns to us the fragmented body of the world, the disjointed reality: a hodgepodge of fragments that are decontextualized among themselves but find a common denominator in their exhibition for eyes ready to enjoy them.

Notes

1. European television is coming closer to this model now, as one can observe in the rapid personalization of newscasts there.

2. The newscasts that emphasize the coverage of immediate events tend to put into place a process of scenographic inscription of the communicative text on the always-constant stage where the newscaster appears at the beginning and end of each report. Understanding this deployment as mere framing would be a mistake. It has as its function the inscription of an absolute present of the communicative act, an inscription that directs the economy of the whole group of reports presented.

3. This is why accepting the reality principle means essentially accepting the necessity for the law.

4. Julia Kristeva points out that "the great commotion experienced by speaking subjects today can be summarized in this way: the truth which these subjects are searching for is the real. A preoccupation throughout history, this experience today becomes, if not something of the masses, then at least something massive and grave, and all the more so since there is no common code that can neutralize it, thereby justifying it" (15).

5. Philip Schlesinger states, "There is an inherent tendency for the news to be framed in a discontinuous and ahistorical way, and this implies a truncation of 'context,' and therefore a reduction of meaningfulness. For news is, after all, not history. It is, if anything, history's antithesis" (105).

For his part, Pierre Moeglin has described "an economy of discontinuity that relies on the juxtaposition of provisional, instantaneous, fragmented, relative and local points of view without reference to what could be a total vision" (16)

A. Weber has indicated how this discontinuity is intensified by the way materials are handled: "Recourse to hyperfragmentation in the montage of archival materials is often explained by the impossibility of lengthening materials filmed thirty years ago. However, rather than keeping them integral, the journalist cuts them up and makes them so brief that they become intelligible only through the commentary of what they are supposed to represent" (53).

6. Luca Balestrini says that "the staging of something nonfictional produces an experience of disorganized time, not only deritualized but traceable to that semantic trauma that had become individuated in the staging of the functions of space. The ritual aspect is recovered in the plane of enunciation. . . . Deritualizing the content, the mise en scène ritualizes itself . . . [and] the discursive time of the event is reconstructed in the unity of the time of fruition. The temporal experience of the events, disorderly and traumatic, is unified in the experience of textual fruition" (45).

7. The "real" should be understood here in a Lacanian sense.

Works Cited

Balestrini, Luca. *L'informazione audiovisiva: Problemi di linguaggio*. Turin: ERI, 1984.

Habermas, Jürgen. *The Structural Transformation of the Public Sphere: An Inquiry into a Category of the Public Sphere*. Cambridge: MIT Press, 1989.

Freud, Sigmund. *Civilization and Its Discontents*. Trans. James Strachey. New York: W. W. Norton & Company, 1962.

González-Requena, Jesús. *El espectáculo informativo. O la amenaza de lo real*. Madrid: Akal, 1989.

Kristeva, Julia. *Loca verdad*. Madrid: Fundamentos, 1985.

Lyotard, Jean-François. *The Postmodern Condition: A Report on Knowledge*. Minneapolis: Univ. of Minnesota Press, 1984.

Moeglin, Pierre. "De l'usage du duplex au journal télévisé." *VVAA: La mise en réprésentation de l'information à la télévision*. Paris: INFORCOM, 1984.

Schlesinger, Philip. *Putting "Reality" Together: BBC News*. London: Constable, 1978.

Verón, Eliseo. *Construir el acontecimiento*. Buenos Aires: Gedisa, 1983.

Weber, A. "Audio-Visuell: montage et contraintes idéologiques du journal télevisé." *Cahiers du CRELEF* 19 (1984): 53–62.

◆ **Chapter 3**
Architectures of the Gaze

Santos Zunzunegui

(translated by Silvia L. López)

I shall begin with something evident. Museums—in particular, fine arts museums—have become in modern societies, at least in those that became what they are under the revolutionary impulse of Enlightenment philosophy, an exemplary space in which unanimous commemoration can take place. They are a space where the secular ritual occurs, through which a community sanctions a number of cultural achievements. Although these achievements bring an individual character to the community, at the same time they are supposed to link it to the whole of humanity in the realm of the spirit. These spaces have been designed for the euphoric exercise of a lay liturgy, a liturgy made possible through the creation of a space for the holding of works, previously defined as artistic, that tries to create a paradigmatic situation that provides for the reformulation of relations between the visible world of present objects and the invisible world of the signification embedded in them.

The museum is a space dedicated to the Muses, and by logical extension it is destined to hold works representative of the human spirit. It is a heterotopic and heterochronic space that through its particular rules of exclusion and inclusion, of openings and closures, allows for the anchoring of utopian illusions of totality and permanence in the contingent reality of selection and in the inevitable usury of time (Foucault 14-15). That same gesture, by inaugurating those *other* spaces, is what facilitated the emergence of what Rudolf Arnheim has called the "necessary frontiers of understanding": alienation (or defamiliarization) as gesture destined to render intelligible all that is isolated, demarked, and, therefore, ordered.

A Pedagogy of the Gaze

In this way, the conditions were created for the emergence of a double polarity that since its origins has marked the museum form. This form is exalted because it tries to isolate and arrange a privileged territory where intellectual and aesthetic experience can occur in what are considered exemplary conditions. This form is condemned because it takes the artwork out of its original locus, thereby altering its original purpose as well as the original conditions of its reception.

These are precisely the presuppositions, and at the same time the limitations, that made possible within rationalist and Enlightenment ideology the creation of a paradigm. This paradigm, while breaking with the privacy and heterogeneity that supported the *Kunstkammern* and *Wunderkammern* of the collectors and amateurs of the sixteenth through the eighteenth centuries, had at its core the idea of order. In this way property went from being individual to being collective. By the end of the eighteenth century, access to the collection began to be understood as a right rather than as a privilege (Pomian, "Collezione" and *Collectors and Curiosities*). The whims of the collector were replaced by the criteria of the expert, and, consequently, the artistic mess of the *cabinet d'amateur* was replaced by an ideology of the visible that had its foundation in the conceptual triad of route, orientation, and order. Through this a true pedagogy of the gaze came into being.

The museum, when constituted as a space of oriented glancing, was therefore understood implicitly as a display of a discourse of manipulation (a making-one-see) constituted by a series of syncretic manifestations that affected all levels of enunciation. These ranged from the significant choice of a particular building to the chosen location, a place made of contiguities and distances, of echoes for works, epochs, styles, and authors. These manifestations were conceived of as details of a global totality capable of conferring upon them an ultimate meaning. The spatial and rhythmic unity is ensured by the emblems of the gallery and by the rooms *en enfilade.* One also must not overlook the whole series of strategic scenographic games of display and concealment.

The space of the museum becomes exemplary and significant through its own strategic and global competence expressed in the construction of one of several tours, which design or inscribe one or several "models of use" in which "a proposal of the gaze" is offered. In the traditional museum, this proposal is based on referential criteria in order to make the History of Art a privileged organizational model exterior to the museum design proper. Only by centering our reflections on the idea of the tour can we adequately consider in the analysis of the museum as text the effects produced by the interrelation of the fundamental constitutive parts: the architecture, the place where it was established, the museographic program—all articulated in the interior of a structure where the formal elements preconfigure the action of the visitors and reveal at the same time the action of the collective subject that directs such a visit.

The Actual and the Virtual

What I have described has much larger repercussions than those of the museum; it affects the totality of spatial and architectonic organization in the broadest sense. Organized space—which has now ceased being "extension" and has become "form"[1] — works as an authentic regulating mechanism of human activity. This premise can be made operative in at least two ways. The first emphasizes the description of empirically observable behaviors displayed by the visitors to the museum. In this case, one would have to make an inventory of behaviors and tours actually produced by museum visitors. The second option is to acknowledge the describability of another kind of "semiotic existence"[2] that we could call actual (and that would refer to the objects that are offered in the present time before the gaze of the analyst). We recognize that together with an actual dimension there is another absent or virtual one that can demonstrate how space implicitly guides human activity, giving rise to the emergence of a group of virtual nonexplicit activities that we can group under the emblem of tours or "guided visits."[3] Only through this perspective does the empirical inventory leave room for a globalizing typology.

The museum constructs (and inscribes in its own material textuality) its ideal visitor in a privileged way through the design and proposal of a tour or a guided spatial traversal. That proposal is to be understood as the virtual organization of one or various itineraries (one global and general, others partial and punctual; the first one expresses the idea of exhaustion, the second the idea of penetration into or of selection as a function of specific interests). All of this, while remaining receptive to the unguided or "wild" visit, is dominated by the pulse of the moment or by the elevation of randomness to an organizing principle.

This is how a "model visitor"[4] is predesigned and how this visitor is presented with a three-part activity. The first activity is a pragmatic one identifiable with the formulation "to visit the museum" and structured in a series of purely physical actions. The second is a cognitive one that involves the action of acquiring a particular historical and aesthetic knowledge that the museum guarantees to include most profound values that characterize culture in a society, that is, its particular "semantic universe." In this sense one can speak of the museum as cognitive space. Finally there is the third activity, in which one can speak of an aesthetic activity related to those pauses during the tour when the body can achieve a singular aesthesis, supposedly provoked by the contemplation of certain works. In short, one can claim that the museum space is presented as a fascinating space, capable of generating the desire for its complete exploration by potential visitors. This exploration demands from the visitor the exercise of an astute intelligence to complete the proposed cognitive program. This fact is linked to its dimension as an initiation rite.

Finally, the museum is constituted as the space of the shortsightedness of the travelers who are forced to begin their exploration without a guide. It is a place conceptualized as the reign of local decision and of continuous calculation. Curiously enough, these are, according to Pierre Rosenstiehl, the three defining characteristics of the figure of the labyrinth.

It is precisely in order to solve the riddle of the maze that classical museums are constituted around the double paradigm of linearity and the predetermined tour. Because the traditional museum is clearly proposed as a labyrinth, even while preserving its character of a "winding tour in which it is easy to lose oneself without a guide" (Santarcangeli 25), it is constructed in such a way that the visitor always finds a way out, both physically and metaphorically. This is the role that the tour plays.

We find ourselves, then, with a typical case of a unidirectional labyrinth, understanding it to mean—as does Umberto Eco ("L'Antiporfirio" 357–60)—that which, if unraveled, would have the appearance of a thread. This is why the museum's very structure guides one to where one should be, and why in its interior one finds a minotaur. The contact with the minotaur is the high point of interest in the tour through the museum. Undoubtedly the traditional museum is an exemplary form of this category of labyrinth, because we find in its organization the form of a thread (as linked to its pedagogical function) as well as the existence of the minotaur (the great works of art that are its basic attraction, such as *Las Meninas* in the Prado or the Mona Lisa in the Louvre).

The Floating Gaze

Modernism, as a radical break from classicist paradigms and as a successful movement since the beginning of the century, presupposes the liberation of visual experience. Modernism creates basic aesthetic and conceptual figures through the assumption of the veracity of retinal experience, of the dematerialization of the visual field, and of progressive dilation. Modernism seeks to replace the guide to perception offered in traditional museology with the floating gaze that claims the emergence of particular architectonic traits like the minimal use of curves, as well as a predilection for straight lines and open clear spaces. Modernism found its most remarkable expression in the so-called International Style.

The design of the museographic and exhibit space was characterized by its insistence on spatial transparency, by its taste for open and amorphous space, and its capacity to be rapidly reformulated through moving panels. It was conceived for the hosting of growing permanent collections, but also for facilitating the arrangement of changing aesthetic and expository criteria. Later, the ideology of direct access replaced the "guided visit" associated with the museum. This direct access coincided with a kind of art that, paradoxically, when presented without intermediaries between the works and the public and when divorced from the implicit didactic mediation of the organizational space of the classic museum, demanded a much higher degree of "making do." The potential danger was to end up with a wandering gaze unable to find points in which to focus its cognitive activity.

The traditional museum can be understood as a direct descendant of Enlightenment despotism. It transmits knowledge through an organized pedagogy supported by a relation of power expressed in spatial terms. The modernist proposal, articulated in the figure of the open room, consists of a space that is always redesignable, adaptable, and changing in its limits and boundaries, and where the contemplation of works comes closer to the act of perusing a catalog than to that of following an itinerary (the motion of display displaces that of the tour). This proposal seems to be situated in the terrain of a liberal-bourgeois practice par excellence when it substitutes, in the ideal visitors of the museum, the oriented gaze with the liberty of relating to art as one pleases.

This type of museum tends to be identified with the negation of the labyrinth, insofar as museums can be inscribed within a rationalist modern architectural project of the nineteenth century. This project was "social, secular, demystifying, and democratic" (Santarcangeli 238), and in it the idea of transparency (both physical and conceptual) was central. The modern museum seems to inaugurate a typology ideally constituted in the absence of "stairs to be climbed, galleries to be toured, walls that interrupt our sight." One does well to remember that the most sophisticated form of the labyrinth is the desert (Borges). The desert, at least in conceptual terms, is where visitors to the modernist museum are left, deprived of points of spatial orientation upon which to fix their cognitive tour.

The Proletarianization of the Model

In recent years the museum has gone from being a territory for celebrating a desacralized ceremony to serving as a privileged space of encounter for the multitudes. From being a realm of quasi-sacred aesthetic contemplation, it has become a forum where people exert their social appearance. Today more than ever, multitudes flock to museums, inundate expositions, and look for their initiation rite into culture, all pushed by a diffuse social obligation. This social obligation brings many who are curious to these institutions where until recently the "great works" of art slept in a distant and closed past.

We obviously live in a time of social compartmentalization where leisure spaces become territories in which human creativity is expanded. This is a world where design precedes the object, fashion precedes behavior, publicity precedes the product, and appearance and simulacrum seem to be constitutive notions. It should not surprise us that one of the most significant manifestations of a society that tries to think of itself as located at the end of a historical journey is an exacerbated cult of the arts in a distinctly "light" way. The most notable example of this practice of massified consumption is the acquisition of museum catalogs and samples, which reveals two things. This "light" consumption is marked not so much by the search for an authentic cognitive or aesthetic experience as by a desperate desire to feel like a participant in the spectacle of culture. In the eyes of people today, this appears to be the last spectacle to offer a kind of social conviviality, even if only in the sad and ephemeral form of sharing the experience of waiting in line.

It is logical to think that the "catalog fever" that has taken over is an authentic operation of pacification that adopts the form of the proletarianization of a certain collection. Through the particular ordering of the pictures of the artworks on heavy paper, as well as through the reminder of the adventure lived in the museum by guides and maps, the public attains a property. Even though this is a degenerated property, it is a tranquilizing one that makes the purchaser the owner of a simulacrum. This simulacrum becomes a central experience, given the weight of mass culture. The phenomenon has reached such proportions that today you cannot conceive of an exhibit that is not accompanied by a catalog unaffordable to the average visitor, a catalog often valued more than the visit and the exposure to the work of art itself.

The Explosion of Typology

If the symptoms described can be situated on a superficial level of social experience, other symptoms reveal more profoundly the collective process. These symptoms give a more substantial account of what we will call "contemporary sensibility."

A pertinent aspect of this sensibility is the consciousness that, at least since dadaism, every object can be considered an object of aestheticization, in a blurring of the banal and the valuable. In a sense, the triumph of aestheticization is the end of a dream that sought to put order into human experience, as long as this experience could go back to a past once and for all established.

With "the end of metanarratives" came the end of Art History understood as the chronological sequence of movements, styles, and authors (Lyotard, *La postmodernité expliqué aux enfants*). A conceptual space has opened up so that we can now think of art in terms of morphological relationships. Where the traditional historical narratives provided a perspectivist illusion capable of situating a principle of explanation above the artistic space, contemporary thought chooses, in the words of Wittgenstein, "to see the facts in their reciprocal relationship and to reassume them in a general image that does not have the form of a chronological development" (28–29).

In considering the formal connection, if not as the only explanation then at least as an alternative genetic hypothesis, the new historiography of art opens up an operative space that will inevitably influence the terrain of museology. When the Mönchengladbach Museum decided to treat a building by Hans Hollein as an artwork in itself, it insisted on the replacement of a chronology with strictly formal criteria. At the time of deciding upon the location of certain pieces, Jonathan Cladders, who was responsible for the exhibit, maintained that the mise en scène has as its ultimate goal the creation of a spatial experience, not a verbal one. His assertion points to the existence of far-reaching changes in the way we have come to understand the museum.

Many recently opened museums put their accent on the spectacular. The Musée d'Orsay in Paris, designed by Gae Aulenti, while respecting the idea of a traditional tour (the central ramp that "ascends" to the light of the impressionists), unsettles scenography by multiplying scenic devices, fragmenting itineraries, and catching the eye in unexpected details that force it to recontextualize the works. In the project for the Art Museum of Catalonia, also designed by Gae Aulenti and Enric Steegman, the tour is broken into three interconnected tours: one chronologically conceived, one symbolically conceived on the basis of the relationship between styles, and a third, typological tour that allows contact with certain artworks in deliberately modified spaces so that the ideal environment in which they were situated may be re-created. In this way, what Calabrese (109–16) has called "bimodal behaviors" are installed in the museum space. Prefigured in these behaviors is an ambivalence on the part of the public, which only serves to provide a better way to negate this ambivalence subsequently. Thus, the contemporary museum is understood less in terms of a pedagogical space and more and more in terms of an explorative space, an experiential space, as source of sensual stimuli, and, above all, as a place where the didactic dimension, while not completely abandoned, is subordinated to the creation of a "tour of sensibility."

One should not be surprised when the recently designed museums present themselves as "singular spaces" that respond to a predetermined typology rather than to concrete and factual necessities. Think of the exemplary case of the double oxymoron (building: unfinished/ruins; collection: *povera* art/baroque art) of the Castelo Rivoli de Turin. Or think of the Museum of Roman Art of Mérida, Spain, that was built to host in situ archaeological excavations and artifacts. Rafael Moneo has taken advantage of the exterior scenographic dimension provided by the placement of the building in relation to the nearby ruins of the Roman theater and amphitheater. He has also adopted certain criteria clearly linked to Roman construction systems (such as the concrete used in brick walls or floor heating so typical of the classic hypocausts) in order to facilitate the nondifferentiation between content and container, as if in a distant future the ruins of the museum were to be indistinguishable from its contents. The scenographic knowledge is displayed in the darkness of the entrance ramp that leads to the interior illuminated by a perfectly calculated regulation of sunlight. All of this is in a building whose severe indifference and exterior discretion do not permit one to predict what it will be like inside, thereby instituting the museum as secret.

This aspect of the museum as secret space is also present in the Museum of Gibellina (Sicily) designed by Francisco Venezia. The museum was conceived to host the only preserved fragment of the façade of the Palazzo di Lorenzo, which was destroyed in an earthquake that laid the city to waste. This museum, open to nature, is an example of the "architecture of dispossession," so much associated with Venice, which brings about a radical rethinking of the relationships between new and old, exterior and interior. The museum is conceived as a patio surrounded by walls upon which, on the interior side, the fragment of the façade is exhibited. On the outside we find simply a white wall with a solitary window through which one can see what is left from the past in the interior. The Museum of Gibellina does not limit itself to expressing its own singularity and its willingness to open a dialogue with the landscape in which it exists; it also illuminates the growing consciousness of the instability that defines a good portion of contemporary art and architecture.

Should we be surprised that in all of these cases there is such a strong expression of a "poetics of fragmentation"?[5] Nothing would be more natural in museums that are "authentic meditations on the catastrophe" (Butor 58) than that these museums prioritize the creation of a space of ruptures. In this space we lose sight of the integrating totality in which we can receive the precise sense of the whole set of real or virtual actions that shape those museums.

The Space of Perplexity

Similarly, one can establish a parallel between contemporary museums and the two other labyrinthine figures identified by Umberto Eco. The mannerist labyrinth is defined as that which presents several options that lead in their practical totality to dead ends (except for the one that leads to the exit); its own design converts the labyrinth into a "path of errors." For the postmodern mentality the same history is an *Irrweg,* a space of confusion that creates a treelike form made of multiple, apparently unending branches. To find the adequate orientation means to identify the adequate response to the "provocation," which constitutes the essence of the museum. The design of the Musée d'Orsay, both linear and alveolar, seems to fit this description. In contrast, one can distinguish another type of labyrinth like those of Mérida, Gibellina, or Rivoli, where the labyrinth is open to infinity, negating the distinction between inside and outside, and where all parts are connected to each other. One of these variations is the "rhizome" (Deleuze and Guattari), which affirms the reversible and dismountable character of the network. The rhizome negates the possibility of global description in spatiotemporal terms, and it creates a real contradiction, in that if any knot can be connected with another, the connection itself cannot be taken for granted.

In all these cases we have a return of the conditions of visibility transformed now into perceptive configurations. The museum in its own architecture acquires a rhythmic configuration that echoes the works inside it. This rhythm relies not on knowledge but on an isomorphic structure with which it constitutes the basis of the aesthetic experience of the works that it holds.

By inverting the traditional priorities we find ourselves subordinating the cognitive to the aesthetic. These museums reveal their intentions in their spatial conceptualization. Their rhythm has little to do with the repetition and regularity of classical museums. We are in the realm of the irregular, of the unexpected (all possibility of prediction is questioned), of local structures (reference to exterior knowledge is avoided), of the improbable, of the surprising.

These expositional spaces represent a profound revaluation of art history. They are conceived for the emergence of a subjectivizing gaze removed from the modernist utopia of nondirectionality. At the same time, they present themselves to their visitors as territories that have been deliberately modified to allow the both terminable and interminable exercise of an aesthetic experience in which notions such as eccentricity, instability, fragmentation, and excess converge to embody the "wait for the unexpected."

Notes

1. On the distinction between "extension" and "space," see Greimas.
2. For a discussion of this notion, see "Actualisation," "Existence sémiotique," and "Virtualisation" (Greimas and Courtés 9–10, 138–39, 420–21).
3. In this way one can recognize the following in the same disposition of space (understood in the broad sense as the intersection of the architectonic dimension and the properly museumistic intervention): (a) the exercise of an assigned competence that predetermines the performances of the individual or collective subjects and (b) the construction of an implicit enunciation for the model user of the formalized space.
4. For the notion of the "model reader" (which I have converted to "model visitor"), see Eco, *Lector in fabula*.
5. The notions of "fragment" and "detail" are derived from Calabrese.

Works Cited

Arnheim, Rudolf. *The Power of the Center: A Study of Composition in the Visual Arts.* Berkeley and Los Angeles: Univ. of California Press, 1982.
Borges, Jorge Luis. "Los dos reyes y los dos laberintos." In *El Aleph.* Buenos Aires: Editorial Losada, 1952.
Butor, Michel. "Le Château de Rivoli." *Techniques and Architectures* 368 (1986): 58.
Calabrese, Omar. *L'eta neobarroca.* Bari: Letarza, 1987.
Deleuze, Gilles, and Félix Guattari. *Rhizome.* Paris: Minuit, 1976.
Eco, Umberto. *Lector in fabula.* Milan: Bompiani, 1979.
———. "L'Antiporfirio." *Sugli specchi e altri saggi.* Milan: Bompiani, 1985. 334–61.
Foucault, Michel. "Spazi altri: I principi dell'Eteropia." *Lotus International* 48/49 (1985/86): 9–17.
Ginzburg, Carlo. *Storia notturna: Una decifrazione del sabba.* Turin: Einaudi, 1989.
Greimas, A. J. *The Social Sciences: A Semiotic View.* Trans. P. Perrone and F. H. Collins. Minneapolis: Univ. of Minnesota Press, 1990.
Greimas, A. J., and J. Courtés. *Semiotics and Language: An Analytical Dictionary.* Trans. L. Crist et al. Bloomington: Indiana Univ. Press, 1982.
Lyotard, Jean-François. *The Postmodern Condition: A Report on Knowledge.* Trans.

G. Bennington and B. Massumi. Minneapolis: Univ. of Minnesota Press, 1984.

_____. *La postmodernité expliqué aux enfants*. Paris: Editions Galilée, 1986.

Pomian, Krysztof. "Collezione." In *Enciclopedia*. Turin: Einaudi, 1978. 3:330–64.

_____. *Collectors and Curiosities: Paris and Venice, 1500–1800*. Cambridge: Basil Blackwell, 1990.

Rosenstiehl, Pierre. "Labirinto." In *Enciclopedia*. Turin: Einaudi, 1976. 8:3–30.

Santarcangeli, Paolo. *Il libro dei labirinti*. Milan: Frassinelli, 1984.

Wittgenstein, Ludwig. *Remarks on Frazer's "Golden Bough."* Ed. R. Rhees. Trans. M. C. Miles. Atlantic Highlands, N.J.: Humanities Press, 1979.

Aesthetics

Chapter 4

The Immutability of the Text, the Freedom of the Reader, and Aesthetic Experience

Rafael Núñez-Ramos

(translated by Susan McMillen-Villar)

> *The problems arising through a misinterpretation of our forms of language have the character of* depth. *They are deep disquietudes; their roots are as deep in us as the forms of our language and their significance is as great as the importance of our language. —Let us ask ourselves: why do we feel a grammatical joke to be* deep? *(And that is what the depth of philosophy is.)*
> —Wittgenstein, *Philosophical Investigations* (111)

One of the features most commonly attributed to a work of art is the union, inseparability, or lack of distinction between form and substance, expression and content. Even though I think that this concept is well explained by some authors (especially Lotman and Mukarovsky), perhaps it would be appropriate to consider it from a pragmatic perspective, for only in that way may we appreciate its true relevance and its influence on the general functioning of literary phenomena. The unity of form and substance is not an autonomous value in the literary text that can be appreciated in itself. It is rather a consequence of the aesthetic character of the kind of perception encouraged by art and a demand on the reader's initiative in order to produce meaning. It is not a factor bound to be recognized in the object, derived from a previous codification (the precise word for the precise meaning), but rather the apparently and paradoxically rigid result of the lack of codification, of the opening of the text to the freedom of the reader in order to establish codes, to produce meanings, and to live experiences.

Let us briefly remember that aesthetic knowledge supposes an unmediated relation between subject and object, a contact that is direct, personal, sensual (not conceptual), and subjective; this contact is not mediated by anything a priori—not even what is a priori in language—through whose system of categories, structures, classifications, and labels the majority of our experiences are filtered and directed. To summarize, in aesthetic knowledge the act of perception is governed solely by the concrete and idiosyncratic nature of the object.

The representative function of language, which is the predominant one in everyday usage, rests on the conventional, social, and conceptual character of the linguistic sign. In this sense, the units and combinations of language constitute an already elaborated, preestablished knowledge that mediates our relation with the world, a knowledge that intervenes between the subject and object of knowledge and that therefore denies the personal initiative of the subject in its disposition to grasp the object directly. Besides, the linguistic sign manifests a conceptual, generic knowledge that makes an abstraction of the individual characteristics of the object and reduces its concrete richness.[1] The representative or referential function of language does not allow, or rather it hinders, aesthetic knowledge and the aesthetic function that, as Mukarovsky points out, "projects onto reality, as a unifying principle, the position taken by the subject with respect to that reality" ("Función, norma y valor estético" 134).[2]

Aesthetic knowledge, then, does not suppose the conceptual assumption of already elaborated information, but the development of a personal response, the formation of an attitude. As a result, the manifestation of aesthetic knowledge cannot grow through the conventional and representative linguistic system. In order to express its aesthetic knowledge, the subject must elaborate its own language, because aesthetic knowledge demands the creation of the language necessary for its representation, even though in practice both might be simultaneous (see Pimenta).

The sign's expressive function seems, in principle, closer to aesthetic behavior, although the comprehension of its role in artistic texts requires some nuances from the classic formulations of Bühler (*Sprachtheorie*) and Jakobson (*Ensayos de lingüística general*). The essence of the expressive function is, for both of them, the fact that the message does not reveal an extralinguistic reality, but rather the speaker's attitude, disposition or posture. It achieves this, not through the sign's conventional value (in which case it would involve a reality expressed referentially), but by other means. Bühler expresses it clearly when he affirms that in this case the sign is not a symbol (which for him means something conventional, codified, preliminary) but a symptom or trace, which as such acquires meaning only in relation to the knowledge and particular experiences of the subject. The following example from Buyssens may clarify this point. When a woman says to her husband, "It's raining," she might mean something like, "I'd rather you stayed at home," or "You'd better take your umbrella." That is to say, the signifier, "It's raining," on the one hand represents conventionally an extralinguistic event, rain. On the other hand, it can be interpreted as a symptom of an intention not directly expressed or recognizable only in relation to psychology or familiar habits, that is, in relation to extralinguistic codes and conventions.[3]

It does not seem too farfetched to conclude that something similar happens to literature. Signs in an artistic text stand for an imaginary reality, and at the same time they are symptoms of a personality, reveal an attitude, imply a subject. This is due to among other reasons, the very fictitious or imaginary nonreferential character of the represented reality. Such a formulation, however, may hint that, in the end, the text works as a symptom of the author's attitude, and that aesthetic perception consists of discovering such an attitude. This implies both a previous codification of the reading and the reader's passive behavior. Both implications are in radical opposition to the aesthetic posture that, in these conditions, would be impossible for the readers (since they would have to limit themselves to an exercise in recognition) and would be reserved for the author.

If this description is valid for everyday linguistic exchanges, in the case of literature and art in general it is necessary to separate the personality, the attitude, and the implicated subject in the text from the empirical author, in order to leave it in a textual form that must be realized by each reader individually. Therefore, if we refer to the expressive function, it is not in order to reduce its aesthetic attitude to a kind of emotive subjectivism of authorial character. In fact, if we resort to the functions of language as presented by Jakobson and Bühler, and if we insist on the displacement of the referential function and the relevance of the expressive function in a literary text, it is not in order to adhere to any kind of theory of expression for art (in this sense, both Bühler's "expressive" as well as Jakobson's "emotive" labels seem bothersome for our ends). Rather, it is because: (1) the indexical or symptomatic character of expression rests on factors and relations that are nonconventional and aprioristic with respect to language and therefore suitable for revealing aesthetic knowledge, which must create its own language; and (2) because, for the same reason, on account of the lack of codes with a prior meaning and the anchoring of the "signifying" units in elements of language that are heterogeneous and not explicitly shown as such, it is the reader's task not only to produce meaning and to develop his or her position with respect to the textual symptom, but also to elaborate the symptomatic signifier itself from material provided by the text. This material is rich, not in meaning—which must be produced by the reader—but in possibilities of constructing "expressive" signifiers. Paraphrasing a sentence from Barthes, employed here for a different purpose, we could say that the play of signifiers may be infinite as long as the literary sign remains unchangeable (266).

In summary, because of the nonreferentiality of the artistic text, its linguistic elements, whatever their level of form or content—from the phoneme and perhaps even the distinctive feature up to the entire text—or whatever their plane, can function as symptoms and acquire meaning in the orbit of a subject (the author, the reader) who inscribes meaning in his or her world and experience. Only in this way is the aesthetic experience possible in the process—passive in appearance only—of reading; the text is not a ready-made language, but simply consists of the materials for its elaboration. The experience of knowledge, the elaboration of language, the production of meaning—such are the conditions (and not phases, since I do not think they are necessarily consecutive; it is not a question of expressing a content given beforehand, prior to language) of aesthetic activity, for the author as well as for the readers. Such conditions are possible, as we see, because of the indexical and connotative value of the linguistic material, and the subsequent identification of the formal elements with the semantic elements, or the indistinguishability of form from content.[4]

The linguistic sign thus is expressive, not because of its representative, conventional, and conceptual characteristics (those of a symbol, in Bühler's and Peirce's sense), but because of the possibility its components (semantic, formal, and material) have of becoming relevant and entering into an active relationship with the vital values ruling human behavior. Let us recall, for example, how a given realization of the word "rain" can refer to vital experiences of given individuals (marriage, for instance) before the extralinguistic event represented.

That meaning, as in connotative semiotic systems and in literature, is nothing more than this is not determined by the form of the plane of expression conventionally associated with it, but rather by the substance of the plane of expression, by the substance of the plane of content, by the form of the plane of expression, by the form of the plane of content, or by any other combination of these.[5] All the aspects of the linguistic material mobilized may become pertinent and have a function that is not simply that of the sign, arbitrary and conventional. And, as all constituents—formal as well as semantic—are functional, the distinction between form and content lacks foundation, and the aesthetic sign presents itself as an unalterable whole.

Now we can see that this unalterability does not proceed from the precision of a content that one can claim to codify, but on the contrary, from the fact that any element, any structure, any aspect of the text, might come to function as symptom, might allow a reader to set in motion a personal attitude toward the world to produce meaning. The possibility that all the planes, levels, and structures of the text may be assumed by the reader is, then, the real foundation of the unity of form and content.

Actually, this operation entails a radical transformation in the role of language, which drifts, to use Susanne Langer's words, from the discursive into the presentational. In language as it exists in literature, there is no previous vocabulary (even meanings function as signifiers), no syntax (the relationships between the parts can be of many different types, and the canonical grammatical relations are useful for instituting higher-order linguistic meanings that, in literature, function as signifiers), nor is there consequently a linear operation (only the whole can make the relations of the text's components perceivable). Even if we could talk of a global and immanent semantic representation, it would not have anything more than a signifier function that would have to react against the receiver's system of values in order to acquire meaning.

Lotman has clearly explained this "motivated" character of the literary sign, which produces the semantization of the extra-semantic (syntactical) elements of natural language; that which is syntagmatic on a given hierarchical level of the text reveals itself to be semantic on another level. Now, given that the syntagmatic elements are those which delimit and divide the text into smaller signs, the suppression of the semantics-syntax opposition causes the erosion of the sign's limits in such a way that the text becomes an integral sign itself in which the minor linguistic signs (which as such have stable, previously fixed values) lose their character of "sign" and become just elements (not parts, since they cannot be easily separated) of the global sign. Phonemes and their extralinguistic combinations, words, sentences, meanings, and so on, play the same role in the literary text as that played by lines, colors, or light and dark areas in a picture. Langer has described their symbolic functioning precisely:

> In isolation we would consider them simply blotches. Yet they are faithful representatives of visual elements composing the visual object. However, they do not represent, item for item, those elements which have names; there is not one blotch for the nose, one for the mouth, etc.; their shapes, in quite indescribable combinations, convey a total picture in which nameable features may be pointed out. The gradations of light and shade cannot be enumerated. They cannot be correlated, one by one, with parts or characteristics by means of which we might describe the person who posed for the

portrait. The "elements" that the camera represents are not the "elements" that language represents. They are a thousand times more numerous. For this reason the correspondence between a word-picture and a visible object can never be as close as that between the object and its photograph. Given all at once to the intelligent eye, an incredible wealth and detail of information is conveyed by the portrait, where we do not have to stop to construe verbal meanings. (94–95)[6]

It is important to stress the presentational character ["a direct *presentation* of an individual object," "that speaks directly to sense; however, there is no intrinsic generality" (96)] that explains the identification of the whole text with a single sign. Lotman, on one hand, explains the identification with a single sign, as the nondiscursive operation that requires a global assumption (since it cannot be simultaneous in literature) of the relations imposed on the constituent elements of the object-sign by the observer. On the other hand, the task of relating, from the aesthetic point of view, does not consist in establishing comparisons between the terms of a relation (a classificatory, conceptual, and discursive activity), but in bringing together different segments with the unity of the ego in a synthesis that is meaningful and revealing for it.

According to Bateson, "aesthetic" means "sensitive to the connecting pattern." "How do all of you relate to this being? Which pattern or guide connects you to it?" (10)[7] These are aesthetic questions (they show the individual's tendency to establish relations of unity and totality with the world), questions we try to answer intuitively and without their being formulated for us, in the processes of aesthetic perception, or rather in the objects' aesthetic experience, to avoid the notion of passivity that "reception" and "perception" seem to have.

Aesthetic objects, and particularly the literary text, are made up of several elements. Isolated or on their own, they are pure virtuality (either they lack meaning, if they treat small units, or they have a general meaning with several possible relations and, consequently, a sense that is vague and imprecise). In the reading experience, such elements may acquire a symptomatic, significant value, if they are capable of involving us, and if we are able to integrate ourselves with them. This can be done, first, by connecting them to other elements from any other level or plane and making them pertinent through the connection we give them (so that from there the object's intangibility as a set of materials whose yield depends on the relations in which they are placed), and second, through the aesthetic sign's connection with the reader's vital values.

To discover the connecting pattern is, in the first case, to construct, in the actual reading experience, a language. In the second, it is to produce a sense (if the experience of knowledge takes place in a positive way, incorporating the result—a new consciousness of things, for instance—into our persona, but the result is not part of the experience any longer).[8] Or rather it is to assume an antisense, a paradox, "changer la vie" (Rimbaud), when the connection does not yield any result but is an oscillation between its extremes, in whose way, "observers are taken to new and intense questions about themselves and about their habitual activity and place in the world. In this way the aesthetic effect takes place" (Pimenta 118).[9]

Notes

1. See Maslow: "What we call knowledge, that is, the placing of an experience within a system of concepts, words or relations, inhibits all possibility of a complete knowledge" (132).

2. "Proyecta en la realidad, como un principio unificador, la postura que el sujeto adopta frente aquella."

3. Semiotics, particularly pragmatic semiotics, has come to account for some of the laws and mechanisms that allow the recognition of nonreferential values in statements. Recanati, for instance, considers that what the statement expresses or evokes may be called its "pragmatic sense" (6). The conditions of the speech acts tell us what the speaker expresses or implies in the act (Searle, *Speech Acts*, 73). Indirect speech acts, the group to which literature can in some way be assigned, have, according to Searle (*Expression and Meaning*, 73), nothing to do with the capacity for inference of the listener and refer to information shared by the interlocutors (they give way to the extrasystemic, in Lotman's terms). My aim is to assign this work to the field of pragmatics. Nevertheless, I prefer to continue talking about expressive function, expressivity, and symptom in order to stress the link between the message and the subject that assumes it, and to give space to all the effects of meaning that do not exist so long as a subject does not base them on a relation established by oneself. See notes 6 and 7.

4. Therefore the text's intangibility—as it is not linked to the manifestation of a precise, univocal, and untranslatable meaning, but rather to the potentially

meaningful condition of the materials of language—can be connected to notions such as disorder, entropy, and unpredictability, which information theory applies to the aesthetic object. It is not the object of the present essay to do so. See, for instance, Lotman.

5. See Zaid: "A poem is a program of vocal, visual and associative acts, which the reader interprets like an actor. Man himself can be thought of as a reading 'machine.' The program (the poem) that would put this reader-machine to work would anticipate the visual stimulus of the word, the click of the unexpected roll of the tongue, the fact that the following word does not begin in a labial position or a position of the tongue that might demand an impossible 'digitation' (for lack of time it gives the terminal position of the preceding word), etc."

6. See also Mukarovsky: "The components of a painting are, then, meaningful, in the same way as the components of a work of poetry: however, in themselves these components are not connected to a determined reality in a direct relation, but rather—as happens with the components in a musical work—they carry a significant potential energy which, emanating from the work as a whole, determines a position with respect to the world" ("El lugar de la función estética" 93).

7. Bateson mentions three logical levels of connection: that among the parts of an individual, that among individuals, and that among the connections of the connected individuals. All of them are operative in aesthetic experience, and remain subsumed in the most fundamental connection expressed in the questions: the connection with the subject.

8. Further on, Bateson says that "the connecting pattern is a meta-pattern" (10), thereby making it possible for the production of sense in the aesthetic experience to be the agent of a transformation in the subject, equivalent to what Watzlawick et al. call $shift_2$, that is, not a shift within the system which, in itself, remains invariable ($shift_1$), but a shift from one system to another. The arrival of $shift_2$ is described by these authors in terms which are applicable to some form of aesthetic experience, "like something uncontrollable and incomprehensible, like a quantum leap, a sudden moment of enlightenment which happens unexpectedly at the end of a prolonged mental, emotional and often frustrating delivery . . . " (43) and that connect it to the mechanism Koestler calls bissociation. Bissociation is defined as something like "perceiving a situation or an idea through two different reference systems, consistent in themselves but normally incompatible," which provokes "an abrupt transference of the course of thought from one associative context to another" (43); such could be the form, to which we made reference at the end of the previous paragraph, in which the observer connects with the meaningful materials of the artistic object.

9. The production of meaning and the assumption of the paradox can be reconciled if we consider the aesthetic experience in literature not as isolated and abstract but as forming part of a series. So, except for the difference which goes between the aesthetic and the reflexive, we could apply the words of Eugenio Trías to poetry and to aesthetic experience: "Philosophy demands as a disposition the passion for admiration and vertigo, a condition of spirited [anímica] or subjective possibility in order to formulate always the same radical interrogations, which are answered philosophically if they allow or open the revalidation—at levels every time more subtle, more delicate, more nuanced and tremendous—of the same radical questions" (27). See also Lorenzo.

Works Cited

Barthes, Roland. *Ensayos críticos*. Trans. Carlos Pujol. Barcelona: Seix Barral, 1967.

Bateson, Gregory. *Mente y naturaleza: una unidad necesaria*. Trans. Leandro Wolfson. Buenos Aires: Amorrortu, n.d.

Bühler, Karl. *Teoría del lenguaje*. Trans. Jena Gustav Fisher. Madrid: Revista de Occidente, 1950.

Buyssens, Eric. *La comunicación y la articulación lingüística*. Trans. Marino Ayerra Redín. Buenos Aires: EUDEBA, 1978.

Jakobson, Roman. "Linguistics and poetics." In *Style in Language*. Ed. T. A. Sebeok. Cambridge: MIT Press, 1960.

———. *Ensayos de lingüística general*. Trans. Jem Cabanes. Barcelona: Seix Barral, 1975.

Johansen, S. "La notion de signe dans la glossématique et dans l'esthétique." *Travaux du cercle linguistique de Copenhague* 5 (1949): 288–303.

Koestler, Arthur. *Act of Creation*. New York: Macmillan, 1964.

Langer, Susanne. *Philosophy in a New Key*. Cambridge: Harvard Univ. Press, 1942.

Lorenzo, G. "Paradoja y experiencia estética (el extraño equilibrio de una esquizofrenia calculada)." *Revista noviembre* (Oviedo), no. 1 (1989): 21–23.

Lotman, Juri. *La structure du texte artistique*. 1970. Trans. Anne Fournier, Bernard Kreise, Eve Malleret, and Joëlle Yong. Paris: Gallimard, 1973.

Maslow, Abraham. *El hombre autorrealizado*. Trans. Ramón Ribé. Barcelona: Kairós, 1987.

Mukarovsky, J. "Función, norma y valor estético como hechos sociales." In *Escritos de estética y semiótica del arte*. 1936. Trans. Anna Anthony-Visová. Ed. Jordi Llovet. Barcelona: Gustavo Gili, 1977. 44–121.

———. "El lugar de la función estética entre demás funciones." In *Escritos de estética y semiótica del arte*. 1936. Trans. Anna Anthony-Visová. Ed. Jordi Llovet. Barcelona: Gustavo Gili, 1977. 139–44.

Pimenta, A. *O silêncio dos poetas*. Lisbon: A regra do jogo, 1978.

Recanati, F. "Le développement de la pragmatique." *Langue française* 42 (1979): 6–20.

Searle, John. *Speech Acts: An Essay in the Philosophy of Language*. Cambridge: Cambridge Univ. Press, 1969.

———. *Expression and Meaning*. Cambridge: Cambridge Univ. Press, 1979.

Segre, Cesare. *Crítica bajo control*. Barcelona: Planeta, 1970.

Trabant, Jürgen. *Semiología de la obra literaria: Glosemática y teoría de la literatura*. Madrid: Gredos, 1975.

Trías, Eugenio. *Filosofía del futuro*. Barcelona: Ariel, 1983.

Watzlawick, Paul, John H. Weakland, and Richard Fisch. *Change: Principles of Problem Formation and Problem Resolution*. New York: W. W. Norton, 1974.

Wittgenstein, L. *Philosophical Investigations*. 3d ed. Trans. G. E. M. Anscombe. New York: Macmillan, 1968.

Zaid, G. *Poesía en la práctica*. Mexico City: Fondo de Cultura Económica, 1985.

◆ Chapter 5

Phenomenology and Pragmatics of Literary Realism

Darío Villanueva

Realism not only has shaped important schools and periods in the evolution of world literature, but also has constituted a basic constant in all literature since the formulation of the principle of mimesis in the *Poetics* of Aristotle. For this reason, it is one of the central points of literary theory most in need of a clarification of its conceptual limits. This effort, in turn, would contribute to the task—often opposed by various authors—of correcting the imprecision, polysemia, and ambiguity with which the realist principle is applied.

This is no easy task, given the diverse implications surrounding realism, all of which are of great significance. The first of these implications is, of course, the philosophical. The very denomination of *realism* has its origins in the old dispute about universals or archetypal ideas, to which Plato conceded full existence. Consequently, to the idealist philosophers poetic imitation appeared to be conditioned, as is argued in book 10 of the *Republic*, by what W. J. Verdenius has called Plato's "conception of a hierarchical structure of reality" (16).

According to Platonic suppositions, there are three levels of reality: that of ideal forms or archetypes, whose ontological completeness is not questioned; that of visible objects or phenomena, which are nothing more than images or reflections of the ideal forms; and a third composed of images proper, where one finds the mimetic arts in general and literature in particular.

These images take as their model a reality, the perceptive reality, which is an imperfect copy of genuine reality. Consequently, the most direct literary imitation is two steps below the essential nature of things. Art truly striving for realism should elevate itself from the ever-precarious material world in order to approach the ideal reality, the essential nature of things, which differs from their visual appearance.

Confronted with this paradoxical Platonic identification of realism with idealism and the consideration of the mimetic principle as something that completely transcends the restrictive realm of art, we refer to the basic extant relationship between the archetypal (*paradeigmatos eidos*) and the sensually perceptible (*mimēma paradeigmatos*). Aristotle's contributions are particularly significant in this regard. Without rejecting the concept of universals, Aristotle does not consider them to be outside the things themselves but rather embodied in them and to be grasped only by abstraction from them. Thus, perceptible reality is no longer an image of anything that transcends that reality, and mimesis is firmly and specifically circumscribed within art and literature. Consequently, for Aristotle, the word "imitation" becomes a term specific to the arts, and "it distinguishes them from all else in the universe, liberating them from any rivalry with all other human activities" (Abrams 25).

In this ordering of things, there is a clear connection among the ontological, epistemological, and philosophical foundations, in general, of what Jan Bruck terms the "bourgeois" realism of the eighteenth and nineteenth centuries. Bruck chooses to view it as something different from and outside of Aristotelian mimesis and the particular conception of reality and art formulated by Aristotle. In effect, however, the traditions of rationalism, sensualism, and empiricism extending from Descartes, Locke, and Berkeley to Thomas Reid's school of common sense, and continuing through nineteenth-century positivism, do not represent any substantial break with Aristotelian philosophy, but tend rather to fortify the full reality of the perceptible objects themselves, outside of the perceiving mind. Derived from this philosophical foundation is a clear aesthetic implication that, in the discussion of literature, allows for purely linguistic considerations.

It is certain that, with rare exceptions, words are not iconic signals. Rather, they are purely symbolic, and their capacity to signify is based on the need to circulate directly with that which they signify. This is not sufficient reason to deny to all undramatic genres their mimetic potential. However, this does introduce a great number of new elements that cannot be ignored. These complicate beyond measure the process of imitative representation of reality, which the verbal art in fact accomplishes.

The empirical theory of language certainly stands quite removed from that which Locke expresses in his *Essay Concerning Human Understanding*, according to which words are direct images of reality, of the things perceived through the senses. The extent to which conceptions like those of Locke's arrive at substantiality are seen in the "first" Wittgenstein (1921), where language is made into a sort of scale map of the entire world, as we read in the *Tractatus Logico-Philosophicus:* "The limits of my language define the limits of my world" (163).

The distance between literary realism constructed from Platonic thought and that founded upon the Aristotelian conception of the world is no greater than that between mimesis according to linguistic proposals like the one we just cited and mimesis according to the "second" Wittgenstein (for whom there exist no essential meanings, only relative meanings). The latter excludes the idea of words as transparent images and concedes to them, on the contrary, full capacity to create—for themselves, for their internal rendering, and for their composition or "language games"—the world of which they speak. In the end, all questions referring to language, among them that of its relation to reality, have been converted into one of the principal concerns—if not the primary one—of contemporary philosophy, in both the "analytic" and "neopositivist" tendencies.

In any case, what is most important is finding a conception of realism that reaches a point of equilibrium between the principle of the autonomy of the literary work as opposed to the determinations of reality and the relationship that is doubtless maintained with it. Without this relationship, literature would not perform its role as an authentic social institution and would lose the interest of the readers of all successive generations.

The lack of that balance produces two fallacies in the estimation of literature that we could well call, respectively, *mimetic* and *aesthetic*. Attached to these are the least pertinent conceptions and practices of the two modalities of realism in which we may summarize the present state of the problem, from the perspective of literary criticism.

In genetic realism everything relies upon the existence of a unanimously accepted reality. This reality is prior to the text, existing before what is situated by long and efficacious observation in the perceptive conscience of the author, which probes into all things hidden. As a result, a true reproduction of the referent is presented, thanks to the transparency or the thinning of the expressive medium of literature, language.

In Zola's essay "Les romanciers naturalistes" we read: "I truly wanted a simple composition style, a clear language, something like a glass house allowing one to see ideas on the inside . . . human documents given in their strict nudity" (11:92).[1] But Zola's idea comes from an earlier work, a letter to Valabrègne of 18 August 1864, in which he develops his theory of the three screens, the classic, the romantic, and the realist; the last is "a simple glass pane, very thin, very clear, which claims to be so perfectly transparent that images go through it and then reproduce themselves in their real states. The realistic screen negates its own existence" (see Alain de Lattre).[2]

What is attempted here is the most complete concealment of the form in order that all of its transparency may favor what Hayek called the "fallacy of conceptual realism." Consistent with this is the belief that behind every word one finds the designated object which corresponds to it; the more imperceptible the word, the greater presence and corporality the object will acquire. It is, likewise, the "propositional phantom" of Wittgenstein's *Tractatus* (which we have already mentioned and which can be related to a neopositivist semantics) that believes in the certain existence of an objective truth and a compact and indisputable world.

In light of the expression of genetic realism represented by the naturalist theory of Zola, it is necessary to expand much of what is usually done in the treatment of the Marxist aesthetic of "reflection," especially in conjunction with Georg Lukács's formulations of this concept. Lukács places the reflection of objective reality in the very center of his aesthetic. There is no direct relation between that reality and the literary text which it represents in the manner of the medieval "aliquid stat pro aliquo," but rather in the manner of the interpretant of Peirce's semiotics, which is situated between the referent object, or *designatum*, and the *representamen*, or sign. Between these two poles is a third discourse which in the thesis of Lukács is an ideology, an essentialist interpretation of reality: Marxism.

In summary, socialist realism is, paradoxically, the faithful reflection by artistic means of a world interpreted ideologically through Marxism. From the standpoint of concrete reality (in which the genetic principle of the work of literature that it intends to represent would reside), it would be more realistic in Lukács's consideration for that work which makes its reflection (the reflection of reality toward the text and the text in relation to reality) to pass by means of the "third discourse" or "interpretant" of the Marxist ideology.

Thus, there is nothing more logical than the identification proposed by Thomas E. Lewis between the concept of referent in the Marxist theory of reflection—exposed more explicitly by Althusser than Lukács—and the semiotics of Umberto Eco, essentially faithful to the principles of Peirce. For both systems, the relationship is established not between the sign and the referent, but between the sign and a convention understood as a "cultural unit" or as an ideology—"a system of representation of images, concretized in specific practices" (Lewis 470)—projected over the referent. Thus, Althusser's Marxist epistemology, the aesthetic repercussions of which cannot be discussed here given the condensed nature of this paper, "subscribes to the same complex of assertions about the relation of thought to the real that figures in the semiotic notion (at least as defined by Eco) of the relation of language to the real, expressed in the concepts of the interpretant and meaning as a cultural unit" (Lewis 469).

The second way of understanding this literary phenomenon displaces its central axis from a reality that precedes the text. This reality is scrupulously observed and reproduced with absolute sincerity by the author to a world created autonomously within the work. This second realism results, more than from pure imitation, from the imaginative creation that cleanses those objective materials that could lie in the origin of the whole process. It subjects them to a principle of immanent coherence that gives them meaning, more by the path of estrangement than by that of the identification of the factual reality itself.

We will speak of formal or immanent realism as opposed to the previous genetic realism. We will attribute to it, instead of a "hermeneutic of reconstruction" (in the mode of Schleiermacher), the principle of aesthetic distinction, developed by Hans-Georg Gadamer (125–28). Implicit in this principle is the abstraction of all that constitutes the root of a work, such as its original vital context, and all functions, religious or profane, in which its meaning could have dwelt: that is to say, of the nonaesthetic moments which are inherent to them—object, function, and the meaning of the content. In this way, concludes Gadamer, "in virtue of the aesthetic distinction by which the work of art is made to belong to the aesthetic conscience, it loses its place and the world to which it belongs" (128).

Gustave Flaubert, with his conception of the novel, exemplifies the fullness of this formal and immanent realism that, in the fashion of Renaissance Neoplatonism, identifies the artist as a creator of worlds along with God. According to Abrams, such an ambitious identification seems to have had its origin in the Florence of the fifteenth century, specifically in the commentaries of Cristoforo Landino about Dante, from 1481 (482–505). Thus Tasso can contend that "Only God and poets deserve to be called creators" (cited in Abrams 483).[3] Since then, Italian and English Neoplatonists, from Sir Philip Sidney on, have maintained that the artist is, like God, creator of a second nature—extremes that are likewise found in Goethe's dialogue *Über Wahrheit und Wahrscheinlichkeit der Kunstwerke* (1797).

In a summary like this we cannot pay much attention to the historical development of demiurgic notions of the writer that have very recently been developed, as in the work of André Malraux in *Les voix du silence* ("Great artists are not transcribers of the world, but *its rivals*").[4] It is enough to cite such a statement as one of the key points for a more solid theoretical characterization of immanent and formal realism. Jacques Derrida wrote about this years ago in a volume dedicated to tracing the theme of mimesis from a deconstructionist perspective: "The Artist does not imitate things in nature, or, if you will, in *natura naturata*, but the acts of *natura naturans*, the operations of the *physis*. But because an analogy has already made, of *natura naturans*, the art of a subject author and, one can even say, of a god-like artist, the mimesis deploys the identification of the human act with the divine act. From one liberty to another" (Derrida, 67).[5]

Thus in Derrida's consideration, true mimesis is established between two producing subjects and two operations of producing, not between two produced realities: one of these (that of the literary work) as reflection of the other (that of nature). The writer imitates nothing but the productive liberty of God, and the analogy established between both "is not only a relationship of proportionality or a relationship between two subjects, two origins, two proportions. The relational process is also returned to the source of the logos. The origin is the logos. The origination of the analogy, that which precedes the analogy and toward which it returns, is the logos, reason and speech, a source, a source like a mouth or the mouth of a river" (74).[6]

From the standpoint of this second realism, as Guy de Maupassant said in a famous prologue (to *Pierre et Jean*), narrative art is characterized, above all, by a sensation of an illusion of truth. This is an idea that has been applied to painting by Ernst N. Gumbrecht with his conception of a wholly antigenetic realism, completely formal and conventionalist, which has influenced beyond measure (through Nelson Goodman and others) literary theory and criticism.

This second appraisal of reality in literature eludes the dangers of genetic mechanicism and interprets the work from within specifically artistic parameters, more in accordance with their essential nature than other external references would be. But it carries in its breast a seed of total disconnection between the created world and reality. This is exacerbated by the most radical immanence, leading us to another dead end with a sign contrary to that called "intentional fallacy" (or "genetic fallacy"), by which the literary work was confused with its own origins. To date, the prevention against this last excess has been generalized in part by theoreticians and literary critics. It is precisely the stimulus that brought us to approach this theme of research and to develop it in the terms that we now summarize.

We will adopt for this task the perspective of literary reception as a third path in the consideration of a problem that has not been perfectly resolved by the other two already implicated in the literary communicative process.

In effect, literary realism bases everything on the relation of writers to the worlds of their orbits, which they conceive through observation and reproduce mimetically as faithfully as possible. Conversely, in formal realism everything centers on literariness: it is the work itself which institutes a reality disconnected from the referent, a "textual reality."

We will arrive, then, at a phenomenology and a pragmatics of realism because both methodological pillars today support all understanding of the literary fact, including the missing perspective of the reader, which is currently gaining in importance. As Roman Ingarden and Wolfgang Iser have shown, included in the dialectic established between the work as a schematic structure and its concretization as an aesthetic object is the fundamental problem of the theory and criticism of literature. Consequently, we also have the fundamental frame of reference for the balanced comprehension of realism that we defend.

For Ingarden, literature has its origin in the creative acts of the intentional conscience of the author. Its ontic base resides in a physical foundation—printed paper or manuscript, magnetic band, computer disk, and so forth—which permits its prolonged existence through time. Its internal structure is multistratified: within it operates a stratum of sounds and verbal formations; another of semantic unities; a third of represented objectivities, intentional correlations of sentences; and a last stratum, that of schematicized aspects under which those objectivities appear. The artistic intention creates a solid union between all of these and thus justifies the polyphonic harmony of the work. Thanks to its double linguistic layer (phonic and semantic), the work is intersubjectively accessible and reproducible so that it becomes an intentional intersubjective object that refers to an open community of readers, both spatial and temporal. Precisely for this reason the work of literary art is not a mere psychological phenomenon; it transcends the experiences of consciousness, as much those of the author as those of the reader.

The work of literature leaves many elements of its own ontological constitution in a potential state; thus, it is its own fundamentally schematic entity. The active actualization of this by the reader fills in these blanks of indetermination (*Unbestimmtheitsstellen*) or latent elements, and if it is realized with a positive aesthetic attitude, it converts the artistic object (the work) into an aesthetic object. In this way, each stratum of which the work is ontologically composed demands different actualizations while avoiding detriment to the concretization of the whole set as a unity. In particular, it emphasizes the reader's process of giving meaning, beginning with the semantic units and the represented objectives. In this task the schematism we have mentioned requires the contribution of those absent or undetermined elements without which the work would not reach true existence.

This schematism leaves open a margin of variability between the inherent artistic values of the work itself and the aesthetic values reached in the concretizations that derive from its total ontological completeness. The fundamental difference between a literary work of art and its actualizations is that in the latter there are concentrated the potential elements with which the blanks or empty spaces of indetermination are filled. The artistic values pertaining to the diverse strata comprise some of those potential elements. Their aesthetic productivity depends in great part upon the system of relationships established between them, that is, the qualitative harmony comparable to the gestalt, or structure.

Thus far we have made use of the idea of literature as a schematic formation and stratified structure in which there is an integration of various levels, including one devoted to the representation of objectives and their actualization as the key element for the ontological completeness of the structure. Husserl's principle of intentionality refers to the activity in which the cognizant "I" extends toward the transcendental phenomenon in order to endow it with meaning. As John D. Boyd reminds us in his work on the function of mimesis, the intentionality that Husserl takes from his teacher Brentano, which is also in Heidegger,

Sartre, and Merleau-Ponty, possesses a long tradition in Thom-
istic thought that continues up until Jacques Maritain. However,
the author of *Logische Untersuchungen* finds a clearly Cartesian
matrix. Thus, in Husserl's *Ideen* we read, *"Over against the expo-
siting of the world, which is a 'contingent' positing, there stands then
the positing of my pure Ego and Ego-life, which is a 'necessary,'* absolutely indubitable *positing. Anything physical which is given 'in person' can be nonexistent; no mental process which is given 'in person'
can be nonexistent.* This is the eidetic law defining this necessity
and that contingency" (108–9).[7]

Thus, for Husserl, Kant's distinction between noumenon
(that which is in the subject) and phenomenon (that which is not
within the subject) is not valid. There are no things unto themselves; there is no being other than the knowable. The value
of this thesis in a theory of literary realism does not escape
us. In an enlightened monograph on the development of intentionality within Husserlian phenomenology, D. Souche-Dagues
clearly explains: "It is henceforth neither the 'I am' or the 'world
is' that can represent the authentic point of departure of a phenomenological ontology, but rather the 'I am—the world is,'
that is to say, the theme of the intentional correlation at the
breast of all experience. It is then really the intention that becomes the director of the stream of the thought, in other words,
of the thought of the being" (240).[8]

In effect, phenomenology studies those things that intentionally point toward an object, real or otherwise, which (in any
case) form a constituent part, as an inexhaustible reference, of
the intentional entity of life. It is for this reason that we study it.
"Cognitive mental processes (and this belongs to their essence)
have an *intentio:* they refer to something; they are related in this
or that way to an object. This activity of relating itself to an object belongs to them even if the object itself does not," we read
in Husserl's fourth lecture in *Die Idee der Phänomenologie* (55).[9]

In this way, intentionality, according to Husserl, is the activity from which the knowing "I" departs toward the transcendental phenomenon in order to give it meaning. This phenomenon could well be reality, such as an image of itself, in the same
way that the conscience makes use of the two ways of representing the world (Durand 8). One is direct, when the object seems

to present itself before the spirit; and the other is indirect: "In all these cases of indirect conscience, the absent object is represented to the conscience by an image, in the largest sense of this term."[10] Durand concludes: "To tell the truth, the difference between direct thought and indirect thought is not as clear-cut as we, in the interest of clarity, just exposed. It would be better to write that conscience possesses different degrees of the image of which two extremes could be constituted by the total equality, the perceptive presence of the most distant inequality."[11] Morse Peckham, in an article about realism with a flashy title—"Is the Problem of Realism a Pseudo-problem?"—considers things as immediate signals that upon being imitated artistically make room for other mediate ones (98).

According to Husserl, the concept of *epoche*, or phenomenological reduction, consists of suspending the belief in the reality of the natural world and consequently placing in parentheses the inductions that it creates in order to exclusively abide by what is given.

This fundamentally phenomenological attitude is the same one that convinces the reader of literature to accept the pact of what has been given the name "fictionality," or, in the appropriate words of Coleridge, "the willing suspension of disbelief." Toward this particular literary epoche there flow three orders of questions, each deserving separate attention. In the first place, the very agreement of fiction in which one suspends disbelief implies the notion of a game, by convention, and also the hermeneutic repercussions of the one on the other. In this respect it will also put forth the pragmatic question of which "speech acts" belong to literary communication. Finally, very directly related to the last question is that of the logicosemantic status of the fictitious or fictional (derived from "fictionality").

The skeptical and phenomenological origins of this epoche are not in contradiction with the ludic component to which we will soon refer. In effect, since Plato the game has been considered fundamental for art and, particularly, for imitation (*Republic* 602b; *Sophist* 234a-b; *Statesman* 288c; *Laws* 796b, 889d-e). In any case this does not identify it with arbitrariness and futility, but with a transcendental exercise, because the imitative artistic game expresses something different, more profound, and compelling than what it appears to represent (see Verdenius). This episte-mological rendering of the game is what justifies the growing interest shown in the game by philosophy and science since the second half of the nineteenth century, as traced by Mihai Spariosu (1982).

Previously, the game, in its double duty as an attitude without transcendence and as a theoretical tool for mediating between inapprehensible reality and reason, had occupied a notable place in Kant's philosophy. On specifically artistic grounds, Schiller, in his *Letters on the Aesthetic Education of Man*, completely identifies art with game.

The question of intentionality, for its part, implies matters of great importance for the literary phenomenon, like imagination, symbol, and meaning. Reality gains meaning through an act of understanding or intentional experience, to which are comparable, in the communicative process of literature, the apprehension of the world by the writer, the production of the text, and the reading of it by its intended audience. Like all intentional acts, the act of understanding constructs intentional objects. It can be said that these are the reality perceived by the author; the work of literature created by this author; and the world which that work creates, projected by the reader.

Also, for Jean-Paul Sartre, "The intention is at the center of the consciousness: it is the intention that envisages the object, that is, that makes it what it is" (27).[12] "Imagination is not an empirical and superadded power of consciousness; it is the whole of consciousness as it realizes its freedom" (358).[13] "There is not a world of images and a world of objects. . . . The two worlds, real and imaginary, are composed of the same objects; only the grouping and interpretation of these objects varies. The imaginary world, like the real universe, is defined by an attitude of conscience" (45–46).[14] The value of this last argument for a theory of realism is unquestionable.

Likewise we encounter a pragmatic emphasis in Sartre's work: "The imaginative consciousness we produce before a photograph is an act. . . . We become aware, somehow, of *animating* the photo, of lending it life in order to make an image of it" (44–45).[15] If we replace the photograph with a literary work, we will have the scheme of a process identical to what we considered in the framework of realism above. Sartre remembers that for Husserl the image was a "remplissement" (*Erfüllung*) of the meaning, and adds; "The image is built up by the intention, which compensates for its shortcomings as a perception" (1940; 64).[16]

The semiotic implications of phenomenology are fundamental, not only in reference to Peirce but also in Husserl. Jacques Derrida has studied these in *La voix et le phénomène*, in which he insists on a key element of the function of realism from the perspective we are applying: co-intentionality. In the first of his *Logische Untersuchungen*, dedicated to expression and meaning, Husserl asserts that the communicative process is accomplished because one listens and comprehends the intention of the speaker, which makes possible, above all else, spiritual intercourse. He characterizes as discourse that which links two people. Established by the physical part of the discourse is the correlation between physical and psychic beings, implicated mutually and experienced by people in respective communication: "Speaking and listening, the relating of psychic experiences in speaking, and the reception of those relistening are mutually interrelated" (1929, 39).[17]

Certainly the type of communication to which Husserl refers is very different from literary communication which concerns us, but for the later development of our vision of realism it is important to leave intact this phenomenological idea of intersubjective intentionality or co-intentionality. For example, S. Y. Kuroda assumes, as does Husserl, that "the essence of linguistic performance consists in meaning-assigning acts [*bedeutungsverleihende Akt*] and meaning-fulfilling acts [*bedeutungerfüllende Akt*]," and that in phenomenological terms meaning is "an intentional object" (130). Nevertheless, "the meaning-realizing act . . . takes place in both the author's and the reader's consciousness" (137), but since between them there exists no contact except through the text and none may exist (which is most often the case), the identity of contexts may fail, but never the co-intentionality of which we speak. This is because of the total identification of this identity with what touches the reader and is particular to the author, as in the fallacy that Wimsatt (1968) and Beardsley denounce.

With regard to the conventions, it is certain that in order to communicate an intention of realism intersubjectively, for example, it is necessary to revert to them. Apart from reality, including its artistic or literary representation, the fictional epoche constitutes a true conventionalist complex, since it is largely the result of social conventions. From this comes the keen assertion of Warning that fictionality is essentially contractual (331).

From the revision of the pragmatic theories of "speech acts" applied to fictional texts, one would deduce that they result not from the presence of certain semantic or syntactic properties but from intentional modifications effected by the agents—emitter and receptor—of the communicative action. In the case in which both realize the same modification, the fictionality will be complete through co-intentionality, but it is sufficient if the authentic owner of the text phenomenologically speaking—the reader—practices intentionality in order that the work be fictionalized in its totality.

Formal logical and philosophical semantics has recently developed a theory of "possible worlds" that has applications to the literary problem occupying us. In effect, the "imaginative worlds, narrative worlds, or worlds of the work of art" in general are a variation of the possible universes in which true assertions are those that adjust to the proposed terms, and false assertions are those that do not.

However, we make note of such a conception of the limitations of the autonomous and immanent character of the possible or artistic world created by fictitious discourse. We are situated in an intentional semantic, mindful only of the game produced by the forms of expression, more than the relationship of reference, which easily causes us to drift toward "formal or immanent realism."

In this respect, we judge the distinction that Gottlob Frege made in his theory of meaning in natural languages to be particularly useful (85–98). Frege proposes the distinction between *Bedeutung,* or referent object of a sign, and *Sinn,* or meaning of the sign (the manner in which the expression designates the object and the information given about it can be identified). One tends to relate both notions to Carnap's juxtaposition of the extensional and the intensional, and to the theories of "reference" and "meaning" proposed by Quine [and we could extend still further the parallels to the *signification/significance* of Michael Riffaterre (in R. Barthes et al. 93–94)]. It does not correspond precisely to the phenomenological linguistic theory included in the first of the *Logische Untersuchungen* (§§12–16), studied by Jacques Derrida (*La voix et le phénomène*). Edmund Husserl also differentiates between the object, *Gegenstand*, or a non-verbal phenomenon denoted by a word, and the way in which the object is presented, or the meaning (for one who employs the term *Bedeutung*, in a sense completely contradictory to that of Frege). Frege's juxtaposition has provoked an expansion of the semiotic scheme of Morris, consistent in distinguishing between semantics, meaning that which is concerned with the relations between signs and their mental representations, and sigmatics, devoted to the relations between signs and the objects to which they refer.

In this way we get closer to the comprehension of realism not from the author or the isolated text, but basically from the reader, with all necessary endorsements of phenomenology that do not consider a work of literary art to be ontologically complete if it is not actualized and a pragmatics that does not consider the meanings only in relation to the merely enunciated, but from the dialectic between the enunciation, the reception, and the referent. Realism in action, in which the activity of the recipient is decisive, and that represents one of the most conspicuous manifestations of the "principle of cooperation," was formulated by H. P. Grice (*Logic and Conversation* 41–58) and was read by Teun van Dijk in an unpublished work (44). The late Jon K. Adams has applied it to the specific field of literary fiction (see *Pragmatics and Fiction*).

The basic idea that animates this principle is that of linguistic conduct as a type of meaningful social interaction, driven by a cooperative willingness that J. Lyons exemplifies, according to Grice, with the sentence "John is a tiger" and the metaphorical key that corresponds to it. In any case, we have come close to a clear formulation: literary realism is a fundamentally pragmatic phenomenon that results from the projection, over an intentional world that the text suggests, of a vision of the external world that the reader—every reader—possesses. Because of this, Paul Ricoeur, in his interpretation of mimesis, to which we have already made reference, highlights its identity— strengthened by the suffix—with poiesis and with praxis, which gives a meaning of productive, not reduplicative, reference to the world.

The pact of fiction, the voluntary suspension of disbelief, renewed by literary epoche, certainly corresponds to Grice's "principle of cooperation." In the same manner, it also obeys the projection of the external field of reference (EFR) over the internal field of reference (IFR) and carries it from the reading of all of that which the schematic structure of the work claims in order to reach its full ontological completeness.

By this same impulse of cooperation readers tend to bring the intentional world of the text near to their own, to the extentional referent. Grice adds that in standard linguistic communication all of the agents expect rational, serious, collaborative conduct from each other. Correspondingly, we propose that the reader who makes, among the varieties of apprehension of the work of literature enumerated by Roman Ingarden, an optimal aesthetic actualization of the work, spontaneously and naturally assumes the "seriousness" of what is written, which, although fictitious in its origin, lends itself to a realistic decodification. This would consist in the hermeneutic task of giving real meaning to the text, distinguishing its immanent IFR from the EFR, which is each reader's vision and interpretation of the multiple reality.

To this third conception of the mimetic literary phenomenon (which we will base on the aesthetic of the Polish disciple of Husserl and on pragmatics) we give the label *intentional realism*. The question lies not so much in the imbrication of the text with reality as in how the readers make use of the text to declare their own reality. Effectively, intentional realism is equal to the giving of realistic meaning to a text of which is made a hermeneutic "of integration," not "of reconstruction" (Gadamer), from the referential horizon proportioned by the experience of the world that every reader possesses.

Karlheinz Stierle, in his theory of the "quasi-pragmatics" of the texts of fiction, begins with the consideration (which we have made our own) in which the fictitious (and the IFR) and the real (and the EFR) interrelate in such a way that one acts as the horizon of the other, without prejudice (313). Thus the essential characteristic of the literary text may be that of a series of unverifiable assertions. But, we add, the reader does not desire such verification, nor could it be reached in a great number of the communicative situations in which it occurs, by virtue of the cooperation illustrated to us by Grice (see *Logic*). "The fiction text effaces itself," continues Stierle, "to the advantage of a textual otherworldliness, of an illusion that the receiver—under the impulsion of the text—produces himself. The illusion (like the result of the quasi-pragmatic reception of fiction) is an out-of-text entity comparable to that of the pragmatic reception" (300).[18]

As we pointed out earlier, Stierle's thesis seems extremely directed. We place his valuative attribution toward the side of ingenuous forms of reception. For us this quasi-pragmatic reading is that of intentional realism. Everything begins with the epoche of the pact of fiction, with the "voluntary suspension of disbelief." Later there comes a process of growing intensity for the represented world that interests us. We identify with the characters, if it is a narrative text (novel or play), or with the lyric enunciator and the enunciator's internal affections, at the same time that we stop perceiving the discourse as a dissolved factor of illusion, even in the act of experiencing it (if the discourse is not "emminent," as Gadamer would say, then everything fails). Finally, let us not regress to the previous epistemological attitude, to our voluntary epoche. The virtuality of the text, and our intentional living of this virtuality, brings us to elevate the rank of its internal world of reference qualitatively until we integrate it, without any reservation, into our own external, experienced world—in a word, realist.

Speaking of art in general, Pablo Picasso talks of "a lie which makes us fall into the reckoning of truth" (quoted in Levin, *The Gates of Horn* 39). The same may be said of literature. It is truth, which, in order to be accepted, does not require us to renounce the autonomy of the artistic text as a construct of all previous reality and of the author's intentions. Realism functions as a nonreintegrated epoche, appropriating this truth and actualizing the aesthetic object for the reader. This suspension of disbelief gives way, without solution of continuity, to the enthusiasm of epiphany.

Notes

1. "Je voulais bien une composition simple, une langue nette, quelque chose comme une maison de verre laissant voir les idées à l'intérieur . . . les documents humains donnés dans leur nudité sevère."

2. "Un simple verre à vitre, très mince, très clair, et qui a la prétention d'être si parfaitement transparent que les images le traversent et se réproduisent ensuite dans leur réalité. L'écran réaliste nie sa propre existence."

3. "Non merita nome di creatore se non Iddio ed il Poeta."

4. "Les grands artistes ne sont pas les transcripteurs du monde, ils sont les rivaux."

5. "L'artiste n'imite pas les choses dans la nature, ou si l'on veut dans la natura naturata, mais les actes de la natura naturans, les opérations de la physis. Mais puisq'une analogie a déjà fait de la natura naturans l'art d'un sujet auteur et, on peut même le dire, d'un dieu artiste, la mimesis déploie l'identification de l'acte humain à l'acte divin. D'une liberté à une autre."

6. "N'est pas seulement un rapport de proportionnalité ou un rapport entre deux—deux sujets, deux origines, deux proportions. Le procès analogique est aussi remontée vers le logos. L'origine est le logos. L'origine de l'analogie, ce dont procède et vers quoi fait retour l'analogie c'est le logos, raison et parole, source comme bouche et embouchure."

7. "Der Thesis der Welt, die eine 'zufällige' ist, steht also gegenüber die Thesis meines reinen Ich und Ichlebens, die eine 'notwendige,' schlechthin zweifellose ist. Alles leibhaft gegebene Dingliche kann trotz dieser leibhaften Gegebenheit auch nicht sein, kein leibhaft gegebenes Erlebnis kann auch nicht sein: das ist das Wesensgesetz, das diese Notwendigkeit und jene Zufälligkeit definiert."

8. "Ce n'est désormais ni le Je suis ni le monde est que peuvent réprésenter le point de départ authentique d'une ontologie phénoménologique, mais plutôt le: Je suis-le monde est, c'est-à-dire le thème de la corrélation intentionnelle au sein de toute expérience. C'est bien donc l'intention qui devienne le fil directeur de la pensée, c'est-à-dire de la pensée de l'être."

9. "Die Erkenntniserlebnisse, das gehört zu ihrem Wesen, haben eine intentio, sie meinen etwas, sie beziehen sich in der oder jener Art auf eine Gegenständlichkeit. Das sich auf eine Gegenständlichkeit Beziehen gehört ihnen zu, wenn auch die Gegenständlichkeit ihnen nich zugehört."

10. "Dans tous ces cas de conscience indirecte, l'object absent est ré-présenté à la conscience par une image, au sens très large de ce terme."

11. "A vrai dire la différence entre pensée directe et pensèe indirecte n'est pas aussi tranchée que nous venons, par souci de clarté, de exposer. Il vaudrait mieux écrire que la conscience dispose de différents degrés de l'image . . . Dont les deux extrèmes seraient constitués par l'adequation totale, la présence perceptive ou l'inadéquation la plus poussée."

12. "L'intention est au centre de la conscience: c'est elle qui vise l'objet, c'est-à-dire qui le constitue pour ce qu'il est."

13. "L'imagination n'est pas un pouvoir empirique et surajouté de la conscience, c'est la conscience tout entière en tant qu'elle réalise."

14. "Il n'y a pas un monde des images et un monde des objets; . . . les deux mondes, l'imaginaire et le réel, sont constitués par les mêmes objets; seuls le

groupement et l'interprétation de ces objets varient. Ce qui définit le monde imaginaire comme l'univers réel, c'est une attitude de la conscience."

15. "La conscience imagineante que nous produisons devant une photographie est un acte. . . . Nous avons conscience, en quelque sorte, d'animer la photo, de lui prêter sa vie pour en faire une image."

16. "Ce qui constitue l'image et suplée à toutes les défaillances de la perception, c'est l'intention."

17. "Sprechen und Hören, Kundgabe psychischer Erlebnisse im Sprechen und Kundnahme derselben im Hören, sind einander zugeordnet."

18. "Le texte de fiction s'efface au profit d'un au—delà textuel, d'une illusion que le récepteur—sous l'impulsion du texte—produit lui même. L'illusion (comme résultat de la réception quasi pragmatique de la fiction) est un hors-texte comparable à celui de la réception pragmatique."

Works Cited

Abrams, Meyer Howard. *The Mirror and the Lamp: Romantic Theory and the Critical Tradition*. New York: W. W. Norton & Company, 1953.

Adams, Jon. *Pragmatics and Fiction*. Philadelphia: John Benjamin Publishing Co., 1985.

Barthes, Roland. *L'effet de réel*. Recherches Sémiologiques: Le Vraisemblable. *Communications* 11 (1968): 20–42.

Boyd, John D. *The Function of Mimesis and Its Decline*. Cambridge: Harvard Univ. Press, 1968. 2d ed., New York: Fordham Univ. Press, 1980.

Bruck, Jan. "From Aristotelian Mimesis to 'Bourgeois' Realism." *Poetics* 2 (1982): 189–202.

Carnap, Rudolf. *Introduction to Semantics and Formalization of Logic*. Cambridge: Harvard Univ. Press, 1959.

Derrida, Jacques. *La voix et le phénomène: Introduction au problème du signe dans la phénoménologie de Husserl*. Paris: Presses universitaires de France, 1967.

_____. *La vérité en peinture*. Paris: Flammarion, 1978.

_____et al. *Mimesis/Desarticulations*. Paris: Aubier-Flammarion, 1975.

Durand, Gilbert. *L'imagination symbolique*. Paris: Presses universitaires de France, 1984.

Frege, Gottlob. *Kleine Schriften*. Ed. I. Angelelli. Hildesheim: Georg Olms, 1967.

Gadamer, Hans-Georg. *Wahrheit und Methode*. Tübingen: J. C. B. Mohr, 1965.

Goodman, Nelson. *Languages of Art: An Approach to a Theory of Symbols*. Indianapolis: Hackett, 1976.

Grice, H. Paul. "Meaning." In *Problems in the Philosophy of Language*, ed. T. M. Olshewsky. New York: Holt, Rinehart & Winston, 1969. 251–59.

_____. "Logic and Conversation." In *Syntax and Semantics, 3: Speech Acts*, ed. P. Cole and J. L. Morgan. New York: Academic Press, 1975. 41–58.

Heidegger, Martin. *Being and Time*. London: SCM Press, 1962.

Husserl, Edmund. *Ideen zu einer reinen Phänomenologie und phänomenologischen Philosophie*. The Hague: Martinus Nijhoff, 1913.

_____. *Logische Untersuchungen*. The Hague: Martinus Nijhoff, 1929.

_____. *Die Idee der Phänomenologie*. The Hague: Martinus Nijhoff, 1958.

Ingarden, Roman. *Das literarische Kunstwerk.* Tübingen: Max Niemeyer Verlag, 1965.

_____. "A Marginal Commentary on Aristotle's Poetics." *Journal of Aesthetics and Art Criticism* 20 (1962): 163–73, 273–85.

_____. *The Cognition of the Literary Work of Art.* Trans. Ruth Ann Crowley and Kenneth R. Olson. Evanston, Ill.: Northwestern Univ. Press, 1973.

Iser, Wolfgang. *The Implied Reader: Patterns of Communication in Prose Fiction from Bunyan to Beckett.* Baltimore: The Johns Hopkins Univ. Press, 1974.

_____. "The Indeterminacy of the Text: A Critical Reply." In *Comparative Criticism: A Yearbook 2,* ed. Elinor Shaffer. Cambridge: Cambridge Univ. Press, 1975. 27–47.

_____. *The Act of Reading: A Theory of Aesthetic Response.* Baltimore: The Johns Hopkins Univ. Press, 1978.

_____. "Akte des Fingierens, oder: Was ist das Fiktive im fiktionalen Text?" In *Funktionen des Fiktiven,* ed. D. Henrich and W. Iser. Munich: Fink, 1983. 30–52.

_____. "Die Wirklichkeit der Fiktion." In *Rezeptionsästhetik: Theorie und Praxis,* ed. Rainer Warning. Munich: UTB, 1985. 277–342.

Kant, Immanuel. *Critique of Judgment.* Trans. Werner Pluhar. Indianapolis: Hackett, 1987.

Kuroda, S. Y. "Reflections on the Foundations of Narrative Theory from a Linguistic Point of View." In *Pragmatics of Language and Literature,* ed. Teun A. Van Dijk. Amsterdam: North-Holland, 1976. 107–40.

Lattre, Alain de. *Le réalisme selon Zola. Archéologie d'une intelligence.* Paris: Presses universitaires de France, 1975.

Levin, Harry. "What Is Realism?" *Comparative Literature* 3 (1951):193–99.

_____. *The Gates of Horn: A Study of Five French Realists.* New York: Oxford Univ. Press, 1963.

_____. "On the Dissemination of Realism." In *Grounds for Comparison.* Cambridge: Harvard Univ. Press, 1972. 244–61.

Lewis, Thomas E. "Notes towards a Theory of the Referent." *PMLA* 94 (1979): 459–75.

Lukács, Georg. *Essays on Realism.* Ed. Rodney Livingston. Cambridge: MIT Press, 1981.

Lyons, J. *Language, Meaning and Context.* London: William Collins & Sons, 1981.

Malraux, André. *The Voices of Silence.* Trans. Stuart Gilbert. Princeton: Princeton Univ. Press, 1978.

Maritain, Jacques. *Bergsonian Philosophy and Thought.* New York: Philosophical Library, 1955.

Maupassant, Guy de. *Pierre et Jean.* London: Harrap, 1966.

McKeon, Richard. "Literary Criticism and the Concept of Imitation in Antiquity." *Modern Philology* 34 (1936): 1–35. Reprinted in *Critics and Criticism: Ancient and Modern,* ed. R. S. Crane. Chicago: Univ. of Chicago Press, 1952.

Merleau-Ponty, Maurice. *Adventures of the Dialectic.* Trans. Joseph Bien. Evanston, Ill.: Northwestern Univ. Press, 1973.

Peckham, Morse. "Is the Problem of Literary Realism a Pseudo-Problem?" *Critique: Studies in Modern Fiction* 12 (1970): 95–112.

Prendergast, Christopher. *The Order of Mimesis: Balzac, Stendhal, Nerval, Flaubert.* Cambridge: Cambridge Univ. Press, 1986.

Reisz de Rivorola, Susana. "Ficcionalidad, referencia, tipos de ficción literaria." *Lexis* 3.2 (1979): 99-170.

Ricoeur, Paul. "Mimesis and Representation." *Annals of Scholarship* 2 (1981): 15–32.

_____. *Time and Narrative*, vol. 1. Chicago: Univ. of Chicago Press, 1983.

Sartre, Jean-Paul. *L'imaginaire: Psychologie phénoménologique de l'imagination.* Paris: Gallimard, 1982.

Schiller, Friedrich. *On the Aesthetic Education of Man.* London: Routledge & Kegan Paul, 1954.

_____. *Hermeneutics: The Handwritten Manuscripts.* Ed. Heinz Kimmerl. Missoula, Mont.: Scholars Press, for the American Academy of Religion, 1977.

Souche-Dagues, D. *Le développement de l'intentionalité dans la phénoménologie husserlienne.* The Hague: Martinus Nijhoff, 1972.

Spariosu, Mihai. *Literature, Mimesis and Play: Essays in Literary Theory.* Tübingen: Gunter Narr Verlag, 1982.

Stierle, Karlheinz. "Réception et fiction." *Poétique* 39 (1979): 299–320.

Verdenius, William Jacob. *Mimesis: Plato's Doctrine of Artistic Imitation and Its Meaning to Us.* Leiden: E. J. Brill, 1949.

Warning, Rainer. *Rezeptionsästhetik: Theorie und Praxis.* Ed. Rainer Warning. Munich: UTB, 1985.

Watt, Ian. *The Rise of the Novel: Studies in Defoe, Richardson and Fielding.* London: Chatto & Windus, 1957.

Wimsatt, W. K. "Genesis: A Fallacy Revisited." In *The Disciples of Criticism: Essays in Literary Theory, Interpretation, and History,* ed. Peter Demetz et al. New Haven: Yale Univ. Press, 1968. 193–225.

Wittgenstein, Ludwig. *Philosophical Investigations.* Trans. G. E. M. Anscombe. Oxford: Basil Blackwell, 1958.

_____. *Tractatus Logico-Philosophicus.* Trans. D. F. Pears and B. F. McGuinness. London: Routledge & Kegan Paul, 1962.

Zola, Emile. *Oeuvres complètes*, vol. 11. Paris: Cercle du livre précieux, 1968.

◆ Chapter 6

The Pragmatics of Lyric Poetry

José María Pozuelo-Yvancos
(translated by Stacy N. Beckwith)

The lyric origins of the poem, as set down by linguistic poetics, have been established on the theoretical grounds that the poem is a linguistic object of a special type. Indeed, as a measure of its "poeticity" (*poeticidad*), one might describe the poem as having been derived from those rhetorical-elocutive origins (figures and tropes) of structural ordering (parallelism, coupling, isotopy, and the like) that I have discussed elsewhere (Pozuelo-Yvancos, *La teoría del lenguaje literario*). Yet until the mid-1970s, very few authors concerned themselves with the pragmatic specificity of the poem, or in other words, with poetry as a special form of communication that takes place between a transmitter and a receiver. This becomes apparent if we go back to Morris's three-fold schema of semiotics, which consists of syntax (the study of relations of signs, both within themselves and to one another), semantics (the relations between a sign and the referent thereby expressed), and pragmatics (the relations between transmitter and receiver, and of both within the context of communication). It can be observed that analyses of the specificity of lyric poetry have confined themselves to the phenomena of syntax, along with studies of rhythm, figures of ordering, and semantics. Very few have approached poetry as a special mode of communication; the pragmatics of poetry have been slow to capture the interest of lyric discourse and its inquiries.

As evidence of this I shall cite two excellent books, both devoted to the specifics of lyric poetry, one by Kibédi-Varga (*Les constantes du poème*), and the other by the Groupe Mu (J. Dubois et al., *Rhétorique de la poésie*). In the first, lyric poetry is regarded primarily as a form of rhythmic ordering; the second contains a brilliant investigation of lyric poetry's semantic-discursive coherence and cohesion in what is actually a monograph on isotopic semantics. Yet neither these works nor many others view their subject from the perspective of pragmatic relations. In fact, it is precisely the quality of the two books in question that highlights the marginalization of pragmatics by structuralist thought, obsessed as it is with textuality in terms of the structure of the sentence or phrase. There are hundreds of studies on the assimilation of lyric poetry to rhetorical figures and to elocution, any one of which could have been cited here.

It is clear that the pragmatic aspects of the definition of lyric poetry have gone unconsidered, so that many of them are excluded from the ensemble of characteristics that constitute lyric specificity. At the same time, it would be a mistake to deem earlier stages of study as "surpassed" or lacking in interest. It goes without saying that areas of inquiry such as phonic-rhythmic structure, tropology, the problem of ambiguity (see Empson), and the special density that motivation or the restructuring of signifier-signified relations acquires in poetry (see Genette, *Figures II* and *Mimologiques*) have brought to light a wealth of textual features, both syntactic and semantic. The same has occurred with respect to the grammatical origins of the syntactic ordering analyzed earlier and with respect to semantic cohesion via isotopy. It is not for the pragmatics of lyric poetry to invalidate these findings, but rather to confirm them as an indispensable "condition" for the particular type of communicative relation established in the reading of lyrical poetry, and also as a "marker," leaning toward the establishment of that type of communication over another (see, for example, García Berrio, *Introducción a la poética clasicista*).

The first pragmatic question involves the actual identification of lyric communication: does lyric poetry constitute a specific mode of relation, with particular features not possessed by narrative or drama? Common sense and experience dictate that there are many pragmatic sides to the expression and reception of a poem that are shared by all other literary messages. They also affirm that there is a culturally sanctified specificity that constitutes a normative horizon (see Pozuelo-Yvancos, *Del formalismo*) and likewise corresponds to an irreplaceable positioning of author and reader. Author and reader alike have their individual, specific attitudes, which should not be despised, and both are intrinsic to the reading and writing of poetry. This specificity will be taken up in what follows, given that some of the pragmatic features that the poem shares with other literary texts have already been discussed (Pozuelo-Yvancos, *La teoría del lenguaje literario*). A question of enormous interest that cannot be fully addressed here is how the pragmatic identity of lyric poetry is partly a phenomenon of normative poetics and how it has constituted itself diachronically along the historical evolution into variable horizons of expectation that every literary culture has gone about selecting for itself.

The notion of "genres," and the singular transformations accompanying the birth of the lyrical, are indispensable for a study of its pragmatics, given that both impinge remarkably on how transmitter and receiver identify with it (see García Berrio, *Introducción a la poética clasicista*; Guillén; and Genette, *Introduction à l'architexte*). The enormous influence of romanticism on the genre we are studying goes without saying, of course, as the nature of "I" as primary source of lyric focalization can hardly be posed in its absence (see also Abrams, Fowler, and Aguiar and Silva). These are all questions that go beyond the scope of this study, but that should be kept in mind as necessary background to what follows.

Stierle has examined the problem of the "identity" of a discourse and affirms that it is governed not so much by formal guidelines (even if these are quite visible, as in the case of lyric poetry) as by the "process of realization of a speech act directed at a speaking subject" (425). In the same vein, this speech act is never a subjective "parole," but a textual realization defined by a public and normative stabilization and by the possibility of an institutional norm.[1] This is the speech act to which Stierle refers as "discourse" as opposed to "text" (*langue*):

What confers an identity on the discourse is not its mere

internal coherence but rather the relation it establishes
with a preexisting discursive scheme, one that extends
itself beyond the individual and concrete discourse at
hand, and that is able to orient both its production and
its reception. And precisely through this reference or
relation of a preexisting discursive scheme to concrete
discourse an ideal value limit can appear in some
measure and can situate itself between production and
reception, promoting the convergence of both. (426)

Stierle repeatedly conveys the extent of dialectic tension that exists between the early outline and the discursive realization, between identity and negation. As Bakhtin has stated, a discourse
defines itself in relation to others; it is the fruit of dialogism.

Stierle's thesis proposes, in no uncertain terms, that the identity of a discourse or genre is a pragmatic question, capable of
orienting the processes of production and reception, whereby it
defines itself. There are critics, such as Culler, who insist that
the definition of lyric poetry is to be found in certain conventions of reading, and that the formal aspects of rhythm, metaphor, and so on, also hold conventional significance (see *Structuralist Poetics*). The peculiarities of lyric poetry are defined by its
effects on readers, as created by determined conventions that
are known to them, to the point where an ordinary piece of journalistic prose written on a page as if it were a lyric poem might
alter the value and meaning of its words or of its blank spaces.
For Genette the ultimate definition of lyric poetry lies in an "attitude of reading" that every poem imposes on its readers:

a motivating attitude which, beyond or short of all the
prosodic or semantic attributes, accords to all or part of
the discourse the sort of intransitive presence and
absolute existence that Eluard calls "poetic evidence."
Poetic language reveals here, it seems to me, its true
"structure," which is not to be a particular *form*, defined
by its specific accidents, but rather a *state*, a degree of
presence and intensity to which any statement may be
led, so to speak, on condition that there is established
around it that *margin of silence* which isolates it from its
surroundings (but not from the gap) of everyday speech.
(*Figures of Literary Discourse* 96; emphasis added)

That state of reading both engenders and is generated by a series of conventions or expectations, four of which are highlighted by Culler in his *Structuralist Poetics*. In addition to "distance and impersonality," which we will analyze later, he points out three that we will discuss below:

(a) The first convention is the expectation of totality and coherence that exacts from poems a guarantee of autonomous totality, allowing them to form a union, or an organic whole (Culler 170–74). An abrupt finish in poetry need not signal the rupture of this totality, but is rather the index of construction in that sense. In contrast to other speech acts that make up part of complex situations, the poem isolates itself as a self-sufficient whole.

(b) Another important and related convention is described thus by Culler:

> To write a poem is to claim *significance* of some sort for
> the verbal construct one produces, and the reader
> approaches a poem with the assumption that however
> brief it may appear it must contain, at least implicitly,
> potential riches which make it worthy of his attention.
> (175; emphasis in original)

This convention implies one of two things: first, that even a trivial anecdote acquires generalized significance and shares in a symbolic ethos of greater purport; or, second, that an obscure and insignificant little poem becomes an "example" of obscure or trivial poetry, posing as metapoetry by dint of the convention whereby poems are taken as declarations on poetry in general, when they are not found to be of greater prominence themselves.

(c) A third convention involves both the attitude of the reader and the effort the reader invests in "shoring up the resistance which the poem mounts against his intelligibility" (175 +). The lyrical process forces readers into a situation of cooperation according to the limits of ease; the more strange and uncomfortable the reading, the more it requires special attention and extra effort.

In conjunction with these conventions set forth by Culler, we might isolate others that affect the very way in which the poem orders itself, in addition to its communicative status. The first of these can be termed *reflexivity*, or the impression that poetry best defines itself as discourse that speaks about itself. Stierle qualifies the norm of the identity of lyric poetry as antidiscursive, as transgressing the discursive sketches that condition the elemental possibilities for organizing the "state of the thing" (*Sachlage*) and its contribution to the "materiality of things" (*Sachverhalt*) (431). Poetry engenders the abolition of temporary schemes and linearity while multiplying and augmenting contexts by way of metaphor and thematic distancing.

Yet beyond this incriminating behavior, Stierle calls attention to poetry's function of revealing its own textual materiality to be the dominant element (435 +). Lyric poetry discursivizes the text in such a way that the text itself becomes an element in its discourse. In terms of "discursive activity," this version of Jakobsonian "autotelismo" in lyric poetry promotes a reflexive function that endows its roles with a significance attached to immanent identity, one that cannot be sought outside the poem itself. Genette discusses a "poetics of language," or a poetic state that resembles the dream and that cannot bill itself as "deviation" from "wakefulness," but rather as its own affirmation of *écart*, of negation, forgetting, illusion, of capturing the hidden side of things, where language and experience are one and the same, not the reflection of one another (*Figures II* 153).

The poem's discursive self-reflexivity, its immanence, its manner of saying things to itself, is a feature revealed by many authors, in different ways, as its principal norm. Not that the poem does not say things. Riffaterre, who has repeatedly opposed measuring the poetic real in terms of mimesis or referentiality, has devised the term "significance," as distinct from "meaning" (*La production du texte* 29). The latter would serve for a heuristic reading of the poem-reality relation, whereas in poetry what matters is the passage from the discourse of meaning to the level of discourse of significance. Here the text contemplates itself as a semantic union, having evolved out of a structural origin or idea. The poetic reading presupposes the heuristic stage of mimetic meaning to arrive at the hermeneutic or retroactive reading of the text's significance as a whole (Riffaterre, *Semiotics of Poetry* 2–10).

Maria Corti, on the other hand, views reflexivity as the incapacity of what the poet enunciates to be replaced by, extrapolated, or separated from the general context of poetic production proper, in the absence of which its reading would lose its specificity. Poetry is a metasemiotic affirmation, which is to say that the communication of poetry and of the poetic text is reflexive, revealing the particular material reality of its organization. The signifying operation is its principal meaning (112–13).

This pragmatic feature of the discursivization of the lyric text cannot be explained without reference to poetry as an "imaginary representation," a general characteristic of all literature, indeed, but one that takes on specific features in lyric poetry. Pragmatic "speech act" theory has established a special norm for literature as activity. S. R. Levin speaks of an implicit dominant oration with respect to poetry, one that can explain the type of illocutive force that the poem may harbor. That oration is the sentence "I imagine myself in, and I invite you to conceive, a world in which (I say that) (I ask you)" (69-70). Poetry invites (perlocutive activity) the imagination; it is, therefore, an act of creation of imaginary worlds, not tied down by the rules of credibility that govern our perceptions of what is real. These are rules that the reader suspends in the act of reading, depending on his or her poetic faith, or by the possibility of entering that imaginary world (73–74). This connection with illocutive action that accompanies the reader transforms poetic communication (and not only lyric poetry) into a special norm.

Already in 1960, long before pragmatic theories of speech acts penetrated the field of philology, Martínez Bonati had rigorously characterized the pragmatic norm of literature, the special relation with its communicative activity, and had spoken in precise terms of imaginary expressions, or pseudo-expressions, in a sense. Unlike real, authentic expressions, these are representations of authentic expressions, but unreal:

> The extraordinary thing is the existence of pseudo-sentences with no concrete context or situation—that is to say, of sentences iconically represented by pseudo-sentences but imagined without any external determination of their communicative situation. *Such is the phenomenon of literature.* The fundamental convention

of literature as a human experience is to accept these
sentences as language and to attribute meaning to them
generally. (80; emphasis added)

Martínez Bonati had already managed to isolate the feature of
text discursivization when he explained that the context of every
poem "is the implicit determination to be a poem" and that our
comprehension unfolds from the immanent situation of the expression: "the author does not communicate with us through
the medium of language, but communicates language to us"
(81). That the imaginary expression immanently signifies its
own communicative situation renders the constant harping on
"the author says" or "the author communicates to us" absurd,
because the speaker of the imaginary phrases is not the one who
expresses, but rather the one who is expressed by them. The
I/you enunciators of the poem form part of the same and are immanent to it (83-84). They are representations of real expressions, imaginary speech.

Every pragmatics of lyric poetry that wishes to explain faithfully the communicative relation originating in the reading of a
poem must be conscious of this characteristic of imaginary expression in order to avoid falling into the simple, vitalist representations of idealist stylistics to which our students find themselves so predisposed and which Martínez Bonati erodes in his
critique of Vossler's idealism. Unfamiliar with Martínez Bonati's
theory, Oomen has arrived at a characterization similar to his, in
affirming that what the poet composes is not a speech act, but a
representation of such: "A poem never talks itself, but recites itself" (174).

Having wrestled with the issue of imaginary speech, we are
in a position to broach the central pragmatic question, which involves the relations between the speakers (speaker-hearer,
writer-reader, you-I) in poetic communication. If we start from
the premise that poetry is a representation of real speech, and is
thereby imaginary expression, we will have to resuscitate the
old questions of the biography of the "author" that enticed
readers to look behind the poetic "I" for an "I" coming from the
life of the poet proper. Allow me to refer to a previous work on
literary reception, and to what is said there with respect to the

"implied reader," in order to draw the same conclusions from the other side of the fence (Pozuelo-Yvancos, *La teoría del lenguaje literario*).

Nevertheless, it would be fruitful to analyze the special aspects attached to the pragmatic question on the relation between the "enunciators" in lyric communication. A story is just as much an imaginary expression as a lyric poem, but in the latter the fundamental question of the "I," and of the identification of the first person, has taken on enormous proportions in theory. This is due, in part, to the weight that the history of ideas has lent the phenomenon of expressiveness in lyric poetry, a phenomenon that romanticism came to sanction definitively. The question of the poetic speaker, of the immanent "I," and of its situation in lyric communication is perhaps the central question surrounding the pragmatics of this genre. In broaching it, we should warn of two distinct questions that often cross one another in the treatment of the thematic of the poetic "I." On one hand, there is the issue of expressiveness or the expressive function of lyric poetry. On the other hand, there is the value acquired by the I-you relation in poetic contexts: that is, the communicative placing of the participants, pronominal or not, in the pragmatic activity unleashed by the reading of a poem.

The treatment of lyric poetry as the realization of the expressive function has been drawn out to the point where the reader is called to identify the lyrical as that genre in which the first person predominates. Indeed, for a long time and through various authors, the theory of literary genres has insisted on the identification of lyric poetry with the first person, narrative with the third, and drama with the second (see Hernadi).

Martínez Bonati has pointed out that the theory of literary genres has mistakenly emphasized the predominance of the "I" in lyric poetry, which is emphasized by Jakobson, among others, and which finds strong support in German romanticism. It has often been interpreted as thematic subjectivity (poetry speaking about the speaker) or in terms of affectivity, volition, or emotive attitude. Martínez Bonati reworks the question by highlighting that the lyrical predominates over expressivity in a very distinct sense, given the fact that it does not constitute a speaking about the speaker (it is indifferent to what is spoken of in a poem), but rather the manifestation of speaking with itself in solitude. Lyric poetry is expression in the sense of being a revelation of the speaker in the linguistic act:

> This makes possible a conception of lyric poetry as the unfolding of the linguistic potential for making something manifest that is *not* said by means of something else that *is* said (or represented). . . . This makes lyric poetry a fundamentally different revelation of being (with different possibilities) from the epic and from philosophy, which are essentially a *saying*, a representative revelation, thematic speech. (88; emphasis added)

The imaginary communicative situation of lyric poetry is that of soliloquies through which speakers feel themselves as beings and know themselves intuitively as inwardness.

In the same way, Kate Hamburger privileged the distinctiveness of lyric poetry, focusing on the particular functioning of the relation of the lyric enunciated in respect to its confrontation with reality. Unlike other elements that "reality evinces," lyric poetry would not have the function of communicating, but rather of constructing a lived experience inseparable from its enunciation. In lyric poetry the subject-object polarity breaks at the moment in which the lyric "I"-object cannot be separated from the enunciation. The object is the subject:

> The limit which separates the enunciated lyric from the non-lyric is not given through the external form of the poem, but rather by the functioning of the enunciated in relation to the object-pole. The fact that we know and sample the poem as the field of experience of a subject of enunciation (and only as such), attests to the fact that its enunciation is not directed towards the object-pole, but rather, that its object is absorbed by the subject's sphere of experience, in which it finds itself metamorphosed. (254)

Once the communicative situation of lyric poetry is configured as fundamentally expressive, it becomes extremely interesting to analyze poetry in terms of the contextual values that the I-you relation takes on. Although the simple, traditional mode of reading has sought to identify "I" = author person, the principal pragmatic feature brought out by all authors today is what Culler terms "distance and impersonality." According to the convention of "distance and impersonality," the value of the shifters and their effects engenders a process of generalization, whereby the I-you of the poem refers not to a real external context but to a fictitious situation that bestows coherence on the reading independent of the external referent (Culler 170–74). Oomen speaks of serious difficulties with the identification of the poetic "I" and "you," in that a variety of different personae can be identified, each apart from reference to the real world, and immanent to the text (141). A similar fault with the "real world" referent sparks a multiplication and extension of the roles, even to the point where, as we shall see, mutual identification of the you and the "I" occurs at one and the same instance, a very peculiar phenomenon in lyric communication.

Obviously, this generalization and multiplication of shifter referents depends on the "speaking situation"; it is not prefixed in the poem as in everyday discourse, nor is it fixed, as in the novel, by the characters' speech and by the activity of the narrator. In effect, referents in the novel are not of the real world either, but, in turn, the narrative fixes the immanent speaking situations of the text, and in that way tends to eliminate its distance with respect to everyday linguistic acting. Of interest in the novel is what Barthes, in "El efecto de la realidad," termed the "reality effect"; lyric poetry often avoids this effect by leaving the speaking situation completely unhinged. It thereby achieves the margin of ambiguity, the generalization of experience, and a process of identification of the reader ("you") with the lyrical "I."

Yuri Levin has noted that in lyrical poetry the character of subjectivity favors the emergence of a "direct" type of communication between the reader, the implicit author, and the explicit characters, who, by way of generalization, become adaptable in terms of role, permitting readers to project the situation of the poem on their experience, personal or imagined, dreamed or desired (206).

Stierle has explained the phenomenon masterfully by pointing out that in poetry the norm of transmitter and receiver has favored the discursivization of the text in such a way that if the subject of enunciation is a function of discourse in all communication; it so happens that it is also produced in lyrical communication, and vice versa. The discourse itself comes to stand as a function of the subject of enunciation, by which the latter, as a role, loses its identity. Stated another way, role and discursive function meld together and become identical. This problematization of the identity of the subject of enunciation causes the emergence of a lyrical subject or role of a lyrical subject, which is not an identifiable entity outside of the poem itself. The discourse itself is a function of the subject of enunciation, and vice versa. A loss of extradiscursive identity is set in motion, and the poem becomes a constant search for that problematic identity of the subject (436+).

The same would happen with the poetic "you," which at times has a referent designated by the actual text, at those moments when the value of the reference is extended to include the reader, and among others, the subject itself ("I"), in a clear process of identification with the one who has written. According to Lázaro Carreter,

> The illocutive force of a poem is always an invitation to the reader to lay claim to its message. This pragmatic relation . . . to me seems fundamental. Only through this does one explain the prominence of the reader in lyric communication. (47)[2]

The multiplication of contexts is not limited, in lyric poetry, to the personal shifters, but extends to the spatial and temporal contexts that undergo an identical process of generalization. The "now" of the poem is not the now of when it was written, but the now of when it is read, its original contexts fading into a multiplication and extension of themselves (see Culler, Oomen, and Stierle).

The extension of place and time is related to the extension of what Oomen terms "space of perception," or a totality of the factors that are given to the participants through the situation, the amount of extralinguistic information shared by the interlocutors in the communicative act (common objects, occurrences present in the speaking communication, and so forth):

> In non-poetic written communication, the speaker has to
> inform the addressee of the circumstances in which the
> latter is writing, in case he wishes to reference the
> situation. In poetry, however, objects and occurrences
> are often mentioned, as if given by a space of
> perception, and as if the addressee formed part of this
> space and were, in effect, familiarized with it. (145)

Through those venues, readers are liberated from their "real"
situation and are introduced into a new perceptive space. The
latter, atemporal and lacking in concrete restrictions, multiplies
the communicative text and extends it to every situation of reading in which one believes oneself to be in the imaginary world,
by dint of the returning presence of those objects and events.

Authors such as Corti and Lázaro Carreter, with extensive
backgrounds in philological studies, have raised the issue of the
inappropriateness of marginalizing the poet and the poet's creative intent from the pragmatics of the lyric text. It makes little
sense, despite anything that the triumph of reception aesthetics
may have obscured. What disappears is the *signatum* of the lyrical sign, which for Lázaro Carreter is to be found in "the meaning created-or-produced-in an individual conscience that the
poet invites us to make our own" (245+).[3] Lázaro Carreter
speaks of two significations and two meanings:

> On the one hand there is the signification that the poet
> has encoded in the linguistic material, and the meaning
> that he has wanted to give it: he has written the orations
> that make up his verses, these being endowed with
> signification—normally so that they might contain the
> meaning he desires to transmit to the reader. . . . Then
> there is the signification and the meaning bestowed by
> the reader that may or may not coincide with those
> contributed by the author. These cannot be marginalized
> in the interpretation of the lyric poem because they make
> up the *signatum* of the sign, and in poetry acquire
> enormous value, corresponding to how the poet has
> coded signification and meaning so that these are shared
> with the reader. Nonetheless, meeting or not meeting
> this objective does not stand in the way of expecting it to
> exist as a goal in studies on semiotics. (46–48)[4]

Maria Corti, although she speaks of a poetic competence, also emphasizes the *pretextual* ("avantesto") process, which does not mean something "outside of the text" but entails a creative energy that functions as input into the text. It is the creative dynamic that spares us from holding a static conception of the text, whether de facto or by contrivance. For Corti, a dynamic conception demands that the creative energy be borne in mind, given that what is termed "creative process" is not only a combination of words but a grammar of the vision, a specific categorizing of reality in which the worlds of desire and of dreams intervene (88–89). So, too, do the states of consciousness and the pretextual, vital elements that are essential in defining the poetic (107+), as do the specific interests of certain extratextual indexes (38–41), such as the biographical ins and outs of certain authors.

In any case, and even if the signifying production is included in the pragmatics of lyrical poetry as part of the communicative event, what Lázaro Carreter and Corti make clear is that the creative instance in no way identifies itself with the real author, whom the biographist tradition has attempted to connect with the category of the poet. Author (as empirical subject) and poet (as creative instance) may be understood as two subjects of differential pragmatic identities.

Yuri Levin has invited an analysis of the communicative norm of the lyric poem in terms of "the structure of the relations between the characters of the text and the characters outside of the text," and he proposes a typology of situations in which there are different forms of the first and second persons: in some the "I" can be identified with the author, with the reader, and so on. In all, the typology would have been more useful had Levin never spoken of the real author, inasmuch as the literary author is always the image of the person who is writing, not of the person who exists. The literary author forms part of an imaginary world, and therefore cannot be the one who imagines and who is imagined simultaneously. Whatever its meaning, the "I"-author of the lyric text, even that one so called and distinguished by Levin, forms part of the imagined of literary fiction; it is a being on paper, a character.

104 ◆ JOSÉ MARÍA POZUELO-YVANCOS

Notes

1. "Institutional norm" is used throughout this chapter to translate Pozuelo-Yvancos's *estatuto*.

2. "La fuerza ilocutiva de una poesía es siempre una invitación al lector a que asuma el mensaje como propio. Esta relación pragmática . . . me parece fundamental. Sólo por ello se explica el relieve del lector en la comunicación lírica."

3. " . . . el sentido creado-o-producido-en una conciencia individual que el poeta nos invita a hacer nuestros."

4. "Por un lado está la significación que el poeta ha cifrado con el material lingüístico y el *sentido* que ha querido darle: ha escrito las oraciones que componen sus versos dotados de significación—normalmente para que quieran decir que (el sentido que desea transmitir al lector) . . . Luego está la significación y el sentido otorgados por el lector que pueden o no coincidir con los primeros (los del autor). Estos no son marginables en la interpretación del poema lírico porque son el signatum del signo, y en poesía adquieren un valor enorme en tanto el poeta ha cifrado significación y sentido para que sean compartido con el lector. Que el propósito se logre o no, no es óbice para atender en los estudios de semiótica la existencia de tal propósito."

Works Cited

Abrams, Meyer Howard. *El espejo y la lámpara*. Barcelona: Barral Editores, 1974.
Aguiar, Branco, and Isabel Maria de Silva. *Teoria da literatura*. 6th ed. Vol. 1. Coimbra: Almedina, 1984.
Bakhtin, Mikhail. *The Dialogic Imagination: Four Essays*. Austin: Univ. of Texas Press, 1981.
Barthes, Roland. "El efecto de la realidad." In *Lo verosímil*. Buenos Aires: Tiempo Contemporaneo, 1970. 95–101.
Corti, Maria. *Principi della comunicazione letteraria*. Milan: Bompiani, 1975.
Culler, Jonathan. *Structuralist Poetics: Structuralism, Linguistics and the Study of Literature*. Ithaca: Cornell Univ. Press, 1975.
Dubois, J., et al. *Rhétorique de la poésie*. Brussels: Complexe, 1977.
Empson, William. *Seven Types of Ambiguity*. 1930. Reprinted, Harmondsworth, Middlesex, U.K.: Penguin, 1973.
Fowler, Alistair. *Kinds of Literature: An Introduction to the Theory of Genres and Modes*. Oxford: Clarendon Press, 1982.
García Berrio, Antonio. "Lingüística, literaridad/poeticidad (Gramática, pragmática, texto)." *Anuario de la Sociedad Española de Literatura General y Comparada* 2 (1979): 125–68.
——. "Il ruolo della retorica nell'analisi/interpretazione dei testi letterari." *Versus* (1983): 35–36.
——. *Introducción a la poética clasicista: Comentario a las "Tablas poéticas" de Cascales*. 2d ed. Madrid: Taurus, 1988.
Genette, Gérard. *Figures II*. Paris: Editions du Seuil, 1969.
——. *Mimologiques*. Paris: Editions du Seuil, 1976.
——. *Introduction à l'architexte*. Paris: Editions du Seuil, 1979.

_____. *Figures of Literary Discourse*. Trans. Alan Sheridan. New York: Columbia Univ. Press, 1982.

Guillén, Claudio. *Literature as System*. Cambridge: Harvard Univ. Press, 1971.

Hamburger, Kate. *Logique des genres littéraires*. Paris: Editions du Seuil, 1986.

Hernadi, Paul. *Teoría de los géneros literarios*. Barcelona: Bosch, 1972.

Kibédi-Varga, A. *Les constantes du poème. Analyse du langage poétique*. Paris: Picard, 1977.

Lázaro Carreter, Fernando. "El poema lírico como signo." In *Teoría semiótica: Lenguajes, textos hispánicos*, ed. M. A. Garrido. Vol. 1. Madrid: Consejo Superior de Investigación Científica, 1984. 42–55.

Levin, S. R. "Consideraciones sobre qué tipo de acto de habla es un poema." In *Pragmática de la comunicación literaria*. Ed. J. A. Mayoral. Madrid: Arco Libros, 1987. 59–82.

Levin, Yuri. "Le statut communicatif du poème lyrique." In *Travaux sur les systèmes de signes*. Brussels: Editions Complexe, 1976.

Martínez Bonati, Felix. *Fictive Discourse and the Structures of Literature: A Phenomenological Approach*. Trans. Philip W. Silver. Ithaca: Cornell Univ. Press, 1981.

Mayoral, J. A., ed. *Pragmática de la comunicación literaria*. Madrid: Arco Libros, 1987.

Morris, Charles. *Signos, lenguaje, conducta*. Buenos Aires: Losada, 1968.

Oomen, Ursula. "On Some Elements of Poetics Communication." In *Pragmática de la comunicación literaria*, ed. J. A. Mayoral. Madrid: Arco Libros, 1987. 137–49.

Pozuelo-Yvancos, José María. *Del formalismo a la neoretórica*. Madrid: Taurus, 1988.

_____. *La teoría del lenguaje literario*. Madrid: Cátedra, 1988.

Riffaterre, Michael. *Semiotics of Poetry*. Bloomington: Indiana Univ. Press, 1978.

_____. *La production du texte*. Paris: Editions du Seuil, 1979.

Stierle, Karlheinz. "Identité du discours et transgression lyrique." *Poétique* 32 (1977): 422–41.

Chapter 7

Reading in Process, the Antitext, and the Definition of Literature

Manuel Asensi

(translated by Laura Giefer)

> *What we have to say in answer to our question is that literature does not exist, or even if it does take place it is like something that does not take place, although an object exists. Language is certainly present, "made obvious," asserted with more authority than in any other form of human activity, but it materializes completely, which means that it merely has the reality of the whole: it is everything and nothing more, ever prepared to pass from all to nothing.*
>
> —Maurice Blanchot (84)

In a previous work, dedicated to a *theoría*[1] of reading, I investigated the paradoxical movement that characterizes the relationship between the language of literary theory and that of literature. One of the core chapters of that work noted the characteristics of identity and difference that mediate between text and metatext. In dealing specifically with the question of difference, the problem of defining language or the literary text was brought to the foreground, a classical problem that was not addressed at the time because the investigation wandered along other paths. Nevertheless, the way was prepared for understanding that the question about the *being* of *literature* ought to remain within the limits of inquiry and the *space* that is extracted from that concept. In this essay I intend to approach the problem of the definition of literature and text based upon assumptions established in a *theoría* of reading. In order to do this, it will be necessary to briefly contrast these assumptions with those that, throughout the twentieth century, have also endorsed certain answers to the *being* of literature (answers to the question "What is literature?").

As a point of departure, I will affirm that literary language (which is not language in the instrumental sense, or *literature*, or text) exploits the potential of the name, not limiting itself to a simple-presence, whereas metalanguage works in the direction of the rigidity of the sign, tending toward the simple-presence. In other words, "when referring to the text we will not discuss the *sign* (a concept conceived in terms of presence, at least in its most structuralist interpretations) but the *hypertrace*. This can be defined as a *hypersignificant element (gramma, between) which composes the space of the T (text), and is never totally present, always being directed toward (and in the function of) the graft—the antitext—and which lends its presence to the metatext*" (Asensi 76; emphasis in original).[2] What are the consequences of these affirmations, which refer to the problem of defining literature? In what way do they confront the question: What is literature?

Let us recognize in principle that the definition of a literary text as trace is excessively general. The "trace" is not the *différance* (see Derrida, "La différance"). The trace opens itself up to the *différance*; it is what transforms the *literary* text into the privileged place of the *différance*, that which names without naming, the introduction to the literary text within the silence of the *différance*. Because the latter is neither a word nor a concept, it stands at the beginning and is either unoriginal or perpetually original. It is precisely the relationship between the trace and the *différance* that makes the given definition "excessively general." However, "excessively general" here does not mean "insufficiently delimited" or "poorly adapted" to the limits of what would be the literary space, as opposed to, let us say, the philosophical, scientific, or natural-language space. This is, above all, because this generality suits the literary text. Here, "excessively general" actually means "untreated," "with little writing about itself." Secondly, we must be aware that the definition of the literary text as trace does not attempt to provoke "literaturity," which is specific to literary language as opposed to other languages—and not only because this definition does not locate itself within the framework of "literaturity," but because it confronts it while at the same time undoubtedly endeavoring to explain the why of "literaturity."

Every day it seems more evident that the attempt to offer essentialist definitions of literature is dissipating.[3] Poststructuralism, from the 1960s until today, and before that certainly semiotics (see Garroni, especially chapter 3), have cast doubt on such essentiality. Looking more attentively at the process points out that the questions of essence ("literaturity") and presence (code, structure, universal grammar) in literature are historically linked to two fundamental facts: on one hand, the adoption of part (and only part) of a theory *of* and *in* the literature of the German romanticism of Jena;[4] and, on the other, the assimilation of the poetic to theory, science, and method in the modern sense, an event in which Husserlian phenomenology played an important part.

It is usually affirmed that with the romantics, literature (and art in general) ceased thinking of itself in terms of "a mirror" (mimesis) but rather conceived of itself as "a lamp" (expression) (see Abrams). In fact, the pair art-reality is replaced by the pair artist-work, from which will emerge an important branch of twentieth-century stylistics. But the concept of expression cannot be understood in a simple way, since "expression," aside from referring to the spirit of the artist, refers to a self-expressed expression, that is, to literature understood as an absolute. Within the scope of literary theory such a symbolic conception of a work combines with the liberation of the signifier employed by the vanguard (and before that by central figures like Mallarmé and Nietzsche, among others) and the so-called Russian formalists at the beginning of the century. In this respect, we remember Klebnikov's hypothesis regarding the self-sufficient word; this word was postulated as absolutely productive in Russian formalist theories. As Boris Eikhenbaum wrote, a fundamental objective of the formal method was "to free the poetic word of philosophical and religious tendencies more and more preponderant among the Symbolists," an objective that assumes "the autonomous value of words" (38-39). Now, this autonomous value permits us to confront the literary work as an object in itself, that is, as an object independent of other objects and other spaces. From this perspective, the principal task of the Russian formalists, and of a great part of twentieth-century literary theory, has been the search for and demarcation of the specificity of literary language.

The second historical fact is the linking of literary theory to the scientific method. Clearly, mention of the scientific method can give way to a polysemy that is difficult to control. Therefore—and this was the course followed in *Theoría de la lectura*—when the scientific method is discussed it must be understood as the scientific method and theory characteristic of the natural sciences and, following Heidegger, of the culmination of Western metaphysics: to think of entity as simple-presence in such a way that it becomes manipulable for scientific (empiric) activity. The simple-presence, the "being there" definitive of the text, is an obligatory pretext (*the* pretext, one would have to say) for an empirical science. Linguistics serves as a clear example. As is well known, literary theory has walked hand in hand with linguistics in attempting to constitute itself as a science. Simple-presence, on the other hand, is perfectly confirmed within the concept of structure. Why? If we think, for example, of the foundations established by Hjelmslev in *Prolegomena to a Theory of Language*, we arrive at the conclusion that the possibility of defining the literary object implies: (1) considering that object as specific and independent of other fields and objects; and (2) thinking of that very object as a total presence capable of being dominated by theory. Only by bringing such presuppositions into the field of literary theory is it possible to achieve "literaturity" and the semantic range that accompanies it.

It would be absurd to demonstrate here why the distinct essentialist positions or predicators of the question "What is literature?" have not proven satisfactory, primarily because it is well known (see Talens). What interests me is: Why is it not possible to satisfactorily respond to the problem posed by the question "What is literature?" The question implies an a priori subjective response at the textual level (literary or not), that is, on the order of presence, organicity, coherence, determinability, and homogeneity (see Derrida, *Disseminations*; Fish; and Pratt)[5] and because at this very moment the "betweens" of the "antitext," the presence-absence of the trace, a space without beginning or end, an impure heterogeneity, are displaced to an inaccessible dimension by the answer inferred from "What is?"

Among the antiessentialist answers that have recently had the widest reception, those given by pragmatics and the aesthetics of reception stand out. Out of them has come a conception of the literary work in which the primary object is to comprehend that every definition is the product of a historical or contextual reading. Thus, the literature of St. Augustine's epoch is not identified by its textual typology, by definitions given at the time, or by public responses to the literature of Castelvetro's, Novalis's, or Eliot's epoch. It follows that any essentialist definition of literature is erroneous for not bearing in mind the historical conditions of every literary conception of being. The concept of literature therefore embraces the historical ensemble of effects and responses given explicitly or implicitly to literature's problem of *being*.[6] Otherwise, it will be framed by certain situations of cooperation or acts of speech (mimetic or nonmimetic).

Now, then, can it be agreed that "literature" is (or is characterized by) the historical answer to the being of literature? With such a definition, an atemporal essentialist (ahistorical) answer is replaced with a historical (relative to the historic moment) essentialist answer: in other words, one continues asking "What is literature?" although now that question may not make claims to universality. But herein lies a fundamental problem: should the attitude of a *theoría* of discourse consist in the acceptance (or in the receptive and passive study) of historical prejudices about the literary space? Do, after all, certain historical concepts and answers to being in literature enclose and institutionalize the sense of that being, perhaps by remaining within the limits of the question "What is?" I must emphasize that I do not deny the implicit importance of knowing these answers, which seems to me of the first order for a literary theory (and I have confirmed this view in *Theoría de la lectura*); what I deny is that the question for literature ought to resolve itself by means of a historical consideration (from and in history) proposed, for example, by the aesthetics of reception. Limiting literature to a historical answer conceals one of the basic questions: Literature? And this is one of the processes I intend to develop in this essay. Rather than ask "What is literature?" I will ask "Literature?" or, stated another way, "Can literature enclose itself within the 'is' of the question 'What is literature'?" In both cases, in the essentialist-universalist answer and in the relativist-historical answer, it is presupposed that literature, that literary writing (if we wish to center the issue more), that the text *is* what is there, susceptible to being apprehended and dominated by theory (see, for example, Ricoeur). It matters little that a theory recognize the impossibility of an exhaustiveness, of a commensurability of the literary object (something common, on the other hand), since the use of the method carries with it an entire historical burden that is not altogether unknown to us.

The criticism I propose clearly bases itself on a Nietzschean and Heideggerian deconstruction of Western metaphysics. In a 1957 conference paper, "The Essence of Speech," Heidegger again insists that the principal effect of method and technique is oblivion of being so that entity might be understood as simple-presence. Therefore, when it is said that something *is*—and saying that arises from the theoretical methodology considered to be the culmination of Western metaphysics—something is alluded to that Heidegger himself expressed very well in his work *Introduction to Metaphysics:*

> We will enumerate a series of different meanings interpreted by means of description. The "being" mentioned in "is" means: "actually present," "existing in a material and constant way," "to take place," "to proceed," "to consist," "to inhabit," "to pertain," "to fall," "to be located in," "to encounter," "to dominate," "to arrive," "to present." By opposing essence, it continues to be difficult and inconclusive, perhaps impossible, to isolate a common meaning, understood as the generic-universal concept, within which one might subordinate, as species, the cited modes of "is." However, a certain unique feature is common to all of these meanings, demonstrating the content-filled comprehensiveness of the verb "to be" within a fixed horizon. *The limitation of the meaning of "to be" remains within the scope of presence, from which it gets its character of being—in the face of consistency and subsistence, residence and arrival.* (Heidegger, "La esencia del habla," 129; emphasis added)[7]

For our part, we could insist that our conception of literature and text continue to be enmeshed in this sense of "being." The question "What is literature?" or "What is the text?" confines the literary object as well as the concrete text recognized as literary (although not only literary) to the limits of a presence shaped by the "is" of the question "What is literature?" Or, in Heidegger's words:

> The word, which is nothing in itself, nothing that "exists," eludes us . . . It reveals what there is but, despite everything, "is" not. In addition, it pertains to what there is, despite everything—perhaps not just "in addition," but before everything—in such a way that, within the essence of the word, what presents is hidden. If we think rightly, we will never be able to say of the word: it is, but rather: it gives (es gibt), not in the sense that words "might occur" but rather inasmuch as the word itself is that which presents. The word: donor (das Gebende): of what does it make a gift? In accordance with the poetic experience and according to the most ancient tradition of thought, the word gives: being. ("La esencia del habla" 171–73)[8]

"What is literature," the question put between parentheses, suspended in the void of theoría, has then affirmed that literature is not, in the same way that Heidegger has written that the word does not exist, but rather presents something. What consequence can a theoría of literature extract from this? The consequence will be not an unveiling of being in poetry, speech, or text in the Heideggerian direction, but rather, to use Levinas's words, an act that "does not consist of equating being with representation, of turning toward a bright light where this adaptation is attempted, but rather, by going beyond this game of lights . . . and by realizing events whose ultimate meaning . . . does not succeed in unveiling" (53).

I have written above that literary theory from the beginning of the century (Russian formalism) assimilated part of Jena's German romantic project, although only part. Of interest now is that part which makes of Jena's proposal a project still being realized. If there is something unedited in the proposal of these authors, it is precisely that which denotes literature a new genre, beyond the differences of classical poetics, capable of resolving innate divisions in the written object (see Lacoue-Labarthe and Nancy). As we will have occasion to show, literature as genre neutralizes not only internal but external divisions as well, those that separate it from science, religion, philosophy, and so on. In fact, literature, as a new genre, denotes the generality and the generativity of literature, apprehending and producing itself in an infinitely unedited work. So then, the fact that literature may be thought of as an absolute, as a self-enclosed entity, does not designate an object with limits, prone to being defined. On the contrary, here the absolute means that literature absorbs theory and does not exclude that into which it is translated. The problem of defining literature is that it remains within the limits of the question, actually the eternally defined question: "What is literature?"

A key concept in German romantic discourse is that of "genre," not a genre subject to the principle of identity, but a genre with no form, no essence, and no possibility of being defined. But is this genre? Can it be? These are questions which must be countered by others: Can there be a genre which is not so? And what is the condition of genre? The problem provoked by these questions is raised in a work published by Derrida in 1980, "La loi du genre." The foundation of this work is its conception of writing. What characterizes any text (be it "written" or "spoken") is its iterability, the possibility of being cited with or without quotation marks. But that iterability breaks with the notion of context as it is conceived by pragmatics, that is, as a saturable element; instead, context must be understood as infinite recontextualization, being only contexts with no center of absolute anchorage.

Returning to the concept of genre, we are assailed with the doubt that it will deal not with a negation or an affirmation of generic character but rather with an infinite difference, a doubt that is quickly resolved when we perceive that the iterability needs repetition as well as difference. And this is where Derrida's work on genre situates itself: Can a literary work (or work of art in general, or of biology) be identified if it does not carry the stamp of a genre or point to it in some way? Such a question does not imply that a work adheres to only one genre (even works that "break" with genre take it as a reference), nor that it ought to make explicit mention of its genre, nor that the stamp ought to be understood as theme, nor even that there be consciousness of genre on the part of the author or the reader. What the question suggests, and this is one of Derrida's theses, is that the law of genre is characterized as an impure law consisting of a counterlaw. In fact, terms such as "impurity," "corruption," "contamination," "decomposition," "perversion," "deformation," and "cancerization" are engendered in the repetition, in the "citation" (Derrida 179–80). The relationship between genre and genericity, to use the words of Jean-Marie Schaeffer ("Du texte au genre"),[9] is emphasized here as being participation without ownership. In this relationship a process of inclusion-exclusion operates in such a way that the commentary that takes place in the genericity, the participating without belonging, cannot simply form part of the corpus. The mention of "novel" is not itself "novelesque"; it does not form part of the body that designates. But neither is it alien to it: "this peculiar *topos,* situated within the work and outside it, on its edge, an inclusion and an exclusion with respect to genre in general, indeed, with respect to identifiable class in general" (Derrida, "La loi du genre," 186).[10] Thus, we have the Law, the closure, the Counterlaw, that is, the enclosure that is excluded from what is included.

I had earlier proposed replacing the question "What is literature?" with "Literature?" As may be observed with this last question, the "nature" or "concept" of literature is not investigated. It is interrogated precisely by the possibility of the "is." And the sense that I attribute to the "is" has been defined above. I believe that I am not mistaken in asserting that proposals like those of Nietzsche-Heidegger, Derrida, or the theoreticians of Jena's German romanticism posit important objectives that replace the "What is?" with the empty question mark "?".

I would now like to return to the definition of "hypertrace" given in *Teoría de la lectura* and mentioned at the beginning of this essay. This term did not seek to establish a concept as much as to introduce the literary text fully within the scope of a presence-absence, that is, within an open field without the limits of what we might call the antitext. As we will see, it is not necessarily opposed to the text, although certainly it concludes with the utopian thought of textual homogeneity as it is presently posed in textual linguistics, beginning with the notion of "coherence." The "trace" designates that condition of the text whose function depends upon a "before," not itself original, and a "for later." Actually, the "for later" is what gives a truthful account of that condition; textualization (a particular organization of traces) always depends upon recontextualization by the reader from the perspective of certain metatexts. And this reading does not refer to only one relationship, that between text and reader, but to the reading-writing of the author, and to the ownership of the text by its reader-interpreter. In the reading, textualization emerges from the paradoxical relationship between text and metatext. The trace reveals that there are elements hidden behind the text that do not occupy space (active-passive producers of the text) and that I call "betweens." These "betweens" form the space of the antitext, a space with neither borders nor edges.

In *Theoría de la lectura*, I attempted to explain that the paradoxical relationship between text and metatext is due to a movement of identity-difference (11–63). I emphasize identity because the metalanguage does not form, cannot form, an exterior with respect to language; the latter is always beyond critics and their limits. From the text-metatext, identity originates all criticism that, gathering fundamentally the theses of Heidegger, Gadamer, and Derrida, was constituted by the identification of the text-metatext with the method. This criticism did not convert the theoretical-scientific-objective proposal into an atheoretical-ascientific-subjective one. But, in any case, the decline (and rehabilitation) of that opposition occurs, beginning with the recognition that text-metatext take place within the metaphoric interior. And as we suggested above, I highlight difference because this metaphoric interior is infinite, in the sense that certain textualities are the privileged, if not unique, space of the dynamization of the name, of the "hypertracing" capacity (if I may be granted such an expression), whereas the metatext works in the shadow of "theory," in the direction of the rigidity of the sign. Thus, the metatext will never be able to saturate the text, will never be able to conceive of it as a semantic self-enclosed

universe, will never be able to fully reclaim its mimetic-repro-
ductive being of meaning (restricted), of the polysemy or the
theme of text. It will surely be the effect of meaning as reflected
in the infinitude of these effects, writing capable of adopting diverse forms, from mimetic-writing to opaque-writing. That we
might contemplate the metatext as an effect of the meaning of
text tells, moreover, of the need for a reading in process that
might discredit its possible authority: Literature? The Text?

It is possible to draw conclusions from what has been said
and suggested up to now. Heidegger used to say that speech *is*
not. How can we carry this idea over to our reflection about the
definition of literature? We can do so by positing, in the first
place, the following difference: the definitions implied by the
question "What is literature?" reveal a technical look at the work
of art, a glance that simultaneously departs from and constitutes
the text, as "artifact" (in Mukarovsky's sense in *Escritos de estética y semiótica del arte*) of the empirical textual material. The text
is modeled around the idea of "presence" postulated by scientific projects and technical metalanguages. Our investigations
have brought us to the conclusion that, in fact, behind the "appearance" of the empirical text is found the "antitext," which
must not be identified with any truth or a face concealed behind
the mask of textual presence but rather precisely with the movement of the trace, a presence-absence that does not fall within
the limits of "being" of the question "What is literature?" or
"What is the text?" So then, confronted with the text and the
signs, we find the antitext and the "betweens." Therefore, if we
propose for the text that it is not a simple-presence, we must accept that any definition of *literature* (or *film*, or *theory* itself, and
the series is interminable) will necessarily be transcended by the
antitext. The trace, due to its "for later" structure, does not permit a definition with beginning and end, nor in the direction of
"literaturity," nor that of a present "code"; the trace surprises
every specificity or codification that might be attributed to it.
Therefore, *literature* (and we continue utilizing this word in ital-
ics, something which should not be given up), from the hand of
the antitext, would be characterized (and decharacterized) by its
utopia (no-place), that is, by constantly avoiding the conceptual
game of literaturity or of the definitions in re of literature (as, for

example, those of reception aesthetics). What is proposed in responding in a determined way (the antitextuality) to the question: "Literature?" is:

(1) That the text (literary and nonliterary, philosophical and nonphilosophical, metalinguistic and nonmetalinguistic) cannot be limited to the presence of "artifact," to the empirically sensible and palpable as a reflection of a supposed orality, nor to the presence of an intelligible object in terms of signs, signifiers and signifieds, forms or contents (see Gasché, *The Tain of the Mirror*, 178+). Surely the very notion of text—in its various meanings—is accomplice to the previous attributions. In this respect I believe that the works of Derrida are sufficiently representative, although we must also refer to Stanley Fish, who, in a now classic work, asserted: "By being so physically convincing the objectivity of the text is an illusion, and moreover a dangerous illusion. It is an illusion of self-sufficiency and completeness. An imprinted line or the page of a book are so obviously *there*—they can be manipulated, photocopied, cut—that they seem to be the depository for all the value and signification associated with them" (Fish 32; emphasis in original).

(2) From the two previous reasons, which are simultaneously inherited from Heideggerian philosophy (as well as Freudian theory), we postulate a distinct "reality" (one would have to say equal and distinct), which we can call the "antitext." This antitext forms part of the presence of all textuality, but at the same time it is an imperceptible movement that retreats toward another space, toward another antitextuality, toward the scope of the trace and the "betweens." This theory of the antitext (which we will develop in various directions in the future) inherits, on one hand, the theory of the graft as explained by Derrida in "La doble sesión" (*Disséminations*) and as practiced by him in *Glas*, but it also inherits what Mary Louise Pratt has called "linguistics of contact" ["a linguistics that would decenter the community, and adopt as an axis the operativity of language through the limits of social differentiation" (68)], the Bakhtinian theory of carnivalization,[11] and the Barthesian proposal about the plurality of codes present, for example, in Balzac's narration (see *S/Z*). Now, then, add to all of these the idea that the antitext does not imply a structure, a harmony, a pacific coexistence of present and absent

elements simultaneously at play, and is not limited to any concrete type of text (the novel or literature itself). Derrida's theory of the graft must make us conscious that the grafted grammas do not retain a relationship of harmony and cooperation, but rather of fragmentation, of the friction of forces, disequilibriums, fractures, and even power relationships. The "writing that refers only to itself simultaneously, indefinitely, and systematically transfers/moves us to another writing," with which it will possibly, we would add, maintain a relationship of conflict. The antitext points to a space without limits [a space of *infinición* "for which a separated being, fixed in its identity, the Self, contains within itself that which it cannot contain, which it cannot not receive by the sole virtue of its identity" (Levinas 52)],[12] for which abound a multiplicity of (meta)texts belonging to our western (Babel) or to another distinct tradition. Barthes called those texts "codes" for reading. We add that they are not limited and do not maintain an internal relationship of organicity.

(3) This "distinct" reality cannot be perceived with a simple gaze/reading, but from an analysis which, like Freud's "case of 'the wolfman,' " never ends. This fact is explained by the fact that the "analysis" (a concept that, like that of the "gaze" or the "reading," one must utilize between quotation marks and with great precautions) cannot avoid the "between" into which it inserts itself, the "between" provoked by the identity-difference relationship between text and metatext. In other words: the antitext, because of its movement and the consequences derived during the process, possesses the characteristics of "parengonality" (Derrida, *The Truth in Painting*), the reason for which the trace-text conflictivity that composes it manifests itself in a double relationship, in the chiasmus of inside-outside: inside (outside) because every text is subjugated by the antitextuality that is prior and posterior to it and that is characterized by a conflictive-grafted indetermination, so that any analysis can only set in motion but not finalize. We speak of outside (inside) because the apparent and empirical relationships between "metatext" and "text" are relationships that at the same time imply conflicts and closures. All this allows the thesis of the metaphor of an organism (such as it has been formulated by Plato and Horace as well as the romantics and structuralists) and Aristotle's

theory of the fable to arise from the oblivion of the antitext, an oblivion that erases borders and fractures and makes apparent the presence of the text as a hierarchical and structured organization. The Aristotelian theory of the fable or the Platonic theory of discourse imply the oblivion of the antitext. At the same time, the antitext exceeds the (dead?) figure of the reader who bases the reading activity on textual coherence, of the reader who encounters a beginning, middle, and end, a structure or meaning. The reader of the antitext does not exist, except as reading in process within the field of *infinición* of antitextuality.

(4) The antitext denies the simple and empirical existence of the text or, at the very least, points to its absolutely insufficient character. Behind this negation, which is not in itself an erasure of the text as artifact, the antitext is included within neither strong nor weak textualism (Rorty; and Blumenberg, especially chapter 19) is not a word liberated as signifier of any signified, nor a word directly related to an external referent. It is instead that which signals the nonexistence of something external to the text. It is the negation of the identity of a self-enclosed text, through which it is possible to introduce the text into the relationships of conflict and power, that manifest this antitextuality. Now, then, if we would like to indicate some ways in which the analysis is introduced into the between of the antitext, we would assert that this "between" talks about the paradoxical relationship between text and metatext, a relationship of interiority-exteriority in which it participates without being able to pause, a between that inverts itself. The "between" refers to the antitext (literary, filmic, philosophical, or whatever); it moves between literality and figuration while simultaneously deleting and maintaining that opposition, understanding that it is not possible to set limits on rhetoric. The "between" alludes to this passage of the literary text between the figural and the discursive (in Lyotard's sense), leading us to understand that the discursive limits (of literature, film, philosophy) come from a historical or actual institutionalization and that, in reality, they permit comparison neither in terms of a theory of the whole, nor in terms of a fixed intertextuality.

The "betweenness" of the antitext transfers and makes possible, in any case, the intertextuality, above all because any theory of intertextuality is finally resolved in a theory of textual coherence or unity of meaning (Kristeva).[13] Is it then possible to affirm an identity between the "between" and Derridean dissemination? This question, according to the hypotheses established in this essay, does not have a simple answer. Derrida states: "And so the thing is written. To write means to graft. It is the same word. The saying of the thing is returned to its grafted being. The graft does not survive aside from the thing. There is nothing but the original text" (*Disséminations* 533). There is nothing but the original text, or else there is nothing but repetition. In fact, it would be impossible to understand a statement without immediately accompanying it with another. The graft is the trace, in other words, what leaves a trace; therefore, "to graft" is the infinitive that points to the noun "trace." In this sense, "betweenness" and "dissemination" point to the same thing: rupture with "literaturity," with the text in its empirical and objective meaning, with polysemy, with semantic restriction, with contextual saturation, with *psicagogía*. It should be added that they point in the same direction, even to posing the relationship between the "trace" and "reading in process." As an active *critical* movement, this rupture has as its end the dissemination of a relationship of more or less absolute closure between text and metatext.

Now, then, in referring to the antitext it is necessary to notice that the "betweenness" even succeeds in imposing itself "between" dissemination and nondissemination in such a way that we cannot forget the "desiring-being," the "direction" of the historical texts. In other words, by glancing more or less attentively over the fixed history of *literature* it is easy to realize that there are texts that have brought about an explosion of the "tracing" process, texts that have evidenced their being-graft, texts that have undertaken a dissemination, and texts that have retained the process of the trace, texts that have emerged with the will to erase the graft, texts that have established the part of dialogue, of psychagogy and not of writing, of logography. It is not difficult to perceive the difference that mediates between certain texts by observing the transcendental meaning around which they are organized. It is clear, on the other hand, that text difference is fictitious, since every text, in the last instance, refers to antitextuality, but this does not mean that differences may not situate themselves regarding such a point. It is therefore pointed out that certain texts (like those by Mallarmé, Artaud, Joyce, or Beckett) have functioned as a deconstruction of all previous textuality. We can carry this affirmation further and say that actually they are the deconstruction of all textuality, subsequent as well as previous, because a large part of the tendency in twentieth-century literary theory can be considered a regression with respect to these texts. Therefore, the "between" of the antitext universalizes the movement that passes between nondisseminating and disseminating text.

The problem of genre is a good example. The "between" would be that which embraces texts that make evident their "will" to be faithful to the identity principle (a good part of twelfth- and thirteenth-century medieval poetics, for example; see Zumthor); texts which make evident a dissolving tendency in the identity principle (the novel as seen by the German romantics and the writing of Mallarmé, Juan Ramón Jiménez, and the like); or texts that tend toward invasion of other types of textuality (an example of this would be Borges, who invades literary, essayistic, and philosophical textuality). And, after all, one must recognize that the "between" of the literary text makes it possible for the disseminating text to be read as nondissemination (text, coherence) and vice versa, although it indicates the relationship of "conflict" that can be present here, the reason for which we prefer the word "conflict" to Pratt's "contact." The "betweenness" recovers the complete scope of writing in such a way that one cannot adjectivize the concept of the text as "literary," since this adjectivization, "literary," consists of a disauthorization of itself, whereas delimitation, specification, or difference consists of a disauthorization assured by the "betweenness" that (de)composes. Along with this is the fact that the "betweenness" covers a more radically historical aspect of the problem of (not) being literary. The disauthorization of the literary as literary reminds us that the "betweenness" makes it possible that a text considered "literary" today may no longer be considered as such tomorrow, and vice versa; this is a case for which the aesthetics of reception could give a good account. This slope of "betweenness" reminds us of Aristotle's condemning the poem that discusses botany (in short, a nonimitative poem); of classical poetics, which did not make way for the novel; and of, more recently, Thomas Mann's introducing questions of botany, psychology (nonimitative questions), or of the novel as a classic genre.

The "betweenness," it is worth taking into account, does not simply deny "literaturity" or, in general, the questions "What is literature" or "What is the text?" The "betweenness" leads both questions to a framework within which they must be thought of as "effects" of meaning of the antitext, to a framework in which they stop serving the "is" of the literary text to dedicate themselves to the "is-is not" of the antitext. The "betweenness" positions them "between"; it leaves them suspended, added to the interminability of the "trace." It can be said that "literaturity" and the question "What is a text?" are displaced as fundamental questions. And so this "betweenness" arises from the separation of literaturity (what is literature) from the literary text: a separation carried out by a reading in process by means of a displacement of general order. There are a multitude of "betweens": the "between" of the relationship text-metatext, the "between" of the infinite interpretation of the disseminated textual body, the "between" of the literary absolute that leaves neither margins nor periphery, the "between" of the antitext that invades (is invaded by) texts-languages, the "between" of the rhetoric that universalizes in the midst of a substitutional vertigo, the unleashing of the voice of the literary text, the "between" of intertextuality and dissemination, the "between" that effaces and institutes linguistic boundaries, the "between" that breaks with genre understood as identity principle, the "between" of the counterlaw, the "between" of a self-effacing literaturity, the "between" of the question "What is literature?" that restores it to the previous "Literature?", the "between" that announces existing conflict and friction in the interior/exterior of the antitext. . . .

Literature? ? Text?

Between.

Notes

1. The author's original word *theoría*, unlike the common Spanish word *teoría*, is modeled directly on the Greek *thēoréō*. To translate the author's word as "theory" would not convey its sense. Hence this word is left in Spanish, accompanied by this explanatory note.

2. It must be emphasized clearly the step that the concept of "trace" (and the chain in which it is implicated: presence-absence, *écriture*, archtrace) gives from Heideggerian discourse (centered on the ontico-ontological problematic of the difference being-entity) to Derridean discourse (the theme of writing, of *différance*), and finally to that which transpires from the cited words objectified in what we will call, throughout the present work, "antitext." This last step does not assume the specificity of the literary, its generality, or its absolute empiricism regarding the "text." See Gasché, "Deconstruction" and "Joining the Text."

3. The author's original word *difuminando* cannot be translated as "disappearing," as is shown by Paul Kiparsky's work.

4. Lacoue-Labarthe and Nancy's work proves to be fundamental with regard to the systematization-anthology of the ideas of the German romantics of Jena.

5. What I am calling "presence," "organicity," "coherence," and so on, is in perfect agreement with what Pratt calls "imaginary community": "Behind the concept of *langue*, behind the diagram of Saussure, is the image of the modern imaginary community, discrete, sovereign, fraternal: a linguistic utopia" (59). ["Detrás del concepto de *langue*, detrás del diagrama de Saussure, está la imagen de la comunidad imaginaria moderna, discreta, soberana, fraternal: una utopía lingüística."] At the same time, what I call "between," "trace," and, above all, "antitext" is sufficiently related to her idea of "contact" linguistics, excepting a few important nuances, which I will indicate later: "The distance between *langue* and *parole*, between competence and performance, is the distance between the homogeneity of the imaginary community and the fractured reality of linguistic experience in modern stratified societies" (59). ["La distancia entre *langue* y *parole*, entre competencia y actuación, es la distancia entre la homogeneidad de la comunidad imaginaria y la realidad fracturada de la experiencia lingüística en las sociedades estratificadas modernas."]

6. In this regard it is important to keep in mind the work of Wolfgang Iser, above all for the analysis to which the matter of the response and effect is submitted.

7. "Enumeraremos la serie de los diferentes significados interpretados mediante una descripción. El 'ser' dicho en el 'es', significa: 'realmente actual', 'existente de modo material y constante', 'tener lugar', 'proceder', 'consistir', 'morar', 'pertenecer', 'caer', 'estar colocado en', 'encontrarse', 'dominar', 'llegar', 'presentar'. Por eso opuesto a su esencia, sigue siendo difícil e incluso quizá imposible, aislar un significado común, entendido como concepto genérico-universal, bajo el cual se pudiera subordinar, como especies, los citados modos del 'es'. Sin embargo, un rasgo único y determinado atraviesa todas esas significaciones. Muestra la comprensión del verbo 'ser' en un determinado horizonte, al partir del cual dicho comprender se llena de contenido. *La limitación*

del sentido del 'ser' se mantiene dentro del ámbito de la presencia y de lo que tiene el carácter de estar—ante de la consistencia y de la substancia, de la morada y del advenir."

8. "La palabra, que no es en sí misma cosa alguna, ningún algo que 'es', se nos escapa. . . . Muestra aquello que hay pero que, pese a todo, no 'es'. La palabra también pertenece a lo que hay, pese a todo, quizás no sólo 'también' sino ante todo, de tal manera que en la palabra, en su esencia, se oculta aquello que da. Si pensamos rectamente, nunca podremos decir de la palabra: ella es, sino: ella da (*es gibt*), no en el sentido de que 'se den' palabras, sino en cuanto sea la palabra misma la que da. La palabra: la donante (*das Gebende*). ¿De qué hace don? De acuerdo con la experiencia poética y según la más antigua tradición del pensamiento, la palabra da: el ser."

9. Schaeffer distinguishes between "genre" as a metatextual concept, a concept pertaining to a theory and therefore an abstract plane, and "genericity" as a textual function, that is, as one of the elements that contribute to the text's being a text. See also *Qu'est-ce qu'un genre littéraire?*

10. " . . . ce topos singulier situé dans l'oeuvre et hors d'elle, à sa bordure, une inclusion et une exclusion au regard du genre en général, d'une classe identifiable en général."

11. "C'est précisément la, dans le rire populaire, qu'il faut chercher les véritables racines du roman liées au folklore" (Bakhtin 21 +).

12. This concept of *infinición* as Levinas develops it seems to be suitable, by way of a not too violent translation of the "antitext." Later he writes: "To contain more than what is possible is, at all times, to explode the framework of the conceived content, to overcome the barriers of immanence. That which erupts as essential violence in the act is the transcendence of being with respect to the thought that tries to contain it."

13. On page 240 she asserts that all of the subgrammas and partial grammas "are an expansion of the function that organizes the text."

Works Cited

Abrams, Meyer Howard. *The Mirror and the Lamp.* Oxford: Oxford Univ. Press, 1953.

Asensi, Manuel. *Theoría de la lectura: Para una crítica paradójica.* Madrid: Hiperión, 1987.

Bakhtin, Mikhail. *Epopée et roman.* Recherches internationales à la lumière du marxisme 76.3 (1973).

Barthes, Roland. *S/Z.* Paris: Editions du Seuil, 1970.

Blanchot, Maurice. *El espacio literario.* Buenos Aires: Paidós, 1982.

Blumenberg, Hans. *Die Lesbarkeit der Welt.* Frankfurt: Suhrkamp, 1981.

Derrida, Jacques. "La différance." In *Marges de la philosophie.* Paris: Editions de Minuit, 1972.

———. *Disséminations.* Paris: Editions de Minuit, 1972.

———. *Glas.* Paris: Galilée, 1974.

———. *The Truth in Painting.* Paris: Flammarion, 1978.

———. "La loi du genre." *Glyph* 7 (1980): 176–201.

Eikhenbaum, Boris. "La théorie de la 'Méthode Formelle.' " In *Théorie de la littérature: Textes des Formalistes russes réunis, présentés et traduits par Tzvetan Todorov*. Paris: Editions du Seuil, 1965. 38–39.

Fish, Stanley. "La literatura en el lector: estilística afectiva." In *Estética de la recepción*, ed. R. Warning. Madrid: Visor, 1989. 32–55.

Garroni, Emilio. *Progetto di semiotica*. Bari: Laterza, 1972.

Gasché, Rodolphe. "Deconstruction as Criticism." *Glyph* 6 (1979): 177–215.

_____. "Joining the Text: From Heidegger to Derrida." In *The Yale Critics: Deconstruction in America*. Minneapolis: Univ. of Minnesota Press, 1983. 156–75.

_____. *The Tain of the Mirror*. Cambridge: Harvard Univ. Press, 1986.

Heidegger, Martin. "La esencia del habla." Conference paper, 1957.

_____. *An Introduction to Metaphysics*. Trans. Ralph Manheim. New Haven: Yale Univ. Press, 1959.

Hjelmslev, Louis. *Prolegomena to a Theory of Language*. Madison: Univ. of Wisconsin Press, 1961.

Iser, Wolfgang. "The Reading Process." In *The Implied Reader: Patterns of Communication in Prose Fiction from Bunyan to Beckett*. Baltimore: Johns Hopkins Univ. Press, 1974. 274–94.

Kiparsky, Paul. "Teoría e interpretación en la literatura." In *Lingüística de la escritura*. Madrid: Visor, 1989. 193–206.

Kristeva, Julia. *Semiótica*. Madrid: Fundamentos, 1972.

Lacoue-Labarthe, Philippe, and Jean-Luc Nancy. *The Literary Absolute*. Albany, N.Y.: State Univ of New York Press, 1988.

Levinas, Emmanuel. *Totality and Infinity*. Trans. Alphonso Lingis. The Hague: Martinus Nijhoff, 1969.

Lyotard, Jean-François. *Discours, figure*. Paris: Klinksieck, 1971.

Mukarovsky, Jan. *Escritos de estética y semiótica del arte*. Barcelona: Gustavo Gili, 1977.

Pratt, Mary Louise. "Utopías lingüísticas." In *Lingüística de la escritura*. Madrid: Visor, 1989.

Ricoeur, Paul. "Qu'est-ce qu'un texte?" In *Hermeneutik und Dialektik: Festschrift für Hans-Georg Gadamer*. Vol. 2. Tübingen: Mohr, 1971. 181–200.

Rorty, Richard. *Consequences of Pragmatism*. Minneapolis: Univ. of Minnesota Press, 1982.

Schaeffer, Jean-Marie. "Du texte au genre: notes sur la problématique générique." *Poétique* 53 (1983): 3–18.

_____. *Qu'est-ce qu'un genre littéraire?* Paris: Editions du Seuil, 1989.

Talens, Jenaro. *De la publicidad como fuente historiográfica*. Working papers, Valencia/Minneapolis: Publicaciones de la Fundación Instituto Shakespeare, 1990.

Zumthor, Paul. *Essai de poétique médiévale*. Paris: Editions du Seuil, 1972.

Subjectivity

◆ Chapter 8

Subjectivity and Temporality in Narrative

Cristina Peña-Marín

(translated by Frances Meuser-Blincow)

Time and the Word

The narrative carried out by a subject that addresses itself and takes itself as the protagonist of its own story raises a series of questions about the relationship between subjectivity and temporality, about the construction of narrative time, and also about the place that narrative occupies in the process of building identity.

Recent studies of temporality in narrative texts resort, almost inevitably, to the distinction between time of the narration and time narrated. However, we must bear in mind that these temporalities do not usually exist as independent and separable entities. Such a dichotomy is intended to account for the difference between the time in which the narrated actions take place and the way in which narrative reorganizes them temporally (referring first to what happened later or accelerating or delaying actions, and so on). The construction of a narrative text is one of the functions attributed to the speaker, the subject responsible for discourse production. The concept of time is necessarily linked, in this respect, to the speaker's voice.

Fictional texts—here I will focus on Clarín's *La regenta*— feature a set of characters whose actions, thoughts, and feelings are reported to us, the readers. One of the most distinctive features of fiction is precisely the fact that those characters may be the "I-Origines" of thoughts, feelings, and actions narrated, in opposition to assertive discourse, where the "I-Origo" is the discourse-producing subject (see Kate Hamburger, quoted in Ricoeur, *Time and Narrative* 65).

But this difference between the real "I-Origo," the discourse-producing subject, and the fictional characters is questioned by the phenomenon of textual polyphony, as it is shown for instance, in the case of free indirect style. In this way, as is well known, especially after Bakhtin's analysis, it becomes impossible to differentiate between the speaker's voice and the character's voice, and to answer questions such as "Who is the 'I-Origo' of the narrated feelings, thoughts, and such?" or "Do they belong to the author or to the character?" Such monologues also introduce another factor of complexity that results when characters construct for themselves a story of their own past. They actually split, adopting several positions: they see their present from the eyes of the other persons they were as children, or they judge themselves, using the values and criteria by which other characters regard or judge them.

The following example of free indirect style in *La regenta* will allow us to analyze the relationship between this form and narrative time, as well as to introduce the study of subjectivity in one of the main characters:

> Still, it was quite an act of resignation to content himself, for the time being, with Vetusta. De Pas had dreamed of better positions, and he had not lost all hope of gaining them. Brilliant scenes, which ambition had painted in his imagination, were stored in his memory like recollections of some heroic poem read with enthusiasm as a youth. He had seen himself officiating in pontificals in Toledo, and at a conclave of cardinals in Rome: even the tiara itself had not seemed excessive. There was nothing that could not be acquired along the way, the important thing was to keep moving onwards. But, as time passed, these dreams had become hazier and hazier, as if they were retreating into the distance. "Such are the perspectives of hope," thought the canon. "The closer we come to the goal of our ambition, the more distant does this desired object appear, for it lies not in the future, but in the past; before us there is only a mirror reflecting the chimerical vision which has remained

behind, at the far-off moment when we dreamed it."
(28–29)

I do not intend to dwell on the analysis of the relationship between the character's voice and the speaker's voice. Sometimes
they seem to be different, as when the character tells us, in his
own words, his thoughts ("Still, it was quite an act of resignation to content himself, *for the time being*, with Vetusta" or
"There was nothing that could not be acquired along the way,
the important thing was to keep moving onwards"). In spite of
the shift from the tense in which the words are uttered by the
narrator, it is obvious that the use of the word has been given to
the character. The responsibility for the fragment's fabric seems
to fall on the speaker (to whom we may attribute the comparison
between the canon theologian's recollections and the way an
epic poem read in early youth is remembered). But the chief
characteristic of the paragraph, as in the case in all instances of
free indirect style, lies in each voice's contamination of the other,
the impossibility of distinguishing clearly to whom content and
expression are to be attributed.

As for time, the distinction between narrated time and the
time in which the events are narrated is likewise problematical.
What is told to us happens during an undefined period of time
(time narrated) in which the canon theologian reflects upon
himself and recalls his own past. But the fragment is also intended to portray the character, to present his thoughts, his
dreams, the wishes that he "kept in his memory" (although
they are not necessarily recalled at the time of narration). From
the present time of the narrated action, we are taken back into
the character's past, not set at any precise point of his biography, but one that colors his discourse with a lasting and progressive aspect: the gradual loss of the force of childhood dreams.
The time of the narrated action, the present of the reflection, and
the canon theologian's remembrances coexist with another temporal construction, the one the speaker uses to portray the character, in such a way that it becomes practically impossible to
reconstruct the time of what is narrated while differentiating it
from the temporal device of narration.[1] Neither is it possible either
to discern whether it is the character that portrays his internal

process or whether it is the voice of the external speaker. Time, as a determination of the word, must necessarily become affected by the contamination of the character's voice and point of view by those of the speaker.

Narration and Subjective Identity

Subjective identity may be understood as the construction of the meaning of one's life which unifies its different "I"'s and its different self-representations into one coherent image. Autobiographical narration, through which subjects select certain events from their biography and organize them as a unified succession of events, plays a fundamental role in this construction of identity carried out by the subjects themselves. Retrospective construction of the character through an autobiographical report inserts itself in the retelling of the character's life as one of the stages in the process toward identity.

La regenta shows some of these stories, told by certain characters to themselves, inserted within the complex process of the protagonists' search for their own identities. It is interesting to examine the temporal framework of these stories, in which the subject is as much narrator as character and addressee of his or her own autobiographical narration. In these stories the entire collection of the subject's many sides coexist, side by side, as we shall see, with many autobiographical stories through which the subject strives to bring coherence and lend legitimacy to his or her different self-images.

In the fragment cited above, the canon theologian opens the direction of his story to the future, to his self-image, which his ambition projects. Bakhtin points out the primacy of the future for the constitution of personal identity. A memory, regarded retrospectively, is summoned and granted a sense from which the subject foresees and wishes to be: "I put my whole self together, not in the past, but in a future that is always before me . . . it is not my has-been-existence unity, but my yet-to-be one" (113–14). "I cannot really believe that I may be only what I am here and now; I become complete out of the yet-to-come, the has-to-be, the wished-for. The reference point for self-definition is located only in the future" (149). Therefore, although such stories perform the function of representing the person as a unit, of granting him or her some coherence, they are always unfinished stories whose "closure" or denouement can be imagined, desired, or feared, but not realized "yet."

In turn, the future, as a projection of present desire, appears here as deeply rooted in the past, in the fantasies of identity dreamed of in youth. The present, as the future of the past, is contrary to the idea that the character had about himself then,[2] and that idea also shapes hope. It is projected into a future permanently unattainable, for it will always have the form of a dream of youth.

We must introduce here succinctly the different identities embodied by the canon theologian in this novel: (a) his public identity as a humble and wise priest, which many people in Vetusta regard as fake and which, in fact, he disguises; (b) a secret identity, revealed only in the presence of his mother and a few relatives or accomplices, of a corrupt priest using his post to get rich; (c) an even more secret identity, not shared with anyone, built up around his ambition for power and prestige, an identity he would like to develop in the future; and (d) a new developing identity that arises out of his relationship with Ana Ozores.

Each one of these identities corresponds to a certain scope of relationships.[3] Before all those who are the canon theologian's "public," he performs his public role automatically, and everything in his words, his gestures, and his manners corresponds with this image of the good priest he pretends to be. Under this identity lies his covert one, which unfolds only before his mother and relatives and in the vicar-general's office, as we shall see presently. But the self-image with which he identifies best is not the latter, in spite of the fact that he cannot possibly part with it, but rather the one shaped by his ambition for social ascension within the ecclesiastical hierarchy. In order to achieve this, he strives to appear as a sage, foreshadowing the recognition he hopes to achieve in the future. Only during brief moments alone can he allow himself to nurture the hope of seeing this project of identity come true some day.

Elsewhere I have set forth the hypothesis that in the core of each of these identities there lies a basic passion that insures its persistence over time and among its various options of being

(Peña-Marín, *Identidad y relaciones*). *Ambition* drives his project of future identity (c) forward; *fidelity* to his mother is the ultimate reason for which he embodies and maintains the identity (b) of corrupt priest; and *love* for Ana Ozores encourages a new type of identity (d), as we shall see. He spends his life alternating among the different identities. Each identity establishes its own past and projects a future, and each of them has a time of its own.

It is also the future projected from the present that inspires a new reflection on the past following the canon theologian's meeting with Ana Ozores:

> Yes, yes, this was something new, something new for his spirit, a spirit weary of living only for its own ambition and for another's cupidity, that of his mother. His soul needed tenderness, gentleness of heart, to compensate for so much asperity. Was everything in life to be pretence, hatred, domination, conquest, deceit?
>
> He remembered his years as a theological student at San Marcos College in León when, full of pure faith, he had been preparing himself to join the Company of Jesus. There, for a time, he had felt the beating of a gentle heart in his breast, he had prayed with fervor, he had meditated with loving enthusiasm, ready to sacrifice himself *in Jesus*. All that was so far distant! He did not seem to be the same man. Might not all those sensations which he thought he had experienced since the previous afternoon be something of the same sort? Might not the fibres which had throbbed within him in the past, on the banks of the Bernesga, be the same ones which were throbbing now, like placid music for his soul? A bitter smile spread over the canon's lips. "Even if it should all be an illusion, a dream, why not dream a little? And who can tell whether this ambition which is devouring me is not a perverted form of another nobler passion? Could this fire not burn for a higher kind of affection, one worthier of my soul? Could I not be consumed in a purer flame than the flame of my ambition? My ambition! How base it is, how wretched! Would the conquest of this lady's soul not be of more value than the battle for a bishop's miter, a cardinal's hat, even the tiara itself?"

The canon theologian found that he was drawing a
tiara in the margin of the paper. (226–27)

The meeting with Ana Ozores breaks the balance maintained
by the canon theologian among his different identities up to that
point. Knowledge gained through Ana Ozores's long "general
confession" unsettles him. The novelty of the sweetness and
spirituality of his relationship to Ana and the wish to actually
become what he represents for her lead him to a state of crisis. In
the above-quoted monologue, the canon theologian speaks al-
ternately from two different points of view: that of the man who
would be the fervent priest he tried to be when he was a student
and that he has represented himself to be for Ana, and, on the
other hand, that of the man who can accomplish such a thing
only in his dreams.

From his new possible identity, the canon theologian judges
his present identity negatively, and returns to a past period of
his life which was until then forgotten. Regarding such a possibility for the future, he constructs a story that establishes a line
of continuity with himself that proceeds from a past now recovered and provided with a meaning, to a present that receives in
its turn its justification and verisimilitude from that past. The
memory is interrupted by the reflections of the "present I" ("All
that was so far distant! He did not seem to be the same man")
that measures the distance between both identities and then
goes another step toward superimposing past feelings on those
he experiences for Ana, to carry out an identification between
the "I" he now wants to be and the one he thinks he was. But,
responding to the period of crisis in which he finds himself, his
split identity reappears, and the skeptic emerges again to warn
him that all of it is but an illusion. And when he persists in believing this dream of a possible new identity, his hand, uncon-
sciously, signals his continuance in the identity characterized by
ambition.

The temporal construction of the two narrative fragments is
different. In the first one, the time elapsed between past dreams
and the present time is regarded as a continuing progression; in
the second, it is represented as a rupture. The present from
which he narrates proves to be unsatisfactory, because his meeting

with Ana has opened up the desire for feelings that are impossible within the identities embodied up to this point. Such feelings acquire meaning as the rebirth of similar ones the subject had experienced in a past that remained isolated without any connection to his present life. This link between past and present entails the creation of temporal brackets that cancel everything that has happened in between, as well as the identity or identities forged during that period. We must take into account the situation, that is, the emotional state of the narrator of this story: the present from which the subject carries out this construction in a moment of crisis, the vacillation among different possibilities of being, and the crisis projected in his discourse. The result is a narrator who is split between believing in and denying the possibility of establishing such a link between present and past.

In contrast to the events characterizing the former fragment, the canon theologian is presented later in the course of his everyday activities when he appears as the vicar-general presiding in his office, accompanied by only those selected by him and his mother as accomplices in his corruption. Against this background, he performs automatically his role of corrupted priest:

> On that morning, as usual, tangled questions came before the vicar-general and he dealt with them, as usual, in a mechanical way, using his own gain as his criterion, with astonishing skill, absolute formal correctness, and apparently exquisite delicacy. More than once, however, his spirit faltered as he decided upon an injustice, an extortion, an expedient act of cruelty (he was feeling nervous, he did not know what had got into him), but the thought of his mother, together with the presence of those daily witnesses of his firm, able defence of his own interests—and in great part, too, the force of inertia, of habit—kept him at his post; and he was the same vicar-general they all knew, he settled all his matters in his usual way, and no one had cause to wonder if he had gone mad nor did he need to make up any stories to deceive his mother about what had happened. Doña Paula could feel well-pleased with her son; yes, her son, not the foolish hare-brained dreamer who earlier in the morning had been embarrassed to

read an insignificant letter and who had felt happy
without any obvious reason at the sight of a resplendent
sun in a clear sky. The sun! The sky! What did they
matter to the vicar-general of Vetusta? He was a curial
officer, wasn't he? A curial officer making himself into a
millionaire so as to pay off sacred debts to his mother
and to slake with cupidity the thirst of frustrated
ambition.

  Yes, yes, that was what he was, and he should not
entertain any illusions or go in search of a new life. He
ought to be feeling satisfied—and he was. (273–74)

"That morning" is immediately assimilated to the time of everyday life, of habit, "just like every morning" (by an omniscient
speaker who, in this first part of the paragraph, describes and
judges the appearance of the canon theologian-vicar-general,
his actions, thoughts, and feelings, and their causes). The canon
theologian's behavior, ruled by automatism and skill, is interrupted by a moral sensibility improper or unsuited to the role he
is performing.[4] The vacillations that the appearance of this new
moral sensibility produces point out the change produced in the
subject after meeting Ana Ozores (see the parenthetical statements introduced by the voice of the character apologizing for
himself).

  But several forces intervene in order to keep him in his place.
First is the recollection of his mother. (Such interference is necessary, for fidelity to her is the passion ruling his identity of corrupt vicar-general that will in the end be revealed as the most
persistent, for it is the most stable of his passions and the only
one that produces in him a certain moral reconciliation with
himself.) Next is the presence of witnesses who expect the
same canon theologian as ever. And finally, habit, stamped in
his body and in his gestures, intervenes through the poses he
repeats every day.

  His own memory, as well as that of others, compel him to
persist: "he was the same vicar-general they all knew, he settled
all his matters in his usual way, and no one had cause to wonder
if he had gone mad." The speaker's voice begins to superimpose
itself on that of the character, who, in his turn, makes the others' points of view and voices his own. Negative enunciations

expose, in order to deny them, the judgments of the others,[5] witnesses, who would have thought him mad, and his mother, who has regarded him as a dreamer and a scatterbrain.

Adopting his mother's voice, her expressions, and her point of view toward him, Don Fermín reasserts himself in the identity created by and for her, according to which all the aesthetic and sentimental sensitivity that affected him a short while before is now improper. He addresses himself with his public name and post ("Vicar-General of Vetusta"), but the identification with the role he adopts for others leads him to the greatest lucidity about himself, about the "I" embodying such a role. The last utterance in the paragraph, the rhetorical question, is the most disconcerting. We may ask: from which point of view can he be considered an official of the curia who becomes a millionaire in order to pay his mother sacred debts and to quench with greed the thirst of frustrated ambitions? Neither his mother, nor his accomplices, nor his enemies know him that well. Not even the canon theologian had judged himself, before this crisis, in such a disillusioned way. Only the enunciator and we, the readers, have been able to judge him in this manner. It happens that, adopting the others' perspective of him, Don Fermín comes to terms with that knowledge in such a way that his own point of view becomes that of an omniscient observer, aware of his innermost motivations and justifications: that of the speaker himself.

This text shows to what extent the speaker's voice and textual time shape each other, becoming two interdependent dimensions. When Don Fermín incorporates the points of view of the other characters as they relate to him, the speaker's and the reader's included, he affirms himself in the lines of continuity and coherence attributed to him by such points of view. And so he ends up by objectifying himself in the way others and we the readers would do. The "*That* is I" (that reinstates the first person in the statement in which a character could presumably express itself) shows an operation of identification between the discourse's subject ("I"), and the image of himself returned by others and one of his past selves ("that"). From this recovered identity he introduces the voice of a former "I" into the discourse, an "I" that he has ceased to be: one who was having illusions and searching for a new way of living. The present "I" assumes his duty: wishing to be what he actually is for the others.

Time in terms of daily activities imposes regulated activities on the subjects, always carried out in the same way. But the subject who endorses a role is not always self-identical. In this fragment, habitual behavior does not expose the internal instability of a subject who now feels different, and for whom activities formerly unquestioned are now a source of (ethical) doubts and hesitation. In this case, the subject decides to reassert himself in the identity that will allow him to play the role without internal conflicts. (The canon theologian has a powerful reason for doing this: his mother. In many other cases, subjects do not have definitive reasons to opt for one identity over the other.)

Internal time shows up as a complex net of personal histories. The subject submerges at times into one of them, whereas at other moments he finds himself in the middle of a crossroads in which several possible paths to the past and the future converge. Several autobiographical narratives serve as a foundation for different options of identity.

The canon theologian fluctuates among several of these stories:

> His mother spoke about the gossiping, as she always did, and he shrugged his shoulders. He heard Doña Paula's hard, dry voice predicting, in an attempt to frighten him, the cataclysm of his fortune and the ruination of his honor as if she were talking about the geological cataclysms of Noah's times. He regarded the vicar-general about whom the public complained as another man. "Ambition, simony, pride, meanness, scandal! What had it all to do with him? Why were they persecuting that poor Don Fermín now that he was dead and buried? Don Fermín was a different man now, a man who scorned his neighbors and did not even take the trouble to hate them. He lived for his ennobling, redeeming passion. But if they insisted on harassing him they would make him lose his patience and then he'd really give them something to be scandalized about." The canon theologian was delighted to find such a man inside himself, stronger than ever, ready for any contingency, and in love with life, which has these

intense, overpowering emotions in store for its favorites.
Reality was acquiring a new meaning for him—it was
more real. (483)

Affectionate passion ("aphrodisiac love," as the canon theologian calls it) shifts the character to a second "I," the one in the
second fragment trying to find in his past an antecedent to his
present feelings, from which he regards all the former ones as
unreal and alien to him. The Don Fermín we saw reasserting
himself in his devotion to the identity he maintained before others is now dead. The new "I" betrays, without the slightest hesitation, all previous loyalties.

The narratives in which the canon theologian represents himself to himself contradict each other,[6] in the same way as the
passion encouraging them is incompatible with the system of
rules and values in which he develops the identities corresponding to each of his own versions of himself. For example, loyalty
to his mother compels him to satisfy her greed, which allows
him to become morally reconciled with himself as a "good son,"
but prevents him from regarding himself as a proper priest and,
especially, as the "soul brother" he pretends to be for Ana.

The construction of identity is not a linear or continuous process, but a constant displacement of elements of itself that the
subject recognizes in the narrations as well as others it dismisses
from them. These narratives are constructed in different moments by the subject according to what the subject plans to become in each case. Those moments of reconstruction of the
meaning of one's own life through stories told to oneself are inserted at different moments in one's life (different moments of
identification with a self-image transmitted through the role per-
formed, be it that of disidentification, of doubt . . .), even when
the so-called critical moments are those that in the end give
more urgent rise to the need for these narratives. Fluctuations in
the subject's feelings and possibilities, ones that take place
throughout life, cannot help being projected onto those narratives and onto the vision and conformation of self-identification
of the narrator, who is at the same time the subject. They will
consequently have an influence on the speaker's temporality,

the representation of continuity or discontinuity between different moments of past and present.

Notes

1. Verbal tenses and adverbial expressions seem to point out the difference that Weinrich would establish between "foreground" and "background" (see Weinrich). The statement "Still, it was an act of resignation to content himself, for the time being, with Vetusta" is to be placed in the present of the fiction; it establishes the moment in which the action is focused. With respect to that "present," the phrases "had dreamed of better positions" and "were stored in his memory" are placed in the background. Ricoeur's discussion, in which he makes Weinrich's foreground correspond to the concept of happening as background does to continuity, *longue durée*, is perfectly pertinent in this context.

2. This vision of the present is a characteristic of Proust's work, as Ricoeur observes.

3. I cannot develop here this concept of identity which, following G. H. Mead, regards the subject as something that is constituted out of its relations with others, though this perspective may be applied to self-consciousness, in which the subject observes and judges itself adopting the position of others with respect to it. Thus, communication and the rules and patterns of interpretation and evaluation of the whole of which the subject is a constituent part give shape to the basis of the subject's identity. In modern society, every individual belongs to more than one field of relationships, and these fields are endowed with different, even opposing, ethical and interpretative codes. Individuals incorporate themselves in these circles representing themselves, and perhaps judging themselves too, according to these different codes. This diversity often places the individual in the position of questioning self-identity, of inquiring "Who am I?"

4. The conflicts of identity give rise, nearly inescapably in *La regenta*, to ethical conflicts (when the rules and values which the subject uses to affirm or judge himself clash).

5. According to Oswald Ducrot, negative statements are a form of quotation. The one who enunciates one of those statements attributes to another speaker, distinct from oneself, the affirmative proposition on which the negative one is constructed. Although this is, in my opinion, an analysis not applicable to all negative statements, it can be applied to those in this paragraph (see also Lozano et al. and Ignacio Bosque).

6. For Ricoeur (*Time and Narrative* 244+), identity is narrative, in the sense that what accounts for the presence of the subject of the action, designated by its name, by itself throughout its life, is the narrative, the story of its life. This is a dynamic model of identity. Narrative identity, Ricoeur states, "may include change, a mutability in life's cohesion"; the history of a life is constituted by a continuation of rectifications applied to previous narratives. According to this author, it is possible to plot different intrigues over life itself, including those that are opposed to each other.

However, it is necessary to consider the moments of crisis to which these different self-narratives and, even more so, those that are opposed submit the subject. What they show us is the impossibility of integrating all these narratives into a coherent story, that is to say, the impossibility of achieving cohesion among the fragments of "I." The rectification to which Ricoeur refers has to be in many cases a *denial* of an "I" that the subject is obligated to recognize, still incorporating it in some sphere, when the subject no longer believes in it (as happens to the canon theologian).

Works Cited

Alas, Leopoldo. *La regenta*. Trans. John Rutherford. London: Allen Lane, 1984.

Bakhtin, Mikhail. *Estética de la creación verbal*. Madrid: Siglo XXI, 1982.

Bosque, Ignacio. *Sobre la negación*. Madrid: Cátedra, 1980.

Ducrot, Oswald, et al. *Les mots du discours*. Paris: Minuit, 1980.

Peña-Marín, Cristina. *Identidad y relaciones sociales: Un análisis de "La regenta."* Madrid: El Arquero, forthcoming.

Peña-Marín, Cristina, et al. *Análisis del discurso*. Madrid: Cátedra, 1986.

Ricoeur, Paul. *Time and Narrative*, vol. 2. Trans. Kathleen McLaughlin and David Pellauer. Chicago: Univ. of Chicago Press, 1985.

──────. *Time and Narrative*, vol. 3. Trans. Kathleen Blamey and David Pellauer. Chicago: Univ. of Chicago Press, 1988.

Weinrich, Harald. *Estructura y función de los tiempos en el lenguaje*. Madrid: Gredos, 1979.

Chapter 9

Subject and Language: Reflections on Lacan and Jinkis

Juan Miguel Company-Ramón
(translated by Susan McMillen-Villar)

The Question of Subject in Language

Jorge E. Jinkis, in his fundamental article "A Topical Distinction: The Subject of the Enunciation and the I of Discourse," follows the split present in Lacanian writings between enunciation and utterance. He analyzes the different conceptual value that Roman Jakobson's shifter, that is, that which articulates utterance with true enunciation, has in Lacanian psychoanalysis. In order to account for the gap between enunciation and utterance, Lacan introduces a first distinction that splits the "I" of the discourse of the subject from the enunciation. What is at stake in Lacanian argumentation is, in short, that the discovery by psychoanalysis of the object as a dissolving function with respect to classical knowledge—that defines the object as the end in itself of a subject's act and as an intentional reference of the subject with regard to things—and the very status of knowledge. The main obstacle that an epistemology of psychoanalysis must overcome in order to be accepted as a science would be, precisely, that elusive character of the object under study—the Unconscious—whose problematic was dealt with several years ago by Jorge Belinski in a memorable seminar.[1]

The epistemological basis of the human or social sciences rests on the clear and sharp assertion that *the subject speaks.* In the study of the Unconscious, psychoanalysis reveals that *the subject is a talked-about being:*

> The linguist says: the "I" of discourse names in the
> utterance the subject of the enunciation. But what is this
> "I" in discourse that in Lacanian and Freudian
> psychoanalytic theory does not agree with the subject of
> the enunciation? In other words: when we speak, who is
> it that speaks? And even before this, why is it "Who
> speaks?" and not "What speaks?" (Jinkis 26)

Psychoanalysis reveals, among other things, that the very notion of subject proposed by social or human sciences—whose
field of study is made up of all those phenomena thought of as
different manifestations of the subject's creative ability—does
not agree with its own notion. And this lack of agreement, this
defect, is precisely what constitutes the field of study of psychoanalysis, its aim. Rejecting the subject of the human sciences—a
constituent of the symbolic world—focuses on what the subject
lacks. Lacan says, "What the subject lacks is not an absolute
lack, but the absolute lack of an object" ("Réponses" 12). Jinkis
adds:

> That is, there is *something* that is truly lacking. . . . When
> we approach the subject, we do not find the subject, or
> rather we just find what the subject lacks. But it is here,
> while borrowing a term from psychological comedy, that
> Lacan reveals the drama of such a wretched being:
> psychoanalysis reveals that this object does not lack a
> subject. The one who lacks an object is the unconscious
> desire.
>   This subversion of the subject-object relationship will
> lead to the questioning of a given epistemological
> treatment that solves the problems by calling them
> metaphysical. Lacan denounces the *persistency* of the
> "revealed truth" in the presupposition of con-naturality,
> of perfect adequacy of the subject, which accepts
> classical epistemology. From now on, the theory of
> knowledge must take into account the point of view of
> analytical truth. (Jinkis 26–27; emphasis added)[2]

The human being is not the subject or the object. The human being
fits into that dimension "in which desire stresses its double lack
for all that has been abandoned on the level of metonymical

chain and for all that has not been able to be carried out on the metaphorical level of metaphor" (Lacan 1970).

Subject/"I"

After questioning the subject-object relationship in the classical theory of knowledge, psychoanalysis faces—as we have already mentioned—one of its most constitutive fractures: the split between the subject and "I." The pronoun "I" (together with its correlative "you") belongs, for Benveniste, to the category of person, and the only reality it refers to is a reality of discourse in the moment it is enunciated:

> I cannot be defined except in terms of "locution," not in terms of objects as a nominal sign is. I signifies "the person who is uttering the present instance of the discourse containing I." This instance is unique by definition and has validity only in its uniqueness. . . . I can only be identified by the instance of discourse that contains it and by that alone. It has no value except in the instance in which it is produced. But in the same way it is also as an instance of form that I must be taken; the form of I has no linguistic existence except in the act of speaking in which it is uttered. There is thus a combined double instance in this process: the instance of I as referent and the instance of discourse containing I as the referee. The definition can now be stated precisely as: I is "the individual who utters the present instance of discourse containing the linguistic instance I." Consequently, by introducing the situation of "address" we obtain a symmetrical definition for you as the "individual spoken to in the present instance of discourse containing the linguistic instance you." (218)

In a word, these pronoun forms refer to the enunciation, unique in each case, that contains them. Their importance lies in direct relation to the nature of the problem that these pronouns serve to resolve: that of intersubjective communication. Such forms, according to Benveniste, are a set of empty signs, nonreferential and in a perpetual state of availability, that become filled only when a speaker assumes them in each instance of the speaker's discourse. They are not tied to the condition of truth—they do not assert anything—and in this way they escape rejection. As Benveniste says:

> Their role is to provide the instrument of a conversion that one could call the conversion of language into discourse. It is by identifying himself as a unique person pronouncing *I* that each speaker sets himself up in turn as the "subject." The use thus has as a condition the situation of discourse and no other. If each speaker, in order to express the feeling he has of his irreducible subjectivity, made use of a distinct identifying signal (in the sense in which each radio transmitting station has its own call letters), there would be as many languages as individuals and communication would become absolutely impossible. Language wards off this danger by instituting a unique but mobile sign, *I*, which can be assumed by each speaker on the condition that he refers each time only to the instance of his own discourse. This sign is thus linked to the exercise of language and announces the speaker as speaker. It is this property that establishes the basis for individual discourse, in which each speaker takes over all the resources of language for his own behalf. Habit easily makes us unaware of this profound difference between language as a system of signs and language assumed into use by the individual. When the individual appropriates it, language is turned into instances of discourse, characterized by this system of internal references of which *I* is the key, and defining the individual by the particular linguistic construction he makes use of when he announces himself as the speaker. Thus the indicators *I* and *you* cannot exist as potentialities; they exist only insofar as they are actualized in the instance of discourse, in which, by each of their own instances, they mark the process of appropriation by the speaker. (220)

The profound knowledge shown by Lacanian theory in these matters can never be sufficiently stressed. Counterbalancing recent and quite remarkable disqualifications (see Catelli),[3] it is worthwhile to affirm the strictly linguistic basis from which Lacan starts, which is confirmed by his analytical practice. Lacan develops, exhaustively and to its ultimate consequences, what was latent in Benveniste's proposal. Let us return, then, to Jinkis's article:

> "I" names the subject of enunciation, but it does not signify it; "I" is not the one who enunciates the discourse that contains "I," but rather the one that designates the subject who speaks in the subject of utterance. . . . It is I who says "I." But the question is: Who is this I who says "I"?
>
> If we say that "I" does not refer to a concept or an individual, but to the whole discourse (in which it names, precisely, the speaker), we are referring to the place where a double deceit has occurred, which is a condition for the introduction of the truth: the dialogue situation, an unmistakable term in Lacan, as removed as possible from everything that reminds us of the liberal and empiricist tradition. When we ask, "Who speaks?" there is always an "I" that initially surfaces in an answer, that persists as a question that constitutes it as an "I." It is always the Other who answers. This condition of dialogue entails an I and an Other, or in discourse terms, an "I" and a "you." "I" and "you" are opposed in a relationship that is neither identical nor symmetrical, but complementary and reversible. *The discourse supposes this situation of dialogue, asymmetrical polarity, reversible, constitutive of the subject.* (29–30; emphasis added)

This brings us to a central question posed by Freudian theory to the rationalist tradition of Western philosophy, which maintains a unitary world conception. Freudian theory's point of departure is the indivisibility of the subject and its isomorphism with respect to "I." Rather than a talking being, the subject is a being *talked about* by language, and sometimes—as we shall see immediately—such language rejoices behind the subject's back. In this way Lacan destroys the Cartesian "cogito," restating the aphorism and transgressing it radically:

> I think where I am not, therefore I am where I do not think. . . . I am not wherever I am the plaything of my thought; I think of what I am where I do not think to think. (*Ecrits* 166)

Truth is framed into a dimension without knowledge. When the "I" is lost in the meaning of its discourse, the lack of meaning of the "I" will ultimately reveal the subject of the enunciation. On the other hand, if it is clear that the subject's desire finds a meaning in the desire of the Other, then, "it is not so much," Lacan says, "that it is because it is the Other who possesses the beloved object, as it is because the first object of the subject's desire is to be recognized by the Other" (quoted in Jinkis 30).

> [The fact is] that the Other cannot offer as an object the subject's desire, but instead another desire, which is what allows desire to be placed beyond necessity. This mediation is precisely constitutive of the subject: upon its recognition of desire, the Other grants the subject the condition of being. (Jinkis 30)[4]

We are now in a position to be able to define this advent of "I" following the Unconscious maturing latent in the Freudian aphorism "Where id was, ego shall be" ("Wo Es war, soll Ich werden") emerging in the subject's alienation from the unity of its image reflected in the mirror (see Lacan, *Ecrits*). It is a tensional "I" trying to repress atomization and the body's shattering in the real space of its proprioceptivity, through the narcissistic, gestaltic constitution of its virtual image, complete and armored, in the mirror. We reach out to the world through this unified gestalt that is the figure in the mirror. And, maybe for that reason, the life of humans—*our* life—works so poorly in its eternal search for an illusory Paradise where personality (unity) is preserved, as was so clearly pointed out by Beckett. That condition of being that the Other grants to us upon recognizing our desire is revealed here as a feature essentially constitutive of "I." To accept the shattering of the subject implies that fellow subjects— and only the Judeo-Christian culture has been able to engender such a deceitful imperative as loving one's neighbor as oneself— may return to destroy us. That is why love, in its origin, engenders tension when it comes into conflict with the narcissistic relation of proprioceptivity—which, paradoxically, is the sine qua non of love—understood as a tendency toward the unified image, opposed to atomization that must be suppressed or at least appeased.

In the field of enunciation, we may conclude by affirming, as does Jinkis, that this is an enunciated enunciation, always revealing the interpretation of the source of its own enunciation, because, in the end, the unconcious always speaks:

> Psychoanalysis reveals that the enunciation that takes into account linguistic analysis is enunciated by the enunciation of the subject as defined by the dimension of the unconcious. (Jinkis 34)

Mistakes of Meaning

Freudian theory concerning the signifier is found implicitly enunciated in three fundamental books: *The Interpretation of Dreams* (1900), *The Psychopathology of Everyday Life* (1901), and *Jokes and Their Relation to the Unconscious* (1905). The fact that the subject is constituted by, among other things, its dreams and Freudian slips and is, no less, structured as a joke, does not keep it from being an antihumanist postulate, a challenge to the logos of a tradition deeply rooted in Western thought. At the beginning of *Jokes* Freud analyzes a remarkable linguistic slip:

> In the part of his *Reisebilder* entitled "Die Bäder von Lucca" ("The Baths of Lucca") Heine introduces the delightful figure of the lottery-agent and extractor of corns, Hirsch-Hyacinth of Hamburg, who boasts to the poet of his relations with the wealthy Baron Rothschild, and finally says: "And, as true as God shall grant me all good things, Doctor, I sat beside Salomon Rothschild and he treated me quite as his equal—quite 'famillionairely.' " (2:14)

Evidently, some of Hirsch-Hyacinth's most intimate truth emerges in his slip, and it is linked, undoubtedly, to the character's diminished social status with respect to his listener in Heine's story. Freud reformulates the protagonist's thoughts:

> "Rothschild treated me quite as his equal, quite familiarly—that is, so far as a millionaire can." "A rich subject's condescension," we should add, "always

involves something not quite pleasant for whoever
experiences it."

Whether, now, we keep to the one or the other of the
equally valid texts of the same thought, we can see that
the question we asked ourselves is already decided. In
this example the character of being a joke does not
reside in the thought. What Heine has put into Hirsch-
Hyacinth's mouth is a correct and acute observation, an
observation of unmistakable bitterness, which is
understandable in a poor subject faced by such great
wealth; but we should not venture to describe it as in
the nature of a joke. (15–16)

The entire weight of the joke in this case lies on the subject of
enunciation or, more precisely, on the place it occupies. The humor of the misunderstanding stems as much from its strangeness with respect to the normal code of language as from the replacement of this code after having been sanctioned by the
Unconscious. We can summarize this in three main points:

1. The word "famillionaire" is incongruous because it does not
appear in the code. It acquires the value of a message precisely
because of being outside the code.
2. This distinction is sanctioned as a joke by the Other, who
places it in the code as such. Freud himself points out in his explanation that a joke is only what is accepted as such.[5]
3. A joke bears a certain relation to truth.

Only if we do not reduce a joke to its literal meaning can we
actually understand its meaning within the level of its expression:

The process by which the joke is formed—that is, the
joke-technique—in this instance might be described as
"condensation accompanied by the formation of a
substitute"; and in the present example the formation of
the substitute consists in the making of a "composite
word." This composite word "famillionaire," . . . is
unintelligible in itself but is immediately understood in
its context and recognized as being full of meaning.
(Freud, *Jokes*, 18–19)

All that is left to explain in order to continue this discussion is the sanctioning function of that Other that makes the joke possible:

> The Other is a demanding-Other, from whom my words proceed. But this demanding-Other grants me only given signs, frozen relations between signifiers and meanings. Yet, however, it has the power to sanction me as a subject, provided that when it ratifies the joke as a joke, not reducing it to its literal meaning, it grants it the value of message. But not of the message of an "I" that is directed to an other, but rather a message of some other thing that is not the "I," which is directed to something that is not the other. It is a message that is not realized in an utterance, a message of impossibility of enunciation, a message in the utterance of an enunciated enunciation, a message of an articulation impossible to articulate: the message is, simply, all of that—a signifier—which in a relation of demand appears as proceeding from somewhere else, like a messenger from *another scene.* This inadequacy between enunciation and utterance is articulated at the level of enunciated enunciation. (Jinkis 35)

Word and Desire

Between enunciation and utterance, the gap of desire is opened. But it is impossible to define such desire according to object-related references, provided it is devoted to and determined by lack, by frustration. Jean Baudrillard, in an enlightening essay on the phallic rituals of striptease, has pointed out that desire's perfection is realized at the fall of the dancer's last veil, in that "something that before being carried out has time to be missed" happens (Baudrillard 166).

Lacan also, when attempting to illustrate how frustrating a love encounter can be—a lover's reproach, "You never look at me from where I see you"—resorts to the legend of Zeuxis and Parrhasius. The former paints a grape bunch so mimetically real that birds come to eat it. The latter paints a veil so plausible that Zeuxis asks for it to be lifted in order to see what is behind it. The problem is not, in any case—as we will explore later on—in the *effect of reality*, but in the deceit of the eye, the triumph over the eye of a glance and its desiring drive addressed toward something beyond which we are spurred to see (Lacan, *Four Fundamental Concepts* 103).

Desire, if not as object, is liable to be apprehended as substance, as in the interjection of the subject. This is the way it is conceived by Spinoza in his *Ethics,* when, after regarding "actions and human appetites as if they were lines, surfaces and solid bodies" (173), he affirms that

> The human body can experience a great number of modifications, and still retain the impressions or traces of objects . . . and, consequently, the same images of things. (174)[6]

According to Jinkis, when we recount a dream, we instinctively describe its degree of reality, we value the impression it has made on us, and so on, giving it the shape of a cited discourse in order to defend ourselves better from the question addressed to us by the dream. Free association about the dream will reveal, uniquely, that latent ideas are the enunciation of a previous utterance that is not identified with the unconscious desire. They are a part of the story and at the same time they are the remains of true enunciation: "A subject's discourse is always an enunciated enunciation of an utterance" (36).

Very possibly, in the example quoted by Freud, Hirsch-Hyacinth's desire is to be treated as an equal by a millionaire. If interpretation were to stop here, we would remain at the level of demand, in the superficial effervescence of desire. We must go farther, searching deeper into the question of how such desire essentially articulates the subject's position. Jinkis finds the answer in the special communicative situation of psychoanalysis, where what is at play for the speakers—both the analyst and the analysand—is not their personalities but rather the (symbolic) place, the topological space that each occupies:

> The object can bear the impossibility of revelation of desire, and the subject, correlatively to the articulation of desire, is deleted. . . . Analysis is possible only on the condition that it follow the signifier's articulations. In this way, it is possible to discover the unconscious desire

that indicates the subject's position. In our example, desire is that of the enunciation enunciated by Hyacinth. *Heine's desire is Hyacinth's unconscious desire and not merely a desire that can either be conscious or not.* At the same time, Heine is clearly presented as the source from which Hyacinth's enunciation proceeds. In Hyacinth's discourse, there is something beyond his own will: a meaning emerges that slips out in a permanent form, independent of the "I" of discourse. (36; emphasis added)

Now we may better understand the formerly expressed statement about the subject's being talked-of by language, and the latter's rejoicing behind the former's back. One last distinction is made by Jinkis to split definitively between subject and "I":

In order not to mistake the subject for I, it is necessary not to mistake demand for desire. Language is that entity which exists in the distance which separates the satisfaction of the necessity of the exigencies of demand; it is that which makes satisfaction impossible and at the same time acts as a tool for all satisfaction. But the necessity can only be articulated in demand on the condition of alienating its object; so, satisfaction would lead to the destruction of the structure of the demand. Destruction or a phase shift: all verbalization supposes a syncopated time, a "temporal" tension, a delay between communication of demand and its satisfaction. That is to say *that demand is articulated by desire,* or to put it another way, desire appears in that gap of demand. Therefore, we may say that desire is the condition, imposed on a subject, that expresses the needs according to the signifier's rules. (37; emphasis added)

In the joke, demand is expressed in accordance with the rules of the signifier, and it is satisfied only at the ideal moment in which the Other sanctions it as a joke. When the subject feels strange about the immediate contents of what has been said, it is because it intervenes in the sanction of the symbolic—the third party in the game—as a possibility. When Lacan says that "subject's desire is the desire of the Other," he implies that desire is the condition through which the subject finds its constituent structure as a desiring subject, in the same possibility it expresses its demand on all those who are, for it, the Other of its demand.

The demand insists, proclaiming a survival of the significance beyond the consistency of signification. With its need for nourishment satisfied, the baby keeps on crying: as *unconditional* demand for the mother's presence. But the arrival of mother's imago provokes a certain strangeness in the baby. Yet it is not that, either. And the appearance of primary forms of self-eroticism—thumb for nipple, for instance—indicates that the subject-object relationship's place is, historically speaking, a disappointing one for the subject, that merely provokes many metonymic slips:

> The more articulated the demand, the more absent from
> the subject's reality desire becomes. . . . Every time
> desire forms a relationship with an object, we discover
> its metonymical nature. They are not abandoned ruins of
> a mythical union of the past—pursued with
> nostalgia—of desire with its object. They are not *remains*
> of an antiquated construction, but a real *building-up* of
> old ruins. It is not something that has been lost:
> something has been lost that could never have been.
> (Jinkis 37–38; emphasis in original)

Beckett is right when he affirms that the only real Paradise is the Paradise that has been lost. Perhaps the fiction that could illustrate best such emptiness of desire is the film *Vertigo* (Alfred Hitchcock, 1958), with Scottie's re-creation of Madeleine's ghost, through Judy's makeup, clothes, and so on. This object, which Scottie attempts to reach, with ingenuity, as a pure object of desire, which never existed, is revealed as such beyond its imaginary metalanguage and the biased fetishistic drive (metonymical) that constitutes it. This yearning for the total object is a sign of an annihilating, absolute desire, close to the drive of death through necrophilia (Scottie is trying to reconstruct a corpse). Against it, Hitchcock reveals, with extreme cruelty and lucidity, the futility of the affective demands of everyday life: the heartbroken tenderness of Midge, the eternal candidate to become the character of fiancée, the vacuum behind Judy's own mask.

In this way, the principal truth in the film is stated from the systematic draining of its fiction. We know, at the end, that the only thing Scottie has achieved after his twisted adventure is to cure himself of his vertigo. In other words, he becomes conscious of the split nature that constitutes him as a subject. There is no other way we are to read the sentence, pathetic to the point of grief, uttered by Scottie in the film's last scene: "How much I've cried for you, Madeleine!" We do not regret, along with the protagonist, the loss of what we always regarded as ours forever. It was only a shadow that came from ourselves, and because of that absolute lack of an object that characterizes unconscious desire and essentially constitutes the subject. In the sexual masquerade of the so-called male-female relationship, the subject does not lack the object (likely to be classified into good and bad according to Kleinian categories), but what lacks the object is the unconscious desire. "It is too late, she can't come back," Scottie says. The final loss of Madeleine—ghost and memory—leaves the main character absorbed in his own vacuum; the glance toward the object of desire, impossible as well, was carried out through borrowed eyes.[7]

Every text is intended to be a parapraxis of writing, a radical nonmeeting between the object and its expression. To theorize such a nonmeeting, such a split between the subject of enunciation and the utterance's subject was indispensable in order to define the space from which this work's primary discursive source emerges as well as to undertake further argumentation. Let us finish this chapter with Jorge Jinkis's lucid words, which he too uses to end his splendid article:

> We have discussed a question of epistemological order. That entity, which the linguist calls the source of enunciation, is something that psychoanalysis cannot admit as the reflexion of its limit. Psychoanalysis questions that source and I have provided an answer: the limit is confused with the intersubjectivity rules that the discovery of psychoanalysis allows us to formulate. Lacan explains that all discourse, while implying a subject, originates from the Other. We know how, from the beginning, a child has no doubt about the adult's knowing his thoughts. "Imitating" the eclipses of that other, the subject itself becomes eclipsed. Repression is

correlative to the need of eclipse, to the subject's disappearance in the enunciation process. This silencing of the subject, called "fading" by Lacan, explains the paradox of the disregard for "I," as the "disregarded I" articulates what it ignores. The subject's going silent allows for the appearance of the gap of something unspoken in the utterance, and, precisely, it is this contradictory demand, this persistence of the unspoken in what is spoken, that obliges us to acknowledge the existence of the unconscious, a silent subject that speaks in every one of us. Essential inadequacy defines negation as a constitutive dimension of the essence, that is, the being (Logos = discourse) of subject: a being that has ceased being and that although it is not, having been because it was determined by a restart previous to every start, has to be, precisely because of the impossibility of being for the first time. (41)

Notes

1. In order to establish the scientific basis of this approach, Belinski begins by asking a double question of psychoanalysis: the question of its object and its origin. This question stems from a perfectly articulated point in the works of Freud, Bachelard, Marx, and Althusser. A first approach to this problem might be defined by the applicability of a scientific model, that of physics, to psychoanalysis. This model has earned the status of "pilot science" from the Renaissance (Galileo) until our century. Freud's historicocritical scope is dominated by physics as the most yielding scientific paradigm. The pragmatism of American psychoanalysis has given in to the demands of physics, the outcome being serious theoretical insufficiencies when the unconscious axis was dislodged by the "I," the latter sometimes conceived as something impertinent, autonomous, and unchangeable (Rappaport). From this deviation, based on Jungian roots by way of American psychoanalysis, Belinski wonders whether the sciences must be named in the singular or the plural. If we privilege either, using physics as a model, we obliterate a central question: that of the territoriality (Bachelard) of a science not due to the empirical object with which it deals, but because every theory is thus. Once this point is reached, a displacement can legitimately be presented: from method to object. The object is not empirical but theoretical: the Althusserian object of knowledge and Bachelard's conceptual theoretical body. The question mark appears then on that object of knowledge departing from reality (different from Hegel and Feuerbach) of chaotic representations and intuitions, a departure point for analysis that is to shatter them to pieces . . . in order to reach simple determinations to synthesize them later into all concrete thought, a *theoretical practice*, according to Althusserian terminology, in which the *product* of this theoretical practice is privileged.

Bachelard says that, when a theoretical corpus is examined and its scientificity is required, it must be questioned according to the rationality of its own doctrinal body (physics from physics; psychoanalysis from psychoanalysis). That is why every epistemology is regionalistic, at least in its beginning. With this, we reach an essential point in Belinski's argumentation for the utmost importance of the economy of our own exposition. That is, psychoanalysis is not merely a territorial science; when it settles, it modifies the whole body of scientificity. Until psychoanalysis, a ruthless subjectivity could be postulated in the observer of a given process, who, once introduced into the mechanism of a given process, polluted it. Investigators are, for Freud, continually absorbed in the field in which they work. From a classic perspective that would be the basic epistemological insufficiency of psychoanalysis—provoking, for instance, Sartre's reticences—that led to endless debates on its convergence with philosophy. If we understand that the investigator is not, in this case, the "contaminator," but the motor that starts a process in which the investigator is included and transformed, we can affirm that the insufficiency has become necessity, and necessity is read from theory. So, as his writings reach maturity, Freud passes from a technical approach (hypnosis as therapeutic procedure) to a method (subordinate technique) for the investigation of psychic processes impossible to reach otherwise. Finally, in the works of *Metapsychology*, we observe the resolution of matters that will give shape to a new scientific discipline. The method has increasingly developed into subordination to theory, drawing from it the elements with which to work. Freud himself has the intuition of epistemological rupture that presupposes, in 1900, the publication of *Traumdeutung*. It is a science—the interpretation of dreams—that arises in a given historical moment, not as a mere accumulation of elements in a chain, but as a gap, a sharp cut with what precedes. In the last chapter of *Traumdeutung*, "The Psychology of the Dream-Processes," Belinski sees the qualitative leap that gives rise to psychoanalysis as a Science. Even in the handling of clinical materials (*Studies on Hysteria, The Case of Dora*), a process of theoretical practice is tested in which medical records become theoretical items. In the studies on hysteria, we notice an element present through its absence—transference—in the Dora case; Freud achieves theorization on transference. In the historical lapse (1895 to 1905) between both texts, Freud has worked out his theoretical object, the unconscious. The analytical relation is a transferential one in which the identity of the object-"I" is strongly questioned.

2. In the last paragraph the author refers to an important essay by Jacques Lacan (*Ecrits*).

3. In an interview, Umberto Eco, the well-known semiotician, declared that he did not understand the Lacanian definition of signifier and regarded it as false. Perhaps the problem lies fundamentally in an understanding of the concept "signifier" strictly linked to Saussure and not to a general theory of discourse. Lacan says that the subject begins in the place of the Other, because there the first signifier appears. Thus the question "What is a signifier?" is answered in the following way:

> A signifier is that which represents a subject. For whom?—not for another subject, but for another signifier. In order to illustrate this axiom, suppose that in the desert you find a stone covered with hieroglyphics. You do not doubt for a moment that, behind them, there was a subject who wrote them. But it is an error to believe that

each signifier is addressed to you—this is proved by the fact that you cannot understand any of it. On the other hand you define them as signifiers, by the fact that you are sure that each of these signifiers is related to each of the others. And it is this that is at issue with the relation between the subject and the field of the Other.

The subject is born insofar as the signifier emerges in the field of the Other. But, by this very fact, this subject—which was previously nothing if not a subject coming into being—solidifies into a signifier.

The relation to the Other is . . . the relation between the living subject and that which he loses by having to pass, for his reproduction, through the sexual cycle. (Lacan, *Ecrits* 198–99)

4. This was expressed in similar fashion by Lacan—and not without humor—to Moustapha Safouan in his Seminar of 1964, in order to make palpable the difference between the object of the drive and the object of desire: "You then say . . . *I love mutton stew.* It's precisely the same thing when you say: *I love Mrs. X*, except that you say it to her, which makes all the difference" (Lacan, *The Four Fundamental Concepts* 243).

5. An example of an unbearable joke was provided me by the filmmaker José María Berzosa after a showing at the San Sebastián Film Festival of his excellent documentary *Chile-Impressions* (1976), filmed for French television. Berzosa interviewed General Augusto Pinochet and his wife at the Palacio de la Moneda about their everyday life. Asked about her opinion of her husband as a politician, Pinochet's wife responded with the following indescribable sample of ingenuity: "I would define him as a sporting president . . . on the grounds that he is so keen on getting people into stadiums." The so-called joke was so ideologically repulsive that Berzosa eliminated it in the final editing.

6. We find here the origin of what Freud called, in his metapsychological writings, the representation of the thing (*Sachvorstellung, Dingvorstellung*): "Representation of the thing consists of a cathexis, if not of direct mnemic images of the thing, at least of more distant traces derived from those images" (quoted in Laplanche and Pontalis 384).

7. We allude, of course, to the well-known fragment of "Les Chants du Maldoror" (4.5; Ducasse 177) in which the poet rebukes his beloved: "These eyes don't belong to you. . . . Where did you get them?" ("Ces yeux ne t'appartiennent pas . . . où les as-tu pris?")

Works Cited

Baudrillard, Jean. *L'échange symbolique et la mort.* Paris: Gallimard, 1976.

Beckett, Samuel. *Proust: Three Dialogues.* London: J. Calder, 1987.

Belinski, Jorge. "Epistemología del psicoanálisis." Unpublished manuscript. Valencia, 1979.

Benveniste, Emile. "The Nature of Pronouns." In *Problems in General Linguistics.* Trans. M. E. Meek. Miami Linguistics Series, no. 8. Coral Gables, Fl.: Univ. of Miami Press, 1971. 217–22.

Catelli, Nora. "El juego del Lector." *Quimera* no. 38 (May 1984): 22–25.

Ducasse, Isidore, Comte de Lautremont. "Les chants du Maldoror." In *Oeuvres complètes*, vols. 4, 5. Paris: Garnier-Flammarion, 1969.

Freud, Sigmund. *Psychopathology of Everyday Life*. Trans. Alan Tyson. Ed. James Strachey, New York: W. W. Norton & Company, 1965.

———. *Group Psychology and the Analysis of the Ego*. London: The International Psychoanalytical Press, 1922.

———. *The Case of Dora*. New York: W. W. Norton & Company, 1952.

———. *Studies on Hysteria*. Trans. James Strachey. London: Basic Books, 1957.

———. *Jokes and Their Relation to the Unconscious*. Trans. and ed. James Strachey. New York: W. W. Norton & Company, 1960.

———. *The Interpretation of Dreams*. Trans. James Strachey. London: George Allen & Unwin, 1967.

Jinkis, Jorge E. "Una distinción tópica: el sujeto de la enunciación y el yo del discurso." *Cuadernos Sigmund Freud*, vol. 1: *Temas de Jacques Lacan* (1971): 23–41.

Lacan, Jacques. "Réponses à des étudiants en philosophie sur l'objet de la psychanalyse." In *Cahiers pour l'analyse*. Paris: Editions du Seuil, 1966. Vol. 3, 12.

———. "Las formaciones del inconsciente." In *Las formaciones del inconsciente*. Trans. José Sazbón. Buenos Aires: Nueva Visión, 1970.

———. "The Mirror Stage as Formative of the Function of the I." In *Ecrits: A Selection*. Trans. A. Sheridan. New York: W. W. Norton and Company, 1977. 1–7.

———. "The Agency of the Letter in the Unconscious or Reason since Freud." In *Ecrits: A Selection*. Trans. A. Sheridan. New York: W. W. Norton and Company, 1977. 146–78.

———. "The Subversion of the Subject and the Dialectic of Desire in the Freudian Unconscious." In *Ecrits: A Selection*. Trans. A. Sheridan. New York: W. W. Norton and Company, 1977. 292–325.

———. *The Four Fundamental Concepts of Psycho-Analysis*. Ed. Jacques Allain Miller. Trans. A. Sheridan. New York: W. W. Norton & Company, 1981.

Laplanche, Jean, and Jean-Bertrand Pontalis. *Diccionario de psicoanálisis*. Trans. Fernando Cervantes Gimeno. Barcelona: Labor, 1979.

Spinoza, Benedict. *Ethics*. Trans. Andrew Boyle. London: J. M. Dent, 1989.

◆　Afterword

Aesthetics and Politics

Tom Lewis

Las Lanzas [The Surrender of Breda *by Velázquez]* is not only
a painting. It is a whole conception of life. Why does Breda
surrender? . . . But the city, the thing whose fate, whose integrity,
whose very existence is at stake, will have been saved. Surrender as
the only alternative to destruction.
> —Luis Goytisolo, *La cólera de Aquiles*[1]

A little socialism, European style, would be just fine with me.
> —Eduardo Mendoza, *El laberinto de las aceitunas*[2]

Today is the day of the nonviolent general strike. Madrid woke up
stiff and empty, like a cemetery where, through the mist, there
move about the bold shadows of the survivors of a bombing.
> —J. J. Armas Marcelo, *Los dioses de sí mismos*[3]

The selection of essays presented in *Critical Practices in Post-
Franco Spain* accurately reflects the balance of forces within
Spanish literary theory since 1975. Fairly specific absences and
emphases help to map the terrain. Gender criticism of Spanish
literature remains primarily the work of scholars residing in
North America. Today, in contrast to the 1960s and 1970s, Marxist theory enjoys little purchase among Spanish literary theorists
or social philosophers. And, having coaxed a turn toward concepts that treat incompleteness, openness, and pragmatics as
opposed to wholeness, closure, and universals, a diffuse but he-

gemonic "postmodernism" now overlies earlier Spanish traditions of linguistic and phenomenological criticism.

Although the editors hint at a uniquely Spanish contribution to contemporary literary theory and criticism, one should dispel the notion straightway that some sort of national identity is etched among the numerous fine insights this volume contains. To be sure, the prominence of phenomenology within the collection contrasts sharply with the critical scene in the United States, where phenomenology occupies a back-row seat among the current "methodologies of choice." And the essays here that rely on semiotics, narratology, and deconstruction—despite being close in tone and spirit to their U.S. counterparts—do balk at embracing the total program of ahistoricity, undecidable reference, and philosophical skepticism associated with poststructuralism. In most respects, however, the volume attests to the full immersion of Spanish critical practices within the same general problematic that shapes the most recent literary theory and criticism produced in Europe, North America, Japan, and a major portion of Latin America.

This problematic, commonly referred to as "postmodernism," has been shown to result from the broad convergence of three distinct but related cultural trends: the reaction against "modernism" in art, the development of "poststructuralism" in philosophy, and the elaboration of the social theory of "postmodernity" (Callinicos 1990, 7). I want first to take account of the latter two trends in relation to the literary and cultural theories included here. My primary aim and interest, however, will be to argue for the social determination of the critical practices on display in this volume. Such an argument will entail substantially enlarging the historical frame provided by the editors in their introduction.

Antirealism and Aestheticism

If any two themes stand out as central both to poststructuralism and to the idea that a new "postmodern" period has dawned, they are surely those of a militant antirealism and a celebratory aestheticism. Philosophical realism, it may be recalled, holds "that the ultimate objects of scientific inquiry exist and act (for the most part) quite independently of scientists and their activity" (Bhaskar 12). Poststructuralists oppose this theory, arguing instead that "reality" is constructed by discourses. The "objects" of any theory are in some profound sense "made up" and can have no status other than that of "discursive effects." Objectivity, knowledge, and truth are thus relativized for poststructuralists, allowing no rational grounds for choosing one theory over another.

Realists such as Roy Bhaskar nevertheless propose a "transcendental" or "critical realism" over and against the anti-realism of poststructuralism. By "transcendental" Bhaskar refers to an argument of the form, "What must the world be like if this or that result obtains?" He thereby conceptualizes the knowledge process as an inferential one involving a distinction between "real objects," which belong to an "intransitive dimension" or ontology, and "objects of knowledge," which belong to a "transitive dimension" or epistemology.

> Transcendental realism explicitly asserts the non-identity of the objects of the transitive and intransitive dimensions, of thought and being. And it relegates the notion of a correspondence between them to the status of a metaphor for the aim of an *adequating practice* (in which cognitive matter is worked into a matching representation of a non-cognitive object). It entails acceptance of (i) the principle of *epistemic relativity*, which states that all beliefs are socially produced, so that all knowledge is transcient, and neither truth-values nor criteria of rationality exist outside historical time. But it entails the rejection of (ii) the doctrine of *judgemental relativism*, which maintains that all beliefs are equally valid, in the sense that there can be no rational grounds for preferring one to another. It thus stands opposed to epistemic absolutism and epistemic irrationalism alike. Relativists have wrongly inferred (ii) from (i), while anti-relativists have wrongly taken the unacceptability of (ii) as a *reductio* of (i). (Bhaskar 24)

Christopher Norris has noted favorably that this argument "enables Bhaskar to defend both the basic rationality of science as an enterprise aimed toward better, more adequate grounds of judgement, and also the need for critique as a process of reflective understanding that questions 'absolutist' truth-claims by revealing their partial, self-interested, or socially motivated nature" (Norris 98).

Whereas "reality" for empiricism is simply given in experience, and for idealism it is something we construct ourselves, for realism "it is the nature of objects that determines their cognitive possibilities for us" (Bhaskar 25). As Andrew Collier explains, "realism follows from the conjunction of two premises: (1) If scientific activity occurs (or makes sense) then there must be real generative mechanisms in nature; (2) scientific activity does occur (makes sense)" (Collier 22). If one is willing to acknowledge the achievements of the sciences, then the debate between realism and antirealism finally settles on the question of scientific revolutions. Scientific revolutions, because they discredit a once secure body of knowledge, often provoke the reaction that there just cannot be any knowledge of the real world. Yet such an apparent spur to antirealism also implicitly affirms that "scientific activity is at least theoretically reputable and practically effective" (Collier 22–23). On this basis, Bhaskar is able to show that "scientific revolutions only make sense on the assumption that they yield deepened knowledge of structures which exist independently of us; and that scientific activity must be both a social process which the human sciences can investigate, and a source of objective knowledge" (Collier 23).

It is important to underscore that the theory of transcendental or critical realism affects the human and social sciences as well as the natural sciences. Society itself, on the realist view, is "a stratified system of structured realities" (Collier 142).

> The scientific, transcendental and critical realism which I
> have expounded conceives the world as being,
> structured, differentiated and changing. It is opposed to
> empiricism, pragmatism and idealism alike. Critical
> realists do not deny the reality of events and discourses;
> on the contrary, they insist upon them. But they hold
> that we will only be able to understand—and so
> change—the social world if we identify the structures at
> work that generate those events or discourses. Such
> structures are irreducible to the patterns of events and
> discourses alike. . . . They can only be identified through

the practical and theoretical work of the social sciences
. . . [through which they] may be hierarchically ranked
in terms of their explanatory importance. (Bhaskar 2–3)

Realism in the social sciences, therefore, is a condition of the
ability to act to transform society. Insofar as antirealism dis-
counts the possibility of identifying "social structures" as anything more than the effects of discourse, and insofar as it refuses
to assign causal primacy to some of these structures over
others—to those precise degrees does it weaken the basis on
which collectivities can move "from unneeded, unwanted and
oppressive to needed, wanted and empowering sources of determination" (Bhaskar 6). Bhaskar's critical realism indeed sits
uncomfortably alongside the traditions of contemporary liberal-
ism in the United States or contemporary social democracy in
Spain. Rather, critical realism comes down squarely on the side
of democratic, revolutionary socialism: "Socialist emancipation
depends on the transformation of structures, not the ameliora-
tion of states of affairs" (Bhaskar 6).

Now, nothing could figure as more alien to the kind of critical
realism I have just outlined than the essays making up the first
section of *Critical Practices in Post-Franco Spain*, "Representation." Actually, Jenaro Talens's essay, "Making Sense after Babel," constitutes a magisterial exploration of the process of
translation, and to the extent that his basic concern stays with
the relation between one text and another text—as opposed to
the relation between a text and the world—his argument proves
unobjectionable in many respects. Yet the essay still manages to
set the antirealist, "postmodern" tone of the entire volume. It
spends its energies, for example, in the attempt to blur the distinction between an "original" text and a "derivative" or supple-
mental translation. It echoes other themes in the Derridean rep-
ertoire when it invokes the issue of "copyright," debunks the
ideal of a "pure" language, and in effect explains translation as a
function of the "graft": "What translation does is to displace
and re/locate a text, making it a new element of the cultural universe where it is now inscribed." And all of this, too, in the context of a hierarchical reversal elevating the "shameful activity"
of translators while still leaving us in the dark regarding the con-

crete mechanisms which make possible their accomplishments. Just how does a person manage to "connect with the text as a living other with whom the translator establishes a dialogue"? The answer: "Anyone who has translated poetry knows."

But it is really with Jesús González-Requena's "The Television Newscast: A Postmodern Discourse" and Santos Zunzunegui's "Architectures of the Gaze" that we enter fully into the orbit of antirealism. For González-Requena "reality" today is a "production of those discourses that constitute it and that make consensus possible." The "present," too, is a production consisting of "the constant rediscursivization of reality." Indeed, "the reality of the world *exists* only insofar as it is submitted/subject to the order of discourse" (my emphasis); the "real," now opposed to "reality," fades into the shadows defying attempts to fathom it.

There is in all of this, of course, a coy nostalgia for the stuff of "real reality." Requena's emphasis on the excitement provoked by the emergence of the spectacular from the "rift from which the real threatens the order of reality" thus resonates with Zunzunegui's enthusiasm for that "subordination of the cognitive to the aesthetic" that enables the museum to be understood less as "a pedagogical space and more and more in terms of an explorative space, an experiential space, as source of sensual stimuli." Although Zunzunegui is concerned to demonstrate that "organized space . . . works as an authentic regulating mechanism of human activity," there is finally for him only "the creation [by contemporary museums] of ruptures" in which "we lose sight of the integrating totality in which we can receive the precise sense of the whole set of real or virtual actions which shape those museums." On his view, "reality" happily escapes systematic formulation in contemporary museumistic space, and knowledge is thereby negated in the name of the aesthetic. Zunzunegui finds this process wholly suitable to the experience of a postmodern "world where design precedes the object, fashion precedes behavior, publicity precedes the product, and look and simulacrum seem to be constitutive notions."

Zunzunegui's essay indeed makes explicit that a key component of the concept of "postmodernism" remains the notion that the world of material production has recently undergone a radical break from its mode of organization in the earlier part of the twentieth century. From "modernity" we have passed to "postmodernity"—a period allegedly characterized by, among other things, the end of Fordism; the priority of the experience of space over the experience of time; the ascendancy of reproduction over production; a numerically shrinking and politically disabled working class; and the unprecedented atomization and destabilization of individual subjectivities. Now, all of these ideas are either wrong or inadequately situated. While I cannot pretend to make arguments for the alternative positions here, I at least want to indicate what the alternatives are.

A significant restructuring of the economy involving strategies of flexible accumulation, for example, certainly has taken place in the advanced capitalist countries, but this shift from Fordism to "post-Fordism" is better understood as "a continuation of trends operative throughout the century" (Callinicos 153) rather than as a push into what some have gone so far as to call "postcapitalism." Critics such as Fredric Jameson, moreover, offer compelling and helpful analyses of the ideological evacuation of historical time from "postmodern" representations (see Jameson). Yet events such as the collapse of Stalinism in Eastern Europe; the return of the national question in the Balkans; the rise of the neo-Nazi movement both in Europe and the United States; the general strikes of 1992 in Italy and Greece; the ongoing wave of strikes and protests in Spain, Britain, and France; the inevitable exposure of the true face of U.S. imperialism in Somalia—all of these events provide a dramatic and unavoidable sense of portentous history.

At the heart of the claim that reproduction has supplanted production is Jean-François Lyotard's claim that "knowledge" and "representation"—as opposed to old-fashioned "commodity production"—now power the economy and otherwise cause the world to go 'round (see Lyotard). Nevertheless, the much-romanticized "postmodern" hacker still must buy a PC, and the much vaunted "postmodern" video still depends on the sale of TVs and VCRs, before any of their effects can be worked! Similarly, the claim that the industrial working class is shrinking remains severely flawed: internationally, the industrial working class is growing (see Kellogg). And the implicit corollary of the notion of a shrinking working class—namely, that secretaries, nurses, schoolteachers, department-store salespeople, bank tellers, data-entry clerks, and so on do not form part of the "working class" because they belong to the "service sector" — is simply false (see Callinicos and Harman).

Finally, the lack of agency that is said to define today's established forms of subjectivity should be immediately qualified by recognition of the demonstrated ability of individuals to join together collectively in order to struggle for and to win significant social changes. Obviously, the 1980s constituted a "postmodern" decade of low levels of working class and student struggle, coupled with an inward-looking focus on "personal lifestyles" and individual consumption in the professional-managerial class. As I shall explain in the next section, those features of the decade resulted primarily from the defeat and demoralization of the Left in the aftermath of "May 1968." It is sheer folly, however, to doubt that collective struggles will return precisely as a response to the increased rates of exploitation and heightened degrees of oppression of the 1980s. It is also folly not to understand that such situations of struggle can produce themselves quite rapidly. The speed with which the initially unforeseen political revolutions in Eastern Europe developed may once again serve as a case in point.

Faced with a set of political experiences that can lead one to lose confidence in organized fightbacks against an oppressive system, intellectuals can tend either to overemphasize the realities that constrain human agency or to locate in aesthetic experience itself the prefiguration, or even realization, of that "realm of freedom" that the "realm of necessity" seems so doggedly to refuse us. Cristina Peña-Marín's "Subjectivity and Temporality in Narrative," for example, examines the vicissitudes of subjectivity in Clarín's *La regenta*. The conditions of representation in free indirect style, as well as the inscription of the "passions" in the serial reformulations of identity through time, determine that both the narrator and at least one of the characters (Don Fermín) prove constitutively incapable of arriving at any sort of coherence as subjects. Juan Miguel Company-Ramón's "Subject and Language: Reflections on Lacan and Jinkis" advances an even more drastic account of the subject's necessary fragmentation and ignorance. Company-Ramón champions Lacanian psychoanalysis as "dissolving . . . the very status of knowledge." Because the possibility of knowledge depends upon the belief that "the subject speaks," linguistic recognition of the split between "the subject of enunciation and the utterance's subject" warrants the Lacanian assertion of "a radical nonmeeting between the object and its expression." The subject is thus rendered ontologically deaf, dumb, blind, and stupid.

This sort of nihilism, of course, is counterbalanced in *Critical Practices in Post-Franco Spain* by the affirmation of the aesthetic itself as the site of the subject's freedom and self-fashioning. For Rafael Núñez-Ramos in his "The Immutability of the Text, the Freedom of the Reader, and Aesthetic Experience," aesthetic knowledge "does not suppose the conceptual assumption of an already elaborated information, but the development of a personal response, the formation of an attitude. As a result, the manifestation of aesthetic knowledge cannot grow through the conventional and representative linguistic system. In order to express its aesthetic knowledge, the subject must elaborate its own language. . . . " Similarly, after conducting in "The Pragmatics of Lyric Poetry" a persuasive critique of expressive models of lyric poetry, José María Pozuelo-Yvancos concludes that through the agency of aesthetic signification "readers are liberated from their 'real' situation and are introduced into a new perceptive space. The latter, atemporal and lacking in concrete restrictions, multiplies the communicative text and extends it to every situation of reading in which one believes oneself to be in the imaginary world. . . . "

I should like both to challenge Darío Villanueva's faulty characterization of Marxist literary criticism (of Lukács in particular) and to explore at some length our own agreements and differences on the question of literary reference. On this occasion, however, I must limit myself to pointing out that his often brilliant "Phenomenology and Pragmatics of Literary Realism" shares Núñez-Ramos's and Pozuelo-Yvancos's apotheosis of aesthetic experience. The "intentional realism" urged by Villanueva does not finally concern the relation between literary texts and the world but rather "how the readers make use of the text *to declare their own reality*" (my emphasis). Indeed, writing as if texts might never involve *ideological* processes of subject positioning and hegemony, Villanueva claims without the least trace of irony that "the virtuality of the text, and our intentional living of this virtuality, bring us to elevate the rank of its internal world of reference qualitatively until we integrate it, without any reservation, into our own external, experienced world. . . . " Once again, literature has become the space of the subject's liberation and self-fulfillment on the basis of its ability to facilitate the reconciliation of the world to the subject's desire.

Manuel Asensi's richly deconstructive "Reading in Process, the Antitext, and the Definition of Literature" clearly strives to avoid "essentializing" the notion of literature in the same phenomenological way that, despite their emphasis on pragmatics, Núñez-Ramos, Pozuelo-Yvancos, and Villanueva manage to do. Yet Asensi himself accepts the contestable distinction between "instrumental language" and "literary language," which always invites the view of aesthetics as a discursive domain in its own right, and he will eventually posit a special status of "betweenness" for the "literariness" he works to displace. Asensi in fact develops Derrida's notions of the "trace" and, in particular, the "graft" in an argument stressing that an "antitext" subtends every text produced in the "literary" mode. And, no matter if he does label it "the between," Asensi's subsequent exploration of the relation between texts and antitexts indeed constructs an essential and proper domain of the aesthetic:

There are a multitude of "betweens": the "between" of the relationship text-metatext, the "between" of the infinite interpretation of the disseminated textual body, the "between" of the literary absolute that leaves neither margins nor periphery, the "between" of the antitext that invades (is invaded by) texts-languages, the "between" of the rhetoric that universalizes in the midst of a substitutional vertigo, the unleashing of the voice of the literary text, the "between" of intertextuality and dissemination, the "between" that effaces and institutes linguistic boundaries, the "between" that breaks with genre understood as identity principle, the "between" of the counterlaw, the "between" of a self-effacing literaturity, the "between" of the question "What is literature?" that restores it to the previous "Literature?",

the "between" that announces existing conflict and
friction in the interior/exterior of the antitext. . . .
  Literature? ? Text?
  Between.

One should note, finally, the religious and even mystical
overtones of this and other portions of Asensi's essay, for they
provide the key to understanding the form of subjectivity projected by Asensi's own version of a celebratory aesthetic: "the
trace," to take another example, "opens itself up to the *différance*; it is what transforms the *literary* text into the privileged
place of the *différance*, that which names without naming, the introduction to the literary text within the silence of the *différance*."
On this view, the subjectivity conferred by the aesthetic is precisely one that keeps faith with Lyotard's apocalyptic call in 1979
to "wage war on totality; let us be witnesses to the unpresent-
able; let us activate the differences and save the honor of the
name" (Lyotard 82). The aesthetic here may not liberate subjects
into some sort of completion or self-fulfillment, as is suggested
by the more phenomenologically based essays in this volume,
but it does serve as the means by which the uniqueness and integrity of the subject is allegedly preserved in the face of what
Lyotard and many other poststructuralists consider to be the
"terroristic illusions" of reason and truth that have become evident in the aftermath of "May 1968."
  Like the militant antirealism that characterizes these essays,
therefore, their authors' turn toward and celebration of the aesthetic as the most efficacious — *and even as the only* — space afford-
ing opportunities for achieving a liberating subjectivity can
themselves be seen as products of the profound disappointment
of revolutionary desires in the late 1960s and continuing
throughout the 1970s. It is this perspective that I should now
like to explore in the context of Spain.

Spain's "May 1968" and Its Aftermath

As the introduction to these essays makes plain, literary theory
was denied a disciplinary foothold within the Spanish academy
during Franco's regime. Growth and modernization of the uni-

versities in the late 1970s and the 1980s, however, created real opportunities for literary theory, culminating in its official establishment as a discipline in the middle 1980s. The 1982 and 1986 electoral victories of the Spanish Socialist party (PSOE)—and especially the PSOE's administrative overhaul of the university system in 1985—were crucial to the subsequent development and ongoing promotion of literary theory in Spain. Both the availability of state funds and the PSOE's careful cultivation of a modernizing, avant-garde image have helped the new discipline to become an institutional meeting ground for the various poststructuralisms on questions of cultural production.

But the political fortunes of the PSOE index much more than just the role of university reform in the rise of literary theory in Spain. It is not feminist or Marxist literary theory, for example, that has won an important acceptance. What requires explanation is thus the particular form that Spanish literary theory has assumed in its institutionalized setting. In other words, why are Spanish critical practices "postmodern"?

Responding to this question returns us to the electric debates of 1974–77 over the *ruptura democrática* versus the *ruptura pactada*. Prior to Franco's death, the majority of the broad Left took for granted the need to break completely with the social, political, and economic legacy of Francoism. Opposition was organized in two main groups: the Junta Democrática, led by the Spanish Communist party (PCE), and the Plataforma de Convergencia Democrática, led by the PSOE. Although the Plataforma was "somewhat more open to the notion of dialogue with the regime reformists than the Junta Democrática" (Preston 75), the Left remained united in its minimal demands of "full political amnesty, legalization of all political parties, free trade unions, the dismantling of the Movimiento and the Sindicatos, and free elections" (Preston 80–81).

Franco died at long last on 20 November 1975, and King Juan Carlos I replaced him as chief of state on 22 November. Throughout the winter of 1975–76, "neither the cabinet nor the king made any serious attempt to dismantle fascism" (Harman 326–27). Only a huge upturn in strike activity and mass demonstrations—thirty-six million hours were lost to strikes in the first two months of 1976 alone, twice the figure for *all* of 1975

(Harman 329)—forced the king and a significant fraction of former Francoists to agree in summer 1976 to call elections before June 1977 and to grant a partial political amnesty. Even so, the government continued to refuse to legalize the Left political parties. The possibility of negotiations seemed as remote as ever in late 1976.

> For much of [1976] a stonewalling conservative bunker had kept alive in the Left its declared objective of a decisive break or *ruptura* with the inherited political order, leading to the formation of a provisional government and the convocation of a constituent assembly. Nearby Portugal had just demonstrated in 1974–75 that a situation of fundamental political instability readily fuels the social aspirations of the working-class masses, raising major ambiguities about the direction of the regime that will eventually emerge from the crisis. (Camiller 9)

In fact, revolution was in the air, and expectations ran extraordinarily high. Membership in the PCE and the far left parties increased with astonishing speed. Swimming with the tide, the reformist PSOE, too, rejected "any path of accommodation to capitalism" at its twenty-seventh party congress in December 1976 (Camiller 9).

The Francoists themselves were organized into two main camps: the *continuistas* or bunker, who opposed any change in the system, and the *aperturistas*, who advocated an accommodation to parliamentary democracy as the way to preserve their political and economic power. Following the army's massacre of workers in Vitoria in March 1976, leading *continuistas* in the government of Prime Minister Carlos Arias Navarro called for measures of repression on a scale equal to that of the 1940s immediately after the civil war. Yet others "who saw what had happened so recently to the Greek and Portuguese dictatorships were not prepared for the risks involved: it might work for a year or two, but the army could not hold down such immense social pressures forever—the eventual explosion would be uncontrollable" (Harman 329). Thus, after receiving U.S. approval, the king demanded the resignation of Arias Navarro in early June, and Torcuato Fernández Miranda engineered the emergence of Adolfo Suárez out of the *aperturista* group to become the new prime minister in July 1976.

Suárez set immediately to work on fashioning a transition to parliamentary democracy that would ensure the survival of the king and key sections of Spain's ruling class. Suárez moved first to legalize the noncommunist Left parties (including the PSOE) in February 1977 and then legalized the PCE in April after obtaining its recognition of the monarchy and a reaffirmation of its "eurocommunist" commitment to the electoral road to social change. In a move designed to "guarantee victory for political parties organized by ex-fascists and the 'moderate opposition' " (Harman 329), Suárez called for quick elections so as to take advantage of disorganization among the most radical oppositional forces. He then staged the elections in June 1977 "on the basis of an electoral system bent to over-represent the less urbanized provinces which had been the stronghold of the CEDA Right in the Second Republic" (Camiller 13).

When his recently formed Center Democratic Union (UCD) won 35 percent of the vote and laid claim to 47 percent of the seats in the new Cortes, Suárez exploited the weakened position of the PCE and the PSOE in order to negotiate a series of economic accords in November 1977. The basic aim of the Moncloa Pacts was to gain breathing space for the new government by involving the Left parties in stemming the rising tide of strike activity and popular unrest. Thus the PCE and the PSOE agreed to 20–22 percent limits on wage increases at a time when inflation was galloping along at 29 percent; the PCE and the PSOE further agreed to monetarist restrictions on credit and immediate cuts in public spending in return for promises of future economic reforms (Harman 334). While these "opposition" parties would indeed go on to sell the unions on the need to muzzle strikes and demonstrations—in effect "making sure the great working-class upsurge of 1975–76 was soon a distant memory"—the government itself would deliver few reforms, unemployment would rise from 7 to 13 percent, and a wave of bankruptcies and factory closings would follow (Harman 334).

By collaborating against the mass challenge to the system from below, the PCE and the PSOE accepted the view that the new "free enterprise monarchy" could in fact "set the parameters for an epochal reconciliation of class interests" (Camiller 14). This was—then as now—an utter illusion. Rather, what became so strikingly evident is that:

> the essential function of the famous UCD-PCE-PSOE Moncloa Accords of late 1977 was precisely to express this renunciation of hegemonic ambitions by the labour movement. Big capital could hardly have wished for a clearer or more rapid vindication of its strategy of replacing the institutional trappings of Francoism. The level of strikes, which had been the highest in Europe, soon fell towards the West German norm of the time; and unemployment began soaring to unprecedented levels as employers took advantage of trade-union flexibility to circumvent the job-protection legislation introduced in the early years of the dictatorship. (Camiller 14)

The Moncloa Pacts thus sealed the fate of the transition. Talk of a *ruptura democrática* after the end of 1977 became stigmatized as immature political fantasy. Although a year later the proposed constitution of 1978 "sanctified the principle of private property, recognized the army's role in 'protecting the constitutional order' and laid down the obligation for any government to maintain relations of cooperation with the [Catholic] Church," the PCE and the PSOE repudiated flat out the political opportunity to pose a clear constitutional alternative during the referendum campaign (Camiller 13–14).

And yet, far from proving exhilarating, the reality of the *ruptura pactada* frustrated and disillusioned many Spaniards. The decisions embraced in the Moncloa Pacts had all been taken in proverbial smoke-filled back rooms. Neither the PCE nor the PSOE had bothered to consult the rank and file of their unions before negotiating harmful wage limits and spending cuts. The voting populace, hungry for democratic debate after forty years of dictatorship, had not been given the chance to hear disagreements or to ratify the final result (Hooper 48). When the balance sheet of the transition was drawn at the end of 1978, it had to be admitted that

the government remained, in the main, in the hands of
those who had run sections of the state machine under
Franco. . . . The key sections of the old anti-Franco
opposition—especially the Communist Party and the
workers' commissions—were prepared to collaborate
with it. The ground was laid for a massive rationalisation
of Spanish industry, which the unions, bound to the
Pact of Moncloa, would not resist. And even when the
Centre Democrat government eventually fell victim to
wrangles of its constituent elements in 1982, a Socialist
Party committed to essentially the same policies replaced
it. (Harman 337)

The precipitate decline of the PCE following the Moncloa
Pacts is a well-known story. Although the Communists experienced a tiny increase in their percentage of the national vote,
from 9.3 to 10.7, between the 1977 and 1979 elections, their percentage fell to 4.0 in 1982. Santiago Carrillo's fawning eagerness
to appear in public praising the Moncloa Pacts severely alien-
ated the PCE's base of support once the economic impact of the
accords on the lives of average working people became clear. Indeed, "throughout much of 1977 and 1978 Suárez skilfully culti-
vated an image of discreet understanding between the UCD and
the PCE, while Carrillo ventilated vainglorious and ludicrous vi-
sions of an epoch of collaboration between the bourgeois and
workers' parties that would carry Spain to the very threshold of
socialism" (Camiller 14). Because the authoritarian character of
the Communist party's internal structure discouraged debate on
the pacts or any other issue of importance, "the discrepancy between democratic ideology and bureaucratic practice was thus
much more sharply felt inside the PCE, and there was little time
for generational or regional annealing once the fatal consequences of 1977 set in" (Camiller 25). Generational and regional
differences in fact led a group of *renovadores* to challenge Carrillo's leadership, with the result that, in 1981, the PCE collapsed
into three separate organizations.

In Spain the years between 1978 and 1981 are popularly
known as the *desencanto,* or the "disenchantment." The Moncloa
Pacts and the new constitution had dashed the revolutionary
hopes of 1975-77, and the new "free enterprise monarchy"

seemed all too familiar and anticlimactic. The *desencanto* came to an end only when the failed military coup of 23 February 1981 jolted the national consciousness. If a general political apathy disappeared with the *Tejerazo*, however, it was to be replaced by a generalized political irony, even cynicism. For the political capitulation of the PCE and the PSOE had been justified by "the claim that any unwillingness to accept the terms stipulated by Franco's heirs would risk military intervention and the cancellation of all prospects of civil liberties" (Camiller 13). This claim, of course, was always bogus (see Camiller 13–14; Harman 337; and Carr and Fusi, 226–27).

Such political disillusionment stands as one of the important avatars of "postmodern" sensibility in Spain. Like the PCF's intervention to end the French general strike of May-June 1968, the sorry performance of the PCE and the PSOE throughout the Spanish transition remains the primary source of the skepticism toward revolutionary politics and organization shared by an entire generation of Spanish intellectuals. Not only did this generation experience the demise of revolutionary situations in France (1968) and Spain (1976), moreover, but it also witnessed the defeat of revolutionary movements in Czechoslovakia (1968), Chile (1973), Portugal (1974), Iran (1979), and Poland (1981), as well as the implosion of the civil rights and feminist movements in the United States in the middle 1970s. By the time the generation that had been radicalized in and around 1968 ushered in the "postmodern 1980s," therefore, "master narratives" and "totality" had become suspect; "change" and "resistance"—when not outright impossible—could be imagined only at the level of micropolitics and personal lifestyle. For this reason postmodernism in Spain, as elsewhere, is appropriately understood "largely as a response to failure of the great upturn of 1968–76 to fulfill the revolutionary hopes it raised" (Callinicos 171).

But a second development also helps to account for the widespread acceptance of the themes of postmodernism among the Spanish intelligentsia. This is the emergence of an increasingly assertive "new middle class," not only in Spain but also in the various Western capitalist nations, as the result of fiscal policies (such as those of Reagan and Thatcher) that redistributed wealth and income from poor to rich. In addition, developments such as the growth of the financial sector (easy credit) and the bull markets of the middle 1980s (mergers and speculation) contributed to a substantial increase in upper-income consumption, best reflected in the rise of "Yuppies" and "Yuppiedom." As Callinicos explains, the generation of 1968 thus usually entered the 1980s

> with all hope of socialist revolution gone—indeed, often having ceased to believe in the desirability of any such revolution. Most of them had by then come to occupy some sort of professional, managerial or administrative position, to have become members of the new middle class, at a time when the overconsumptionist dynamic of Western capitalism offered this class rising living standards (a benefit often denied the rest of the workforce: hourly wages in the US fell by 8.7 percent between 1973 and 1986). This conjuncture—the prosperity of the Western new middle class combined with the political disillusionment of many of its most articulate members—provides the context to the proliferating talk of postmodernism. (Callinicos 168)

In Spain, of course, it is the PSOE that has served as the "vehicle for bringing to power a 'new class' of upwardly mobile professionals whose only rapid road to the top—to private wealth and social status—was through politics" (Petras 16). The regime of Felipe González has fashioned "a new power bloc of bankers, multinationals, importers, tourist and real-estate speculators" (Petras 22). It has outfitted itself, moreover, with "an army of ex-leftist intellectuals . . . [whose] job has been to sell the pro-investment, anti-labor programs of the Socialists as the only 'possible' realistic program open to Spain, given its constitutional system, the need to integrate into Europe, Spain's underdeveloped nature, the threat of a military backlash, the problem of modernizing the country, etc." (Petras 18). As the party of great entertainment spectacles that celebrate its own political success, the PSOE has inspired the social phenomenon of the *movida*, or "happening," whose crass consumerism and frenetic lifestyles represent an attempt to ape "not only the wealthy and powerful in Spain, but even more so their European counterparts" (Petras 17).

The list of PSOE- and PSOE-connected "new rich" includes such personalities as Mario Conde, Juan Abello, the "Albertos" (Cortina and Alcocer), and Miguel Boyer—all of whom have risen on the basis of "nonproductive, speculative, and financial dealings." Nepotism is a routine practice of the González regime: in 1990 four "Socialist" families—the Solano, Fernández Ordóñez, Yáñez Barrionuevo, and Rodríguez de la Borbolla—occupied twenty-one high governmental positions and funneled other appointments and promotions toward relatives and friends. The PSOE has in fact accomplished nothing less than the wholesale socioeconomic assimilation of members of the new ruling class to the old ruling class in Spain:

> Once in power, the Socialists dropped their early antioligarchic rhetoric against the Francoist elite, bankers, industrialists, and generals, and rebaptized their new coalition partners as modernizers and democrats. Henceforth, to attack the "oligarchy" was to be against "modernity" or to be un-European. The essential point is that the class resentment voiced by Spanish socialism's professionals expressed not opposition to class domination, but their desire to *escape from* the dominated class and *become part of* the dominating class. (Petras 16; emphasis added)

The typical career of a PSOE elite indeed progresses from an initial period of involvement in popular mobilizations, to one of electoral victories and office holding, "followed by the use of public office to enter elite circles, make investments, and reap fantastic incomes" (Petras 16).

Despite its rhetoric justifying the imposition of Reaganesque and Thatcherite austerity on the Spanish masses in the name of "modernization," the PSOE has actually presided over a decade in which real development of national technology and means of production has been sacrificed to outside interests. Generous concessions to foreign capital; the creation of low-skill, low-pay jobs; and other aspects of its industrial reconversion policy "have led to massive closings of industrial firms with no commensurate development of new industries" (Petras 16). Not an increase in the competitiveness of Spanish enterprises but the replacement of Spanish goods with European products has been the result of entry into the European Economic Community. Of course, "the upwardly mobile professionals have brushed off these failures as part of the costs of becoming 'modern' and 'European'—meaning a 20-percent unemployment rate and a dependence on both cheap, non-unionized labor and tourist earnings resembling those of early 'developing' countries" (Petras 16). Yet the disconcerting reality remains that today what growth there is in Spain "is based on a fragile and shrinking productive base and is increasingly dependent on external financial and technological sources" (Petras 22).

Spain's economy is currently a mess: among other horrors, a massive flight of foreign capital in September 1992, two devaluations of the peseta between September 1992 and May 1993, and growth rates of 2.3 percent in 1991, 1 percent in 1992, and a projected-0.8 percent in 1993. Spain has the highest unemployment rate in the European Union: an already brutal 16.3 percent in 1991, it is expected *by government forecasters* to rise to 22.4 percent in 1993 and 23.4 percent by the end of 1994. The PSOE, of course, has responded by attempting to squeeze Spanish workers even harder. The present state of affairs is perhaps best captured in the following story:

> At the end of October [1992], González celebrated ten years in power by announcing his intention to stand for reelection in 1993 at a massive PSOE rally in Madrid's main building. The day before, nearly one thousand out-of-work steelworkers who had walked from the Basque country and Asturias were joined by another ten thousand protesters outside the Ministry for Industry. INI, the state industrial building company, announced plans to eliminate another twenty thousand jobs over four years. (Wooller 456)

Conditions are expected to deteriorate further as the European single market kicks into gear, and, indeed, the fiscal 1993 government budget is the "most restrictive in years" (Wooller 454, 455).

Like President Bill Clinton of the United States, González hopes to solve his country's economic crisis by making deficit reduction his top priority. The government has rejected any rise in unemployment benefits for 1994, stiffened requirements for those who might qualify for unemployment benefits, and limited pension payments to a 3.5 percent "cost-of-living" increase. Salaries for active public employees will be frozen in 1994, and public sector hiring will be reduced. At the same time, indirect taxes will go up. Value Added Tax revenues are scheduled to rise by 16 percent, and revenues for "sin" taxes on items such as tobacco and alcohol will rise by almost 8 percent. Revenues from corporate taxes, however, will be allowed to fall by 29 percent. The limit on the business investment tax credit will move generously upward from 25 to 35 percent, and substantial tax breaks will be on offer to stimulate the creation of small businesses. A new law will eliminate the exemption of unemployed persons from paying income tax. Another new law will most likely allow temporary employment agencies into Spain for the first time, thus permitting employers to fire full-time workers with benefits and replace them with part-time workers at low wages and few if any benefits.

None of this should prove the least bit surprising from a party with the PSOE's history of opportunism and demonstrated lack of principle. In 1974 the PSOE was a party of just 4,000 members with few roots in the Spanish working class. Bankrolled by Bonn and other members of the reformist Socialist International, it was able to establish "an impressive network of offices throughout Spain" after Franco's death (Camiller 9). Yet the PSOE failed by a long shot to match the PCE in membership and leadership during the great upsurge of 1975–76. Recalling the role of Mario Soares and the Portuguese Socialist party in dissipating the energies of the Portuguese revolution of April 1974, Suárez gave González and the PSOE "the go-ahead to organize openly throughout the country" in autumn 1976 (Harman 329). At the same party congress in which the PSOE paid lip service to renouncing "any path of accommodation to capitalism," therefore, it also made clear that it "would take part in the [June 1977] election even if parties to the left of it, such as the Communists, were still banned" (Harman 329).

The PSOE went on to acquiesce to the pro-big business Moncloa Pacts in a manner "equally complicit" with the PCE, despite the fact that an astute González "preferred to adopt a lower profile" when taking credit for the pacts than Carrillo (Camiller

14). Later, under pressure from a red-baiting campaign launched by Suárez as part of the 1979 election campaign, González did not hesitate to exploit "his own [personality] cult to the full" in order to batter the PSOE into dropping its designation as a "Marxist" party (Camiller 16–17). Since winning a sweeping electoral victory in 1982, "what the late Franco and later the Suárez regimes could not or would not do—reduce living standards, introduce permanent insecurity into the labor force, subsidize employers to hire nonunion workers—the Socialist government [has] pursued with zeal . . . in the name of the working class" (Petras 15).

There was nothing "postmodern," of course, about the general strike of 14 December 1988, in which ten million Spanish workers and small business people communicated their anger to a PSOE hopelessly absorbed in its own bureaucratic world. Yet it is easy to understand how the decade of the PSOE has helped to spawn the decade of "postmodernism" in Spain. The ironic attitude toward Marxist politics acquired by most of those who experienced the disappointments of 1968–76 has received heavy reinforcement from the sad spectacle of a "socialist" party administering capitalism just as efficaciously for the times as the avowedly capitalist parties. No wonder there is a crisis of representation! So it is that the 1968 generation remain suspended between, on the one hand, a revolutionary experience that gave them significant insight into the rotten dimensions of capitalist society and, on the other hand, a subsequent experience of profound disillusionment with the professed alternatives.

On this account, "talk about postmodernism turns out to be less about the world than the expression of a particular generation's sense of an ending" (Callinicos 171). One can thus appreciate—though perhaps not endorse—the historical reasons that have led contemporary Spanish intellectuals to overestimate the extent to which reality is "created" in discourse, as well as to seek in "aesthetic" experience the realm of freedom that is denied them in everyday life. Of course, this is not the place to mount an argument concerning why it would be a mistake to presume that there will occur no more upheavals in the advanced capitalist countries rivaling those of 1968–76. Nor is it really the place to debate what is to be done in order to avoid repeating the betrayals and missed opportunities of that period. One can only express the desire that the window into which *Critical Practices in Post-Franco Spain* invites us to venture might become less of a surface reflecting an aestheticized subject and more of a window opening onto the world.

Notes

1. "*Las Lanzas* no es únicamente una pintura. *Las Lanzas* es toda una concepción de la vida. ¿Por qué se rinde Breda? . . . Pero la ciudad, aquello cuya suerte, cuya integridad, cuya existencia misma está en juego, se habrá salvado. La rendición como única alternativa a la destrucción."
2. "A mí un socialismo tipo europeo ya me viene bien."
3. "Hoy es el día de la huelga general pacífica. Madrid amenecío rígido y vacío, como un cementerio en el que, entre brumas, se mueven las sombras arriesgadas de los supervivientes de un bombardeo."

Works Cited

Bhaskar, R. *Reclaiming Reality*. London and New York: Verso, 1989.
Callinicos, A. *Against Postmodernism: A Marxist Critique*. New York: St. Martin's Press, 1990.
———, and C. Harman. *The Changing Working Class: Essays on Class Structure Today*. Chicago: Bookmarks, 1987.
Camiller, P. "Spanish Socialism in the Atlantic Order." *New Left Review* 156 (1986): 5–17.
Collier, A. *Scientific Realism and Socialist Thought*. Boulder, Colo.: Lynne Rienner Publishers, Inc., 1989.
Goytisolo, Luis. *La cólera de Aquiles*. Barcelona: Destino, 1979.
Harman, C. *The Fire Last Time: 1968 and After*. Chicago: Bookmarks, 1988.
Hooper, J. *Los españoles de hoy*. Madrid: Javier Vergara Editor, 1987.
Jameson, F. *Postmodernism; or, The Cultural Logic of Late Capitalism*. Durham, N.C.: Duke Univ. Press, 1991.
Kellogg, P. "Goodbye to the Working Class?" *International Socialism* 2.36 (1987): 105–11.
Lyotard, J.-F. *The Postmodern Condition: A Report on Knowledge*. Trans. G. Bennington and B. Massumi. Foreword by F. Jameson. Minneapolis: Univ. of Minnesota Press, 1984.
Marcelo, J. J. Armas. *Los dioses de sí mismos*. Barcelona: Plaza y Janés, 1989.
Mendoza, Eduardo. *El laberinto de las aceitunas*. Barcelona Seix Barral, 1982.
Norris, C. *What's Wrong With Postmodernism?* Baltimore: The Johns Hopkins Univ. Press, 1990.
Petras, J. "Spanish Socialism: Neither Social nor Democratic." *Against the Current* 28 (1990): 15–23.
Preston, P. *The Triumph of Democracy in Spain*. New York: Methuen, 1986.
Wooller, M. "Spain." In *1993 Britannica Book of the Year*. Chicago: Encyclopaedia Britannica, Inc., 1993.

Contributors

Manuel Asensi. Associate professor of literary theory at the Universitat de Valencia. He has published several articles on rhetoric, deconstruction, and literary history, and is the author of two books, *Teoría de la lectura* and *Deconstrucción y crítica literaria*.

Juan Miguel Company-Ramón. Associate professor of literary theory and film at the Universitat de Valencia. He has published on literary history, film, and psychoanalysis. His more recent books are *El trazo de la letra en la imagen* and *Ingmar Bergman*.

Jesús González-Requena. Associate professor of communication and film theory at the Universidad Complutense of Madrid. He is the author of *El discurso televisivo* and *S. M. Eisenstein*.

Tom Lewis. Professor of Spanish and comparative literature at the University of Iowa. He has published numerous essays and reviews on Marxism, semiotics, and nineteenth-century Spanish literature. His book *Fiction and Reference* is forthcoming, and he is currently writing on the Spanish novel of the 1980s. Lewis is a member of the International Socialist Organization.

Silvia L. López. Doctoral candidate in comparative literature at the University of Minnesota. Her dissertation focuses on theories of literary modernity in peripheral contexts. She has published articles on the work of Walter Benjamin, on contemporary Central American fiction, and on the historiography of *modernismo*.

Cristina Peña-Marín. Associate professor of communication at the Universidad Complutense of Madrid and researcher at the Fundación Ortega y Gasset. She has published widely on sociology, semiotics, and feminist theory, and has coauthored *Análisis de discurso*.

José María Pozuelo-Yvancos. Professor of literary theory at the Universidad de Murcia. He has published, among other books, *Teoría de lenguaje literario* and *Del formalismo a la neoretórica*. He has published widely on rhetoric, literary history, and narratology. He has been a visiting professor at numerous European universities.

Rafael Núñez-Ramos. Associate professor of literary theory at the Universidad de Oviedo. He has written on general semiotics, the semiotics of sport, theater, and literary theory. Among his books are *Política semiológica, El "Polifemo" de Góngora,* and *La poesía.*

Jenaro Talens. Professor of literary theory and film at the Universitat de Valencia. He has been a regular visiting professor at the University of Minnesota since 1983, and has also taught at other U.S. and European universities. He has authored fifteen books of poetry and has translated many classics of German and English poetry into Spanish. His more recent books are *Through the Shattering Glass: Cervantes and the Self-Made World* (coauthored with Nicholas Spadaccini; Minnesota, 1993) and *The Branded Eye: Buñuel's "Un Chien andalou"* (Minnesota, 1993).

Darío Villanueva. Professor of literary theory at the Universidad de Santiago de Compostela. He has been visiting professor at the University of Colorado at Boulder. His more recent books are *El polen de las ideas* and *Teoría del realismo literario.*

Santos Zunzunegui. Professor of communication and film theory at the Universidad del País Vasco and dean of the College of Information Sciences. He has published widely on film history, semiotics, photography, and mass media. His more recent books are *Pensar la imagen* and *Metamórfosis de la mirada.*

Index

communicative function xxi, 95;
complexities of poetic discourse
xxi; contexts, multiplicity of xxi;
distance and impersonality 100;
enunciation xxi; expressivity
xx-xxi, 98-99; lyric xx, 90-105;
peculiarities and effects on
readers 93-94; pragmatic identity
xx; reflexivity 95-96; romanticism,
influence of 90; spatial and
temporal contexts xxi
Polyphony of characters xxiii, 130
Pomian, Krisztof 44
Portugal 172, 176, 180
Postmodernism: and international
critical perspectives 161; and
newscast discourse xii, xv-xvi;
and poststructuralism xii, 161;
and social determination 161-170;
political disillusionment as avatar
of 176-178
Pound, Ezra 12
Pozuelo-Yvancos, José María xii, xix-
xxi; and *Del formalismo* 92; and the
expressive models of lyric poetry
168; and *La teoría del lenguaje
literario* 90, 92, 98
Prado Museum xvii, 47
Pragmatics and Fiction (Adams) 83
Pragmatics of meaning xix
Pratt, Mary Louise 109, 117, 121, 123
(note 5)
Preston, Paul 171
Proust, Marcel 141 (note 2)
Psychoanalysis ix, xi-xii, xxiv,
143-144, 146-149; and American
pragmatism 156-157 (note 1); and
the body's shattering 148-149;
and empiricism 162-165; and
emptiness of desire 154; and
fetishistic drive 154; and free
association about dreams 152;
and illusory personality unit 148-
149; and the narcissistic gestalt
constitution of one's own image
148-149; and necrophilia 154; and
phallic rituals of striptease 151;
and philosophy 157 (note 1); and

proprioceptivity 148-149; and self-
eroticism 154; and transference
157 (note 1); as a scientific model
156-157; desire and frustration
151; Freudian slips and the joke
149-154; the object and its origin
156-157; subject as originating
from the Other 155-156;
unconscious desire characterized
by lack of an object 155;
unspoken, persistence of in what
is spoken 156; Western
philosophy and Freudian theory
147
Publishing: explosion x; houses x-xi

Quine, W. V. 83

Rappaport, Julian 156 (note 1)
Reagan, President Ronald 176
Realism: and aesthetic actualization
84; and archetypal ideas 69-70;
and autonomy of artistic text 85;
and co-intentionality 80-83; and
consciousness of author and
reader 81-82; and criticism 76; and
cultural unit 73-74;
deconstructionist perspective 75;
and democratic, revolutionary
socialism 164; and empiricism
162-165; and epiphany 85; and
fictionality 79, 81-82; and game,
notion of 79-80; and God 74; and
illusion 85; and imagination 80;
and literary communication 81;
and literary reception 76; and
literature as a schematic
formation and stratified structure
77; and the missing perspective of
the reader 76-77; and the novel
74; and the ontological
constitution of literature 77; and
phenomenology xix, 76; and
philosophical implications 69-71;
and psychological phenomena
76-77; and reality in literature 75;
and reality versus the real xiv-xvi,
xviii-xix; and suspension of